100 Wonders of China

REBO PUBLISHERS

COPYRIGHT PAGE

© 2005 Greenland International Books Co. Ltd.
© 2006 Rebo International b.v., Lisse, The Netherlands

Project Editor: Hsiu Chin Chen
Coordinating Editor: Wei Wei Ge
Created and produced by Greenland International Books Co. Ltd.

Chief Designer: Hsin Ying Lin
Designers: Chia Ling Chiou,Su Wen Chen,Li Zhen Chen
Editing of English text: First Edition Translations Ltd, Cambridge, Great Britain
Proofreading: Sarah Dunham

ISBN 978 90 366 1660 7

Foreword

China is an enormous country with a long history. It boasts numerous world-famous historical relics. These include the 4000-mile (6400km) Great Wall, one of the Seven Wonders of the World–which extends from the Shanhai Pass to the Jiayu Pass–the Potala Palace in Tibet, the Mogao Grottoes in Dunhuang, the Forbidden City in Beijing, and the Longmen Stone Grottoes in Shanxi. Having gone through historical turns and twists, they fully deserve to be treasures shared by all humanity and are thus listed as World Cultural Legacies by the United Nations.

China's picturesque and mysterious landscape has attracted millions of explorers and travelers both at home and abroad. Natural wonders include the Yellow Mountain in Anhui, Lushan Mountain in Jiangxi, the Jiuzhaigou Gorge and the Huanglong Area in Sichuan, the Lijiang River in Guangxi, West Lake in Zhejiang, the Tulufan Basin in Xinjiang, and Shangrila County and Luguhu Lake in Yunnan. The enchanting natural scenery and unique cultures add more luster to the country.

As a matter of fact, China boasts more scenic spots and historical sites than what has been collected in this book. These one hundred attractions present a panoramic picture of the ancient towns, beautiful landscapes, and modern cities of China. We are fully convinced that each one will pleasantly surprise as you explore this vast land, filled as it is with mystery, vigor, and charm.

Contents | 4

Jiuzhaigou

FAIRYLAND ON EARTH

NATURAL WONDERS

Hukou Falls

Dragon Ridge Terraced Fields

IMPERIAL REMAINS

The Forbidden City

ANCIENT TOWNS

Qufu

Yili

CULTURAL HERITAGE

Potala Palace

CITIES THAT CHARM

Hong Kong

BEAUTIFUL VILLAGES

Hongcun Village

Mount Huangshan (Anhui)
The finest mountain of all

Beihai viewing platform, Mount Huangshan (main picture)

Huangshan pine tree (top, right)

Stone Monkey looking at the "Sea of Snow," Mount Huangshan (below, right)

The footprints of Xu Xiake, the great traveler of the Ming dynasty, covered almost all the great mountains in China. Descending from Mount Huangshan, he proclaimed Huangshan to be the finest mountain of all, dwarfing even the Five Holy Mountains.

The four signature features of Mount Huangshan are its grotesquely shaped pines, its spectacular rocks, the sea of clouds, and the hot springs.

The Huangshan pines are considered remarkable for four reasons: the high places where they grow half a mile (800m) above sea level; their evolution from traditional Chinese pine species to Huangshan pines as they have adapted to Huangshan's unique geology and climate; the rocks including granite, in which they are rooted, sprout and grow; and the variety of ways in which they are shaped. Normally pines grow upward. Huangshan pines, in contrast, are found growing downward. Since cliffs and rocks constitute the geology of Huangshan, these pines have to perch precipitously on the cliffs and break out of rocks, which gives rise to their extraordinary shapes as they grow sideways, lie flat, wind about, or suspend. Despite the adverse environment, Huangshan pines, when they do grow upward, assume an attractive appearance, with straight trunks, flat canopies, and layer upon layer of verdant green foliage. There is no such ting as ordinary-looking Huangshan pine. The ten most well-known Huangshan pines include the Welcoming Pine, the Farewell Pine, and the Phoenix Pine.

The rocks in Huangshan are spectacular too, with their odd shapes that can be taken for human beings, birds, animals, and so on. They attract attention also because they look very different from alternative perspectives. For example, when viewing the Tiandu peak from the Banshan Temple (a temple at the midpoint of the mountain), you might compare the rock on the peak to a rooster flapping its wings in readiness for flight. When ascending to the peak and turning around for another look at the rock, you may find the rock seems to turn into five old men with long fluttering robes. Oddly shaped rocks, over 1200 of which are individually named, may be found all over the mountain. At every turn, you come across a new view with imposing peaks and convoluted rocks, as if classical Chinese

LOCATION
Mount Huangshan is
located in the south of
Anhui province, where
it shares a border with
Zhejiang province.

CLIMATE
Conditions are subtropi-
cal and monsoonal,
with four distinct sea-
sons: a warm spring,
a pleasantly cool sum-
mer and fall, and a cold
winter. The mean tem-
perature in July is 69°F
(20.7°C). It is quite cold
in the mornings and
at night up in the
mountain.

OF SPECIAL INTEREST
The mountain has been
proclaimed a site of sce-
nic beauty and historic
interest by the State
Council, and was
inscribed on the
World Heritage List
by UNESCO in 1990.

MAIN ATTRACTIONS
Hot springs, the Human-
shape Waterfall, the
Paiyun Pavilion, the
Shixin peak, the Wel-
coming Pine, the Lotus
Flower peak, the Tiandu
peak, the Yixian Tian,
and the Nine Dragons
Waterfall.

paintings were rolling out before your very eyes.

Almost every high mountain offers a view of a sea of clouds, and the one from Mount Huangshan is one of the most spectacular. More than two hundred days of the year are cloudy and foggy on Mount Huangshan. Peaks in Mount Huangshan rise high and low, interrupted only by clouds. Therefore, clouds can be seen almost everywhere on the mountain, with different views at different heights. The seething clouds between the peaks are turned into flickering waves in an upsurging sea. Visitors can feast their eyes on a spectacular sea of clouds, sometimes calm and tranquil, sometimes surging and sweeping, sometimes cascading all the way down, and sometimes lingering gently through the peaks. If the sun shines on the clouds, the whole scene becomes even more dazzling and glorious.

Hot springs are located at the foot of the Ziyun peak in Huangshan, the first stopover of the Mount Huangshan scenic site. The hot springs maintain a temperature around 107.6°F (42°C). Apart from the springs, attractions include waterfalls, streams, and ponds, all of which provide visitors with various delights.

Mount Huangshan is miraculous. Seventy-two imposing peaks tower aloft in an area of 59 square miles (154 square kilometers), among which the three major peaks, Lotus Flower peak, Tiandu peak, and Guangming (Everbright) summit, are higher than 5900 ft (1800m). The mountain has many perilous roads, one of which leads up to the peak of Tiandu. To reach its summit, visitors have to take the Sky Ladder and walk through what is known as "The Back of a Crucian Carp." The Sky Ladder is the name for a flight of stone steps 1017 ft (310m) long, and the steps have a variety of dimensions. Some are so steep that they are almost vertical and climbers have to clutch the iron chains and climb up using their hands. The Back of a Crucian Carp is a rock 5807 ft (1770m) above sea level that is 33 ft (10m) in length and only 3 ft (1m) in width, and it has a slope of 85 degrees. Flanked by cliffs on both sides, the rock does indeed look like the back of a carp emerging now and then in the waves. Traversing this huge boulder is the only way through to the summit of Tiandu peak .

There are abundant scenic spots along the way up Mount Huangshan, such as the bamboo woods beside the Ciguang Pavilion, the tranquil Banshan Temple, Three Islands of Penglai, the North Sea, the Welcoming Pine of Yuping, the sea of clouds viewed from the Paiyun Pavilion, the sunset viewed from Qingliang platform, and so on. In a word, Mount Huangshan is the finest of all mountains.

The source of Wuling (Hunan)

Unique peaks and elegant waters in Zhangjiajie

Zhangjiajie is a ready example of the dramatic changes in the world's geological history. People have just come to know Zhangjiajie in the last 20 years or so. In 1979 Wu Guanzhong, a famous oil painter, wrote a short essay awaking Zhangjiajie natives to its hidden beauty. The photographer Chen Fuli was stunned after visiting it in 1981, saying that the scenery was first rate.

When arriving at Zhangjiajie, you are sure to make your first arrangement that of seeing the mountains. Zhangjiajie is renowned for its peaks. They share grandeur with Taishan, grotesqueness with Huangshan, elegance with Lushan, and ruggedness with Huashan. You might say that all the mountain sights on earth are concentrated around here. A term used to refer to the sights is "2800 pillars," revealing something of the spectacular nature of the sights. With nearly three thousand grotesque peaks, running in an extraordinary continuous chain of thousands of mountains and forming a stone forest, among them there are more than two hundred summits above 2625 ft (800m) high.

To enjoy the mountainous scenery, tourists have three angles of view. The Gold Whip Stream extends 4.7 miles (7.5km) and is a very beautiful canyon indeed. Following the stream, take the stone slab path that winds up into the distance to enjoy the beautiful sights, including the single log bridges, the old trees reaching into the sky, and so on.

The Gold Whip Rock, an eyecatching landmark 984 ft (300m) high is as steep and smooth as if it had been split with an ax from above. The square pillar is certainly like a giant whip. Alongside the waters there are many more such peaks, such as Drunken Arahat, Treasure Lotus Lantern, Jade Bamboo shoot, and so on. The fascinating scene slides in and out of view with every step.

Straight ahead is Yellow Stone Village, which has an elevation of 3280 ft (1000m). The sights here are not to be missed. The sightseeing platform is built on the summit of the rock, to which the only access is either through the front or the back entrance, for there are precipices on four sides that descend 984 ft (300m). From the platform, the peaks can be seen as stones in a raging sea, jumping tigers, or rolling dragons. The sea of clouds surging from halfway up the mountains to their tops is like hordes of troops and horses surging in every direction. After rain, clouds and mists drown out the mountains, leaving lonely peaks standing here and there.

At the summit of the Emperor Mountain, look down. At an elevation of 3940 ft (1200m), you are overlooking the chains of mountains. The most extraordinary sights, beyond description, gather before your eyes. When looking upward, the mountains appear as a continuous chain. Looking down presents a different view, for now they are stalagmites, like forests, tall, graceful, and dignified. It is not possible to see the bottom of the valley owing to the clouds and mists lingering halfway down the mountainsides, and this may make you feel extremely giddy. It is strange that pines take root on the otherwise bare tops of the peaks. No wonder people say that the mountains of Zhangjiajie rewrite the concept of a mountain.

Strange stones call for water as a companion. The saying here is, "Eight hundred waters girdle three thousand peaks." To speak of eight hundred waters is no exaggeration. Take the Gold Whip Stream as representative. Here the pure green water flows through-out the year, even in long droughts, curving up and down, the glory of which pictures can never reveal. The red, white, and green pebbles at the bottom, the freely swimming rock fish, and the water all shimmer and gleam under the sunlight that filters down through the swaying woods. The numerous rivulets of this ancient ecosystem zigzag through the forests and link Gold Whip Stream, Flower Stream, Pipa Stream, and some of the other larger waterways, all of them reflecting the surrounding peaks and strange looking stones. When they meet gentle slopes, they become deep ponds or shallow pools. When they reach precipices, they transform into flying falls, some majestic and others charming. They set off the mountain sights and separate them from the world of mortals, giving you inspiration to become a hermit.

LOCATION
Wulingyuan is located in the heart of the Wuling mountain range, within the jurisdiction of Zhangjiajie city, 237.5 miles (380km) from Changsha, the provincial capital.

CLIMATE
The area has a moderate climate, with an annual average temperature of 60.8°F (16°C) and a subtropical mountainous zone monsoon climate.

OF SPECIAL INTEREST
The scenery combines lofty peaks, winding rivulets, thick forests, deep caves, and waterfalls. These features are elegant, tranquil, wild, and also hazardous. The natural scenery here is listed as a World Natural Heritage site by UNESCO.

MAIN ATTRACTIONS
Zhangjiajie National Forests Park, Emperor Mountain, Suoxi Valley, Yangjiajie Scenic District.

Emperor Mountain at Wulingyuan (top)

Yellow Stone Village, Zhangjiajie, Hunan province (below, left)

Gold Whip Stream, Zhangjiajie, Hunan province (below, right)

Lushan Mountain (Jiangxi)

The mecca of Magic Mountain and River

LOCATION
Lushan Mountain is situated to the south of Jiujiang, in the northern part of Jiangxi.

CLIMATE
Climatically, it is in the subtropical monsoon area, which features a short summer and a long winter, a late spring, and an early fall.

OF SPECIAL INTEREST
This is a world-famous mountain with rich cultural connotations.

MAIN ATTRACTIONS
The Immortalis Cave, Song Meiling's villa, the Wulao peak, the Yuyuan Pool, the Huangya Waterfall, and the Bailudong Academy of Classical Learning.

Bai Juyi, one of the greatest poets in the Tang dynasty, praised Lushan Mountain in his line: "Its beautiful landscape comes first in the world." Bai's ode rings true, for the well-known mountain has Boyang Lake to the east, Tengwang Tower to the south, and the Yangtze River to the north. The river, lake, and mountain unite to present one of the most magnificent views under the sun. What is more, that view changes for each season.

Thousands of writers, artists, hermits, and statesmen have visited Lushan Mountain – it has been admired since ancient times. Their tours have left a rich cultural legacy, which has made the mountain even more famous near and far.

Reaching an altitude of 4836 ft (1474m) and covering an area of 108 square miles (280 square kilometers), Lushan Mountain boasts 16 natural wonders and 474 scenic spots. You may come across famous lines from a number of writers. An example is by Su Dongpo, the renowned poet of the Song dynasty: "It looks like a ridge from a horizontal perspective while it may turn into a peak from a lateral view. The view may change from different distances and heights."

The charm of Lushan Mountain extends from its natural features to its cultural ambience. Poets have spared no effort in praising the mountain since the Dongjing dynasty (265-420 AD).

It is estimated that more than four thousand poems have been written to describe Lushan Mountain, which deserves the honor of being one of the best-known scenic attractions immortalized in the country's landscape poetry.

"Watching Zhuqiao from the top of Lushan Mountain" by Xie Lingyun in the Dongjing dynasty and "Watching the Stone Gate" by Bao Zhao in the South dynasty (420-589 AD) are regarded as the earliest Chinese poems featuring landscape. In addition, Tao Yuanming pioneered pastoral poetry, which he based on Lushan Mountain, exerting a far reaching influence on Chinese poetry after his time. Another great poet, Li Bai of the Tang dynasty, left

14 poems about Lushan Mountain, written during his five visits there. One poem, entitled "Watching the Waterfall at Lushan Mountain" is very well-known in China. Two lines from this ancient masterpiece run as follows: "It rushes down as long as nine thousand chi as if the galaxy poured to the earth." You may not find any more exact and powerful words to depict the waterfall at Lushan Mountain. Moreover, Su Dongpo's philosophical poem entitled "Words on Xilinbi" is full of wisdom. Take these two lines: "You may fail to know about what the Lushan Mountain really looks like because you are in the mountain."

Chinese landscape painting featuring Lushan Mountain has become well established in the history of traditional painting. For instance, Lushan Mountain by Gu Kaizhi of the Dongjing dynasty is thought to be the first landscape painting made in the entire country.

Lushan Mountain is the crystallization of Chinese landscape and traditional culture. Consequently, it was listed as a World Cultural Heritage site by the United Nations in 1996. Experts from UNESCO aired their views after touring the mountain. Their claim is that the historical sites on Lushan Mountain are merged into an extraordinary natural beauty of its own, which results in the outstanding cultural attraction it offers. It features an incomparable combination of beauties, conveying the spirit of the Chinese nation and its cultural life.

It is a rich cultural heritage that gives a new lease on life to Lushan Mountain, now a world-famous tourist highlight.

Tiechuan peak in clouds, Lushan Mountain (above)

Lulin Lake, Lushan Mountain (below)

Jiuzhaigou (Sichuan)
A fairyland tucked away in a deep valley

LOCATION
Situated in the Aba Tibetan Autonomous Prefecture, Sichuan, Jiuzhaigou is over 250 miles (400km) away from Chengdu, the capital city.

CLIMATE
Jiuzhaigou has frozen soil and melting snow before April. Average temperatures range from 66°F to 71.6°F (19°C to 22°C) in summer and from 44.6°F to 64.4°F (7°C to 18°C) in fall. A drastic temperature change occurs between day and night. It is very cold in winter, and its rainy season lasts from July to August.

OF SPECIAL INTEREST
Jiuzhaigou boasts dust-free picturesque scenery and unique Tibetan customs and culture.

MAIN ATTRACTIONS
Wucaichi Lake, the overlapped waterfalls, Nuorilang Waterfall, Heye village, the colorful primitive forests, and the floating icebergs.

This is an amazing place, which seems to exist as if in a fairytale. It is a mysterious land full of natural wonders.

Deep in the valley of the Mingshan Mountain in the Aba Tibetan Autonomous Prefecture of Sichuan, nine Tibetan villages are hidden. Three gorges named Shuzhen, Rize, and Zechewa are perched in a Y shape; the name Jiuzhaigou means "a gorge with nine villages in scenic countryside."

Covering an area of 510 square miles (1320 square kilometers), Jiuzhaigou boasts 114 lakes, 47 springs, 18 groups of waterfall, 11 rapids, 5 calcsinter (travertine) sports centers, and 9 Tibetan villages.

There are five treasures in Jiuzhaifou. These are green lakes, tumbling waterfalls, colorful forests, snow-capped mountains – and Tibetan folklore.

The water of the lakes is green and clean all through the year. On fine days the blue sky, the white clouds, the distant mountain, and the nearby trees are reflected in the lake. Fish seem to swim in the clouds, and birds to fly in the sea. The colorful lake, a product of sunshine, seaweed, and sediment, sometimes presents numerous geometrical patterns in yellow, green, gray, red, and emerald hues. Fanciful compositions mingle, resulting in an infinity of designs. Some sunlit lakes look like a burning sea in the distance while others seem to have dragons moving fast across the bottom, an illusion created by submerged calcified reefs. Overall, these are most beautiful lakes, many of them linked by torrential waterfalls.

Rhinoceros Lake, Jiuzhaigou (below, left)

Shuzhen Lakes, Jiuzhaigou (above, right)

Fall scenery at Changhai Lake, Jiuzhaigou (below, right)

It is fascinating to discover that all the overhanging waterfalls in Jiuzhaigou splash down from the dense forests. The Nuorilang Waterfall, the widest in the area, rushes down from Cuiyan peak like a huge silvery curtain, majestic and spectacular. Some waterfalls cast an expanse of water drops in the wake of the plunge from the high points, foggy or misty in the distance. They are called overlapped waterfalls and those in Jiuzhaigou are unique.

Jiuzhaigou has 74,000 acres (30,000 hectares) of primitive forest, home to more than 2000 species of plants. The forest changes its colors from season to season. In fall the forest presents a panoramic view. The yellow fir, the red maple, and the gray elm are dotted here and there. They are reflected in the lakes. In winter the green lakes are like sapphires against the pure and white forest.

Three gorges in the area are encircled with high mountains. Atop Gaierna Mountain there are more sinuous mountains looming in the distance, more serpentine valleys extending in the green. You may experience the illusion of floating. In addition, the snow-capped mountains shine so brightly in the sun that you may become dizzy.

Jiuzhaigou is home to Tibetans, whose culture is mixed with that of the Han, the Qiang minority, and the Hui minority nearby. Therefore, the architecture is markedly different from that of the Tibetans in western China. Its private houses feature the Han fashion of adopting elevated corners and circular gates. On the other hand, it is common to see white stones used for door and window frames, evidence of some imitation of Qiang architecture.

Nowadays, Jiuzhaigou is listed as a World Natural Heritage site and a World Human and Biological Protection Area by the United Nations.

Huanglong (Sichuan)

The most magnificent karst scenery in the world

Known as the largest, the most complete, and the most unusual karst area in the world, the Huanglong scenic area is a rarely seen geographical attraction, of high value for both sightseeing and scientific research.

Situated at an altitude of 9840 ft (3000m), Huanglong is in fact a calcified gorge which measures 4.4 miles (7km) long and 984 ft (300m) wide. The surface of the huge gorge is covered with many layers of golden scale-like calcsinter (travertine) compound, which shines brightly in sunlight. In the distance water flowing rapidly over the golden surface looks like a gigantic yellow dragon rushing down from the snow-capped mountains. The dragon zigzags through the primitive forest and valleys. The colorful calcified lakes of a variety of sizes on its waist and back constitute the dragon's scales. As a result, the name of this area is Huanglong, which means a yellow dragon in Chinese.

Surrounded by high mountains, this area offers a perfect example of the prevailing geological conditions, and reveals traces of Ice Age occupation as well as geographical features relating to the water source. In addition, in its primitive ecological environment it boasts some very rare species, which offer the possibility of finding hitherto unknown animals and plants.

Huanglong is a unique scenic miracle in the country. Praised as the museum of natural calcification, Huanglong is famous for its grotesque structures, rich colors, primitive surroundings, and abundant species. Its calcsinter section extends as far as two miles (3600m), with the longest part reaching 4265 ft (1300m) and the widest 558 ft

(170m). What is more, 3400 colorful lakes are scattered along the length of the gorge. One waterfall, called Zhaga, is as high as 306 ft (93.2m). All these figures make this an outstanding area in the country.

Huanglong Gorge faces the Fujiang River, with the snow-bound Mingshan Mountain in its background. The snowmelt water from the high mountains is mixed with water from underground. Together they make a creek running down the stalactite slopes. In the course of jumping from one slope to another, the creek produces many calcsinter cascades along the way. By contrast, in some places it slows down,

blocked by dried branches or huge rocks. Then its calcium carbonate starts to settle, creating a calcsinter dam after a long time has passed. As a result, clusters of colorful ponds appear along the course of the creek.

The thousands of colorful ponds together make a mind-blowing natural picture – a miracle in Huanglong indeed. Situated on the terraced slopes, they are revealed in a number of forms. Some are as big as 11 square feet (1 square meter), while others are as small as a cup, a bowl. The golden pond walls seem like they are made of magnificent yellow jade. In the process of sedimentation carboniferous elements are mingled with organic or inorganic materials, producing a large number of calcific compounds. Changes of scenery and the different angles of the sun make the calcsinter ponds look like an artist's palette. The dried branches mixed with calcsinter look just like stalagmites in the distance.

The Huanglong scenic area is renowned for its rich reserves of fauna and flora. Subtropical evergreen forest, broad-leaved forest, coniferous and broad-leaved forest, coniferous forest, and mountainous grassland all grow at different altitudes, from the foot of the Huanglong Valley at 6560 ft (2000m) above sea level to the top at 12,470 ft (3800m) above sea level. Over ten rare species of animals, including the panda and the golden monkey, live in the area. Therefore it is listed as a World Natural Heritage site and World Biological Protection Area by the United Nations.

LOCATION
Huanglong is situated in Songpan county in the northwest of Sichuan.

CLIMATE
There is a long winter with an annual average temperature of 44.6°F (7 °C). This area receives ample sunshine, however it is foggy in the morning and at night. The rainy season lasts from May to August.

OF SPECIAL INTERESTS
Huanglong boasts the biggest, the most complete, and the most grotesque karst scenery in the world.

MAIN ATTRACTIONS
Yingbin Pond, Hongxing Rock, Erdaohai Pond, Xuebaoding Mountain, Zhage Waterfall, and Huangdong Temple.

The famous colorful ponds in Huanglong scenic area (below, left)

Enchanting natural scenery: Huanglong covered in thick mist (below, right)

Daocheng (Sichuan)

The soul of Shangri-la in Sichuan

LOCATION
Situated on the south of the Ganzi Tibetan Autonomous Prefecture in the southwest rim of Sichuan, the county of Daocheng is 500 miles (800km) away from Chengdu, the capital.

CLIMATE
At an altitude of 12,303 ft (3750m), Daocheng receives a great deal of sunshine. Its low temperature is intensified by the drastic temperature range within a single day. Daocheng experiences its rainy season from June to August and has its winter from November to March. The best touring seasons are from April to May and from September to October.

OF SPECIAL INTEREST
The area boasts a great variety of fauna and flora, and charming natural scenery. The Yading Nature Reserve in the county of Daocheng is well maintained and regarded as land untouched by humans.

MAIN ATTRACTIONS
Yading Nature Reserve, Chonggu Temple, Tibetan villages, magic peaks in Daocheng, and the Pearl Lake.

There is neither sorrow nor pain. There is only the singing of birds. This is where the immortals live.

Were this true, it would be said of Daocheng in Sichuan province.

Joseph Rock, the explorer, noticed three snow-capped mountains when he toured Lijiang in Yunnan in 1926. After consulting the local people, he found out that they were called Nianqingonggarisonggongbu in the Tibetan language. That was what is known as the Daocheng scenic area today. In the following four years, Rock explored the mountains with the help of local Tibetan officials. His words and pictures were published in the National Geographic in June, 1931, and they made a big stir in the United States. The readers there had never imagined that there existed such a world of amazing landscapes in the Far East!

Daocheng had scarcely been visited since ancient times, for it is tucked away in the hinterland, inaccessible to the outside world. Its local people have had a loving heart toward life and nature, hoping to maintain the local religious culture, which holds that any form of life should be protected. This belief has made Daocheng one of the regions in China that boasts the best preserved primitive vegetation, and is also one of the last unpolluted territories.

Since Rock's time, many tourists have been amazed by the splendid landscape of Daocheng – after they have soothed away the numerous obstacles they met on the way there.

In 2002 a road to Daocheng was completed, and this has made the scenic area accessible to the rest of the world. Photographers have been busy exploiting the enchanting natural scenery, the primitive local customs, and the mysterious cultural relics.

The Daocheng Plateau is composed of Gongga Mountain and Haizi Mountain. Situated in the north and south respectively, the two mountains account for one third of the whole area, which stretches from north to south, and from west to east, in terms of geographical features. High mountains follow one after another, presenting a dramatic view. There are three principal rivers, called the Daocheng River, the Chitu River, and the Dongyi River, and all of them empty into the Jinshajiang River.

Originating at the foot of Haishan Mountain, the Daocheng River runs over 75.6 miles (121km). The Dongyi River, which comes from Echu Mountain, extends as far as 69 miles (111km). The county of Daocheng has nearly 30,000 people, over 96 percent of whom are Tibetan. The rest are Han, Naxi, and Yi.

The Yading Nature Reserve is regarded as the last Shangri-la. When you ride a horse from Yading village to the Chonggu Temple, you may spot a Tibetan village hidden in the flowers and among the extensive crops. You will come across the fathomless primitive forest, through which a jingling creek merrily runs. In addition, colorful lakes change their aspect from time to time. The snow-capped magic peak stands out, with the green forest extending around its slope and foot. What a pure and clean world this is!

If you want to experience how friendly and kind the local people

are, drop in at a household in the Tibetan village. The hospitality of the people there may make you reluctant to leave.

It is said that one thousand feelings arise from one thousand tourists who return from Daocheng.

The famous scenery
of the "Sea of Red-grass"
in Shangri-La (above)

Yangfangyong ice peak
(bottom, left)

Sparkling stream under
the blue sky with white
clouds above (bottom,
right)

Luguhu Lake (Yunnan)

Lake area where a matriarchal community exists

A distant view
of Luguhu Lake
(above, left)

The spring scenery
of Luguhu Lake
(above, top)

A unique local boat,
just like an eating
trough used by pigs
(above, center)

A Mosuo woman
standing by Luguhu
Lake (below, right)

Situated in the northwest of Yunnan province and covering an area of 19 square miles (50 km²) with an average depth of 295 ft (90m), Luguhu Lake has very long, serpentine banks, dotted with numerous islands. The area near the lake is remarkably different from the outside world, in that the local people maintain a matriarchal tradition to this day.

These people are called the Mosuo, and are perhaps the last matriarchal community in the world. There are many special customs among the Mosuo people. They are very different from other communities with regard to such things as clothing, food, housing, and transportation. One unique feature is that they still have primitive marriage rites called zouhun. These have added a somewhat mysterious luster and atmosphere to the region, which has long been regarded in the East as the Kingdom of Girls.

The kingdom is characterized by tenderness and love. The Mosuo attach the utmost respect and importance to mothers and girls. The most striking feature lies in the fact that a big family is built up and strengthened by maternal blood ties, not the usual paternal ones. It is the grandmother that presides over family affairs and has the final word in every important thing. What is more, the significant family members are the daughters, while sons are regarded as uncles to nephews and nieces. In addition, women are dominant in such aspects as farming and community affairs.

Perhaps the most interesting is the zouhun ("walking marriage"). A man and woman do not marry and live under the same roof. If a man is attracted to a girl, it is cus-

LOCATION
Luguhu Lake is situated in the Ninglang Yi Autonomous County, Yunnan province. It is at the juncture of Sichuan province and Yunnan province, on the Dianxibei Plateau.

CLIMATE
Luguhu Lake area is cool in summer and warm in winter, owing to the surrounding mountains and the big lake. Its annual average temperature is less than 68°F (20°C), with not a great deal of rainfall all the year round. The best touring seasons are spring and summer.

FEATURES
The Mosuo people are said to be the only group around Luguhu Lake who still live in a matriarchal community.

HIGHLIGHTS
Luguhu Lake, the Mosuo people around the lake, three islands in the lake, the Yongning hot spring, and the Zhameishi Temple.

tomary for him to walk to her house in the still of night, perhaps after making some overtures to her in advance, and have a heart-to-heart talk with her. If everything goes smoothly, he is allowed to stay overnight, leaving before daybreak.

In practice, both men and women attach a greet deal to love. They are free to continue their relationship or to continue on their own in that they live in their respective mothers' houses. However, once their relationship is settled, they remain loyal to each other. If their relationship produces a baby, the baby naturally belongs to the woman, who takes on the responsibility of caring for the child and bringing it up.

No matchmaker or parent is ever involved in these arrangements. In the community very few disputes occur. Villagers are friendly and kind hearted, and have a calm attitude toward people and things around.

In addition to the local customs, which make this ancient land charming and mysterious, the natural scenery is eyecatching.

In the Kingdom of Girls you can take a boat on the lake and visit the Mosuo villages nearby. The log cabins and the compound courtyards are worth touring. Besides, it gives you a good opportunity to observe zouhun in practice. You may consult the local people if you are interested in the folklore as well.

There is a village called Luoshui on the west bank of the lake. It is a typical scenic spot with a primitive landscape, and it is a must-see place, accessible thanks to easy transportation and its convenient location.

Another attraction is Yongning, 12.5 miles (20km) north of Luoshui village. There you may visit the Zhameishi Temple and the Yongning hot spring, where you have the chance to learn about the daily life, history, religion, culture, and folk art of these people.

Xinjiang Uygur Autonomous Region
• Urumqi
Turfan
Gansu Province
Qinghai Province

Turfan (Xinjiang)

A basin of flame, grapes, and culture

LOCATION
Situated in the east of the Xinjiang Autonomous Region, Turfan has Tianshan Mountain to the north, and is not far away from Urumqi, the capital city of the region.

CLIMATE
Known as the Land of Flame, Turfan is the place that has the highest temperatures in the whole country. From June to August its average temperature reaches over 100.4°F (38°C).

OF SPECIAL INTEREST
Turfan has striking geographical characteristics. Its unusual features are seldom seen elsewhere.

MAIN ATTRACTIONS
Jiaohe ancient town, Gaochang ancient town, the Qianfu Grotto at Bozikelike, the Kanierjing wells, Flame Mountain, the grape valley, Aiding Lake, and the Zero Point landmark.

Turfan prides itself on having the sweetest grapes and the most beautiful girls. It is the land of flame, wind, desert, and oasis as well.

Turfan, which means "the land of abundant resources" in Turkish, is situated between Tianshan Mountain and the Takalamakan Desert. It is indicative of western China on account of its unique natural environment and colorful local customs.

Situated on the ancient Silk Road, it is an important town that links Xinjiang Autonomous Region with the hinterland of the country, Central Asia, and Europe. Turfan used to be one of the military, political, and economic centers of western China.

Turfan has an annual rainfall of only 0.6 inches (16mm), with evaporation amounting to 11.8 in (300mm). Moreover, it has drastic temperate changes within a single day. As the saying goes, "You put on a fur coat in the morning, then you have to wear a shirt at noon." Perched in the Tulufan basin, the town has a rich reserve of underground water, which makes it possible to grow fruits such as grapes and watermelons in large quantities. These fruits have a very high content of sugar, thanks to the dry climate. Renowned as the land of grapes, the town is the main producer of the seedless white grape, famous both at home and abroad. With their green

color they are a distinctive and excellent local product.

In the town a special street has been constructed so that tourists may pick their own grapes and enjoy the atmosphere of gathering the fruit. The whole street is a sea of colors; grapes are one of the pillars of the local economy.

The city is on a terraced area. It is positioned on a 13,000 ft (4000m) plateau in the north, on 3250 ft (1000m) hilly land in the west, the south and the east, and also on the Gobi Desert and a plain with an altitude of less than 1300 ft (400m). The lowest section is 508 ft (155m) below sea level. What is more, centered round Aiding Lake, the Turfan basin has three circular belts: the plain oasis, the Gobi, and the snow-capped ridge.

In addition to the variety of fruits and the dramatic geography, Turfan boasts 14 cultural relics of significance at regional and state level. The famous historical sites include the fresco in the Qianfu Grottoes, the Athtana ancient tombs, and the Islamic Sugong Pagoda of the Qing dynasty. The Flame Mountain depicted in the well-known classic novel *The Journey to the West* is located in Turfan. What is more, the spectacular Kanierjing well system, a specialist irrigation project, is connected with the underground river here. This region has also attracted attention because of the large 24-million-year-old fossils found here. The local silk

and the ancient classical books recording important historical research attract widespread interest too.

Turfan boasts over 1100 Kanierjing wells, which run more than 312.5 miles (500km). These are part of the outstanding water system that makes the most of local water. The residents are able to use water conserved underground in the wells, a practice that reduces the loss of water by vaporization in this area with its very low rainfall. The longest well extends 5 miles (8km) and has as many as three hundred outlets. Imagine how extensive the amount of digging work involved was! The Kanierjing well is the spring of life in this city.

Turfan is a place where modern progress meets ancient civilization in a harmonious way. It is a fascinating place in western China, and a visit there will bring you many pleasant discoveries.

Harvest time for Turfan grapes (above)

The Flame Mountain in the Turfan basin (below, left)

A Kaníerjing well in Turfan (below, right)

Tianchi Lake (Xinjiang)

A tranquil lake crouching in towering mountains

Russia
Urumqi
Tianchi Lake

Xinjiang Uygur
Autonomous Region

LOCATION
Tianchi is located on Bodga peak in Xinjiang, 69 miles (110km) from Urumqi on the east.

CLIMATE
There is a temperate continental climate, with ample rainfall and snow. Weather conditions are quite unpredictable.

OF SPECIAL INTEREST
In the Tianshan mountain ranges the natural landscape consists of high mountains and a tranquil lake.

MAIN ATTRACTIONS
A cruise around the lake, Bodga peak, the view at sunrise on the Dingtian Rock, waterfalls in Xiaotianchi (Little Tianchi Lake), and so on.

Sprawling 1560 miles (2500km) in total length across Central Asia, the Tianshan mountain ranges serve as a natural demarcation line between the Tarim and Junggar basins. Tianchi Lake is located midway up the Bogda ice peak, which is part of the Tianshan ranges. A natural half-moon alpine lake, 6494 ft (1980m) above sea level, it is 11,155 ft (3400m) long, 4920 ft (1500m) wide, and 344 ft (105m) in the deepest place, and it covers an area of 1.9 square miles (4.9 square kilometers). The crystal-clear lake is encircled by lush green mountains covered with spruces and pines, while the snow-capped peaks are reflected in the lake below.

Tianchi was formerly known as Yaochi (Jade Lake). In Chinese myths, this was where the Peach of Immorality Gathering was hosted by the Queen Mother. The lake was named Tianchi during the Qing dynasty, when it was declared "the mirror for heaven and the lake for the immortals." Thawing snow from high mountains feeds the lake that plunges to more than 33 ft (10m) in its deepest place, and lends it a clean, untouched look.

To the southeast of Tianchi is the towering Bogda peak (meaning Peak of Holy Spirit or Heavenly Peak in Mongolian), 17,864 ft (5445m) above sea level, with one peak on each side of the Bogda peak. Looking up from Tianchi Lake, you will see three peaks standing side by side, like a huge penholder that thrusts into the

thick clouds. The glaciers and snow on the peaks, flickering in silver light, and the blue and crystal-clear water of Tianchi add radiance and beauty to each other, and give rise to a spectacular natural landscape of high mountains and a tranquil lake.

Geologically a moraine lake, Tianchi gave birth to magnificent glaciers about 200,000 years ago, when global cooling occurred with the advent of the Ice Age. Glaciers, carrying gravel with them, rubbed fiercely against and eroded the valleys in their slow downward movement, resulting in diverse ice-eroded topographical forms. Tianchi Valley was turned into a huge ice-house. Later, as the global climate gradually warmed and glaciers

began to melt away, a lake became today's Tianchi Lake. Every summer, wild flowers bloom on the lush green grassland around the lake. Yaochi, the best scenic spot in the Tianshan Mountains, has become a paradise for fans of alpine skiing in the winter. Every year, as the frozen period approaches, athletes from all over the country gather here for training and contests on the frozen lake.

Scattered on the mountains around Tianchi are specimens of the snow lotus (Saussurea involucrata). Snow chickens dwell above the snow line, while in the pine woods mushrooms and herbs such as dangshen (Codonopsis pilosula), Astragalus mongholicus, and Fritillaria thunbergii grow. Fauna of rare species can be found in the valleys, fish swim in the lake, and aquatic birds flock around. Glaciers shine on the peaks. All these define the Tianshan Mountains as a scenic place with outstanding charm.

A large-scale cluster of rock drawings were discovered in recent years in the Tianshan Mountains. It is considered to be the most outstanding rock art discovered so far. For the first time in China, rock drawings featuring birds, topographical maps, and horse-drawn carriages were found. Among them there were a large number of drawings of birds in lines, carved using stones. Other rock drawings were made by chiseling or rubbing. Rock drawings are quite rare in China. It was estimated, on the evidence of the shape of the carriages in the

drawings, that they were made about three thousand years ago. The discovery of this cluster of rock art was significant in that it was possible to identify the period of time in history when the drawings were made. In addition, archeologists excavated, about 3 miles (5km) west of the rock, drawings and ceramic pieces from the Neolithic Age.

Mount Tianshan and the Tianchi Lake scenic area is a state-level forest park and has been proclaimed by UNESCO as the Bogeda Biosphere Reserve.

The enchanting winter scenery of Tianchi Lake in the Tianshan mountain range (above)

A distant view of the lush green forests on Tianshan Mountain (below)

Shangri-la County (Yunnan)

A dust-free magic land in Yunnan

Instead of being simply a part of Yunnan province, Shangri-la county is really a secret place enclosed since ancient times. Its mysteries may bring you fantasy and wonder. A painter says that each inch of this land will serve as the subject matter of a painting. Then a poet comments that each flower grown here is a poem. Finally, a musician concludes that its every river may produce a melody. As a result, any immortal that is moved by the land is happy to regard Shangri-la as his own home.

Yunnan is the only province in the country with three rivers running parallel to each other, and Shangri-la is perched on the area where these rivers roar forward day and night. Its enchanting natural scenery makes a deep impression on tourists, who often stand and marvel at this paradise on earth.

Situated on the Zhongdian Plateau, Napahai Lake and Bitahai Lake are the most beautiful lakes in Shangri-la. In May, when the sea of azaleas along the lakes is in full blossom, the fallen petals are scattered and drift in the breeze. They settle on the water and become an attraction to the fish. Consequently, tourists may enjoy the unique scene of the Fish in the Bitahai Lake intoxicated by fallen Azalea Petals.

Moreover, the hand of nature has produced the terraced field,

a miracle comparable with any in the world, which attracts numerous travelers from across the land and further afield. They may prefer to be called "pilgrims" rather than travelers since they take a long route to find the home for their souls in Shangri-la.

It is said that the biggest mystery may lie in the snow-capped Meili Mountain, which is regarded as a holy mountain by the Tibetan people. Up till now, no climber has ever conquered the mountain, in spite of all their painstaking efforts. Enshrouded in thick cloud or heavy mist all through the year, Meili Mountain has seldom lifted its veil to the local people. Even the few lucky witnesses find it difficult to describe how they feel about the mountain.

Lying at an altitude of more than 6560 ft (2000m), the Baishuitai scenic area is another attraction in Shangri-la. But there is a serpentine road running to Baishuitai. Looking upward, you may enjoy its very special geological feature. It is composed of calcium carbonate deposits in the water, which are then exposed to the sun for long periods. Eventually, the white sedimentation piles up, one layer upon another, resulting in the outlandish geology. Its surface shines brilliantly in the sun.

In Shangri-la there are many other scenic spots and historical sites. They include the Buddhist temple, Gedansongzanlin Temple, Dabao Temple, No. 1 Bay on the Yangtze River, and the Xiage hot spring.

What is more, tourists may have the opportunity to enjoy the extensive azalea bushes in full bloom, the pastoral melodies to be heard on the prairie, and the uncontaminated snowmelt water from the high snow-bound mountains.

Tibetan Buddhism is the main religion in this area. A subdivision of the main stream of the religion, it has a good many sections that flourish alongside each other and attract different groups of local believers.

Shangri-la, paradise on earth (above)

Ice peaks under clouds, Shangri-la (below, left)

The golden roof of an ancient temple in Shangri-la (below, right)

Xishuangbanna (Yunnan)

A golden phoenix in tropical rainforests

A typical scene in Xishuangbanna (below, left)

Xishuangbanna's Tropical Botanical Garden (above, left)

A pretty resident of Xishuangbanna (below, center)

Xishuangbanna Water-sprinkling Festival (below, right)

Xishuangbanna means "a wonderland of promises" in the language of the Dai. One of the very few precious lands of lush rainforests in China, Xishuangbanna is noted throughout the world for its spectacular natural landscape of tropical rainforests as well as for the unique lifestyles and customs observed by the minority groups that live there. It is also the only oasis to be found further north than the Tropic of Cancer.

Stepping into Xishuangbanna region, visitors feel as though they are immersed in a world of thick greenness, consisting of virgin forests, rubber plantations, banana plantations, tea plants, and trees of luxuriant greenness with twisted roots and gnarled branches. As one of the regions in China that has the most densely distributed and richest biodiversity, it has enjoyed the reputation of being "a floral kingdom" and "a kingdom of herbs." In the 115,316 acres (46,666 hectares) of wild forests stretching far and wide, there are over 20,000 species of flora, 5000 of which are of the highest grade. About three hundred are indigenous, rare, or surviving species.

Thus this is also referred to as the "archive of floral genes." These species, having survived for over a million years, are also referred to as "living fossils." The rich vegetation and moderate climate have created an ideal environment for various animal species to prosper. So far, Xishuangbanna has been identified as having almost 400 bird species, 67 animal species, and 1437 insect species. Among them, species like the Asian elephant, bald eagle, and leopard are under protection. Species such as the slow loris and apes are under first-degree state

protection. Besides, it has a number of rare mammal species such as goanna, python, and so on, earning itself another title, that of "kingdom of animals." This region accommodates a large peacock population and is hence also known as "home to peacocks." With their elegant style and dazzling colors, peacocks symbolize good luck, beauty, and happiness to the Dai people. No wonder almost every young girl of Dai is capable of peacock dancing. The peacock park in Jinghong city has become the largest breeding ground for peacocks in Asia.

Xishuangbanna is where the Dai people live in compact communities. In Banna visitors will be impressed by the thick bamboo woods and the Dai bamboo houses in the woods. The bamboo houses look like peacocks boasting their dazzling plumage, or like young Dai girls performing the peacock dance with pride.

The typical Dai bamboo house is a two-story elevated building with railings. In order to avoid the damp earth, the lower floor is not intended for people to live in but for raising domestic animals. The inhabitants of the house live on the upper floor, which is the center of the building. The living room is usually at the entrance, where the wooden ladder from the ground stops. At the center of the living room is a large piece of bamboo matting on which people eat, rest, or receive guests. Outside the living room, there is a balcony and a corridor where odds and ends such as bamboo tubes and water tanks are stored, or where the Dai women do some needlework. There is a stove in the living room on which an iron rack is placed for pots and kettles. Next to the living room is the bedroom, also with bamboo matting on the floor. The bamboo house is usually spacious and well ventilated, perfectly adapted to the humid and rainy climate of the region. The Dai people live in these bamboo houses, eating rice and drinking wine from bamboo tubes. Sometimes the Dai girls, with trim figures and long hair, perform the peacock dance, striking graceful postures for their audience.

LOCATION
Xishuangbanna is located on the southern tip of Yunnan province. Jinghong, the capital city, is 430 miles (692km) away from Kunming, the capital city of Yunnan province.

CLIMATE
Conditions are tropical and monsoonal with plentiful sunshine and rainfall, and an annual average temperature of 69°F (21°C).

OF SPECIAL INTEREST
A natural landscape of tropical rainforests, this is home to the Dai people who have a unique lifestyle and customs.

MAIN ATTRACTIONS
Tropical Botanical Garden, Virgin Forest Park, Ganlanba (olive plain), Ethnic Culture Park, Park of the Dai Ethnic Culture, Wild Elephants Valley, and so on.

Heilongjiang Province

Jilin Province

● Changchun

Mount Changbaishan

Liaoning Province

Korea

Mount Changbaishan (Jilin)
A dreamland of spectacular peaks and lakes

LOCATION
Changbaishan is located in Baishan city in the southeast of Jilin province.

CLIMATE
The winter is long and cold, while summer is short and cool. Weather conditions are unpredictable. The annual average temperature varies between 19.4°F (-7°C) and 37.4°F (3°C).

OF SPECIAL INTEREST
This is a state-level forest nature reserve with mixed mountain, forest, and river scenery, and it is rich in natural resources.

MAIN ATTRACTIONS
Tianchi Lake, Changbai Waterfall, hot springs, Underground Forest, Heifeng Mouth (mouth of Black Wind), Grand Canyon, alpine ski fields, and so on.

Tianchi Lake, Mount Changbaishan, in spring (below, right)

The snowscape of Mount Changbaishan (top)

A white birch tree in fall on Mount Changbaishan (below, left)

"White Mountain and Black Water" is another name for northeast China. Black Water refers to the Black Dragon River and White Mountain stands for the Changbai mountain ranges in the three northeastern provinces of China. While the water in the Black Dragon River is not at all black, the mountain ranges are truly white. Mount Changbaishan is white all year long, partly because of the pumice stones that cover its slopes. The whiteness is also often caused by snow, which covers the peaks for as long as nine months every year, wrapping the mountain in silver white and making it look pure and pristine.

It is said that the place where the mountain is now was an ocean hundreds of millions of years ago. Then volcanic eruptions occurred. In the process of thousands of changes, nature put in this place a huge mountain instead.

Changbaishan covers an area of 3090 square miles (8000 square kilometers), with its main peak 9019 ft (2749m) above sea level, and it has altogether 16 peaks above 8200 ft (2500m). Those peaks are in various shapes, effectively forming a scroll of Chinese painting featuring stately and graceful, steep and sprawling peaks. Starting from the mountain foot, four landscape zones and different floral types were formed as the altitude rose from the temperate zone to the frigid zone, all described in the saying: "there are four seasons within a mountain and weather varies within a distance of ten *li*." Going up from the mountain foot, you would first come across coniferous forests with tall trees and thick shrubs. Gradually the conifers become smaller and disappear. As you climb above 6560 ft (2000m), you come to the lichen area, where only azaleas grow. If you are visiting in June, you will see enormous azaleas, bright and wild, in full bloom.

Changbaishan is a dormant volcano, and it is surrounded by more than a hundred other volcanoes. The largest crater is 8530 ft (2600m) above sea level, measuring 3 miles (5km) in diameter and 2625 ft (800m) in depth. According to historical data, it has erupted three times since the sixteenth century, and the latest eruption occurred over three hundred years ago. Trees turn the mountain luxuriantly green, and they even grow inside the crater where magma bubbled out, transforming it into an underground grove or a sea of forests on the valley floor of pines and cypresses in thick green. What would take your breath away is the King Korean pine near Tianchi Lake. It takes three people to stand with their arms stretched to embrace this 480-year-old pine that has witnessed the three volcanic eruptions. Having weathered natural disasters without withering away, this pine has become a living emblem of Changbaishan.

The most famous scenic spot in Changbaishan is Tianchi Lake – a crater lake, blue and tranquil, that perches on top of the mountain as a result of the tumultuous volcanic activity. The lake is 7182 ft (2189m) above sea level, so high that from below it looks as if it is hanging up in the sky, hence

its name of Tianchi Lake (Heavenly Lake). The lake is hemmed in by mountains like a hidden gem. The sun shows up now and then behind drifting clouds and shines through mists, brightening or dimming the peaks around the lake apparently as it wills. The lake covers an area of 3.86 square miles (10 square kilometers) and the deepest place measures 1224 ft (373m). The water in the lake is blue and clear all year round. Though strong winds are quite common on the mountain top, the tranquility of the lake is not at all disturbed and the unruffled water continues to reflect the peaks around. However, finding a fine day when this view is attainable does not come easily, owing to the capricious weather conditions caused by the high altitude. When it is sunny and clear at the foot of the mountain, you may come to the top only to find that it has turned to rain there, with clouds and mists all around, obscuring the lake and lending it a foggy yet beautiful grandeur.

While Tianchi Lake represents beauty in tranquility, the waterfalls in Changbaishan are symbols of power. Leaking from a gap on the north of Tianchi Lake, streams begin to form the Chencuo River on the cliffs above, 6560 ft (2000m) high. After flowing 4100 ft (1250m), the river gushes out from the mountain top and forms a waterfall over 197 ft (60m) high. The cascading waterfall seems like a suspended river whose deafening roars may be heard miles away. The waterfall is considered the most spectacular sight in Changbaishan. Besides this one, a number of smaller waterfalls in various shapes have been formed around Tianchi. Among them, some are extensive and magnificent while others are smaller and more graceful.

A group of hot springs varying in size bring yet another surprise to visitors. Some are as big as a bowl while others are as small as a finger. These hot springs are scattered in an area of 10,800 square feet (1000 square meters) where spring water flows forth with a temperature up to 140°F (60°C). The springs here glitter in different colors. The rising steam bathes the stones below the springs and adds to them radiant hues of golden yellow, dark blue, bright red, and jade green.

Qinghai Lake (Qinghai)

A mirror embedded in high mountains

LOCATION
Qinghai Lake is located on the Qinghai-Tibet Plateau, 94 miles (150km) from Xining, the capital city.

CLIMATE
The climate is continental and highland, with low temperatures, scarce rainfall, and plenty of sunshine.

OF SPECIAL INTEREST
There is alpine lake scenery.

MAIN ATTRACTIONS
Bird Island, Mount Riyue (Sun and Moon Mountain), and so on.

Qinghai Lake, with clear water and numerous birds, is the largest inland saltwater lake in China. Formerly named the Western Sea, it is called "Koko Nor" in Mongolian, which means blue sea, and "Tso Ngonpo" in Tibetan, standing for blue lake. The lake is hemmed in by four big mountains in four directions – the majestic Mount Datong to the north, the towering Mount Riyue to the east, the undulating Mount South of Qinghai in the south, and the steep Mount Xiangpi in the west. The four mountains provide a natural defense that embraces the Qinghai Lake. Miles of grasslands sprawl from the foot of the mountains to the banks of the lake. Qinghai Lake is just like a huge gem embedded between mountains and grasslands, giving rise to a magnificent landscape that integrates mountains, lake, and grasslands.

The four seasons at Qinghai Lake present totally different views. In summer and fall, both mountains and grasslands are covered in lush green and dotted with wild flowers in various colors. A pastoral picture can be seen everywhere, with yaks and goats roaming freely, as described in the famous folk lyrics: "grasses bend their heads in a breeze, only to expose cattle and sheep grazing." In a breeze, the wheat grown on the banks of the lake waves and the yellow flowers of vegetables shine in the sunlight. Small waves are formed on Qinghai Lake, rippling toward the horizon in the far distance. In cold winter, the lake's surface is frozen like silver white jade glittering under the sunshine.

The lake covers an area of 1720 square miles (4456 square kilometers) and is over 225 miles (360km) in circumference, more than twice as big as the famous Tai Lake. With a distance from east to west longer

than the distance between north and south, the lake is roughly oval shape and looks at first glance like a wide aspen leaf. With an average depth of over 62 ft (19m), the lake plunges to 92 ft (28m) in its deepest place. Its surface is 10,696 ft (3260m) above sea level, higher than the two mountains of Taishan put together. Even under the blazing sun in hot summer, the average temperature in the daytime does not exceed 59°F (15°C), making the place an ideal place as a summer resort.

Bird Island on the west of Qinghai Lake is indeed fascinating. The island, 33 ft (10m) above the lake, is known as the "kingdom of birds." The best time to visit it is in late spring and early summer, when hundreds of thousands of birds, some of rare species, flock to the island, and then engage themselves in building their nests all over the land. White or green eggs, or brown ones with dots, are scattered about. As long as a suitable spot is identified, the female bird hatches her eggs in the nest while the male bird watches closely nearby. If disturbed, tens of thousands of birds are startled into taking a sudden flight, blurring the sky and making calls and twitters that can be heard far away. Birds' droppings pour down like rain. It is a rare and spectacular scene. Before winter comes, most of the birds have migrated to warmer places, leaving behind swans, wild ducks, and larks on the lake. With its population depleted, the lake offers a different yet no less charming view.

In the scenic area of Qinghai Lake, there are many historical and cultural relics on the famous ancient path linking the lands of the Tang dynasty and Tibet, as well as on the roads that converge to make the famous Silk Road. About 1300 years ago, Princess Wencheng of the Tang dynasty made her way through the area to Tibet to marry. Further back, in ancient times, this was an important place for the breeding of cattle, horses, and goats. The horses from Qinghai Lake were quite widely known, as the Horses of Qin, during the Period of Spring and Autumn and the Period of Warring States. Later in the Sui and Tang dynasties, the horses of Qinghai Lake were cross-bred with other species such as the Wusun horse and Xuehan horse to improve their performance, giving birth to a refined hybrid horse species with unique characteristics. They were famous not only for their handsome looks but also for their competence in war.

A distant view of Qinghai Lake (below, left)

Groups of wild birds at Qinghai Lake, by the shore (center, right)

Offering a sacrifice to the Qinghai Lake (below, right)

Lijiang River (Guangxi)
Passionate and dreamlike water

Sailing down the winding Lijiang River, you might suddenly think of the verses written by He Jingzhi, a modern poet of China: "Gods in clouds, Immortals in fogs, Divine posture of Mountains in Guilin! So passionate, and so dreamlike, You waters of Lijiang!" Xu Xiake, a traveler of the Ming dynasty, once took a journey from Guilin to Yangshuo. Greatly fascinated by what he saw, he said, "Here is a world of green lotus and jade bamboo." By boat, one can fully enjoy the graceful and touching landscape of Lijiang River.

Lijiang River is part of the Zhujiang water system, originating in the Cat Mountain (Maoer Shan) of Xinan county, to the north of Guilin city. Within the boundaries of Xinan county there is a canal that was dug in the Qing dynasty. The first one of its kind in China, it is called the Xinanling Canal. It is at this point that the Xiangjiang River runs northward, while the Lijiang runs southward. Called "the diverging point of Xiang and Li," the Lijiang River gets its name from this phenomenon. *Li* in Chinese also means "lucid" and "transparent." The Lijiang River is like a sparkling, sinuous jade band, there being shallows at every bend. Some have counted the number of shoals in the river from Guilin to Yangshuo. They amount to 3605 in the 52 miles (83km) of waterway. The water at both ends of each shoal is shallow, producing a gurgling sound as it flows – like celestial music in a heavenly palace.

The visitor can take a boat down from Guilin to Yangshuo to enjoy the 52 miles (83km) of river landscape of Lijiang River. This is a typical area of karst topography. Here you can see the numerous ridges and peaks, and their reflections in the ever flowing blue water. It is like making your way through a hundred-mile (160 km) long spectacular art gallery. The reflections have their own special charm, hazy and swaying. The mountains in the water seem clear compared with the real ones, and it seems as though they flow together with the water. When tourists go boating on the ever winding Lijiang River, they can enjoy the landscape from different angles, each of which presents a picturesque scene. On arriving at the Zhulin scenic point, see along the precipices the stalactites hang down from above, gigantic as well as imposing, looking like dragons bending down and drinking the water. After that you come to Yangdi scenic point, and there you can see the lofty mountains and the floating clouds. Yangdi is a place that offers urbanites the opportunity to enjoy moments of leisure and to experience a carefree state of mind.

In the imposing mountainous chain, there is a set of eight peaks that very much resemble the Eight Immortals of ancient Chinese myth. Further on, there is another peak coming up, long and big, across the Lijiang River. It has the appearance of a carp, and on its back stands a small hill somewhat like a fin. Local people call it "Carp going against the River." Traveling along the Lijiang River, tourists not only appreciate the beautiful mountains, they also relish the roaring waterfalls, the flowing streams, the dangerous shoals, and the bamboo forests.

The Paintings Hill is a sheer cliff that features shades of different colors. Seen from a distance, the precipice seems to present a picture with faintly discernible horses. Tourists are invited to count the number of horses. It seems that no one is able to give the exact answer.

When traveling by boat along the Lijiang River, you will feel as if the scenery is sliding by too swiftly to allow you to catch sight of everything you want to see. Eventually you reach your destination, Yangshuo. As the old saying goes, "Guilin's landscapes are the finest under heaven, but Yangshuo's landscapes are even finer than Guilin's." From the Green Lotus peak (Bilian Feng), it's possible to get a bird's eye view of Lijiang River, embracing the Lijiang scenery. At Yangshuo, you seem to draw to a perfect stop on your journey. Halfway up the Green Lotus peak, there is a scenic path. Along this path, you can enjoy the unique landscape of Yangshuo, as well as the scattering of farmhouses and the ancient carvings on the precipices. There is also an ancient ferry, named the Banyan Shade Ancient Ferry, which is a good place from which to appreciate the scenery nearby. The banyan tree is imposing, as it is more than a thousand years old. It is several arms' lengths in circumference and its roots cross each other on the ground, offering dark shade for those beneath.

LOCATION
Lijiang lies between Guilin and Yangshuo, in Guangxi province.

CLIMATE
The area belongs to the mid-Asian tropical moist monsoon climate. It is temperate with plentiful rainfall. There is a saying about it: "Three winters without snow, four seasons with flowers throughout."

OF SPECIAL INTEREST
With its elegant mountains and charming waters, this is typical karst topography.

MAIN ATTRACTIONS
Dragons playing with Water, the Gongs and Drums Yuanyang shoal, Elephant Trunk Hill, Paintings Hill, Jianshan carvings, and many more.

Scenery of Xingping, recognized as the most beautiful part of the Lijiang River (left)

Huangbu shoal (Yellow Cloth shoal), Lijiang River (below, right)

The West Lake (Zhejiang)
Ten great views to delight your eyes

LOCATION
The geographical position is in the southeast of China, specifically the southern part of the Yangtze delta. The West Lake is west of Hangzhou.

CLIMATE
This is a temperate and moist area. March, April, September, and October are the best seasons to visit.

OF SPECIAL INTEREST
The reputation of West Lake is that of "Paradise in the World." It is the key tourist city and the most famous city for history and culture.

MAIN ATTRACTIONS
Su Causeway, Bai Causeway, Lingyin Temple, and Hubin Walk. Also the scenes depicted in Three Pools mirroring the Moon, Lotus in a Breeze at Qu Courtyard, Viewing Fish at Flowery Harbor, Sunset at Thunder Peak Pagoda, Sunset at Thunder Peak Pagoda, and Listening to Orioles singing in Willows.

If we say that Hangzhou features the West Lake, then West Lake features the Ten Views. "The Ten Views of West Lake" is the title of a series of landscape paintings produced by artists of the Southern Song Imperial Art Academy. They shone a spotlight on the essence of West Lake, and since then the lake has attracted artistic interest that can never be lost.

Spring Dawn by Su Causeway: This painting shows a long causeway in the middle of the lake, with willows and six picturesque bridges crossing intermittently and linking the causeway. Spring dawn is the best time to appreciate the charm of this scene. Then a variety of fresh flowers are in full bloom and birds of unfamiliar species sing and fly among the green twigs.

Lotus in a Breeze at Qu Courtyard: The courtyard used to be the imperial brewery of the Song dynasty. *Qu* in Chinese refers to the yeast used in making wine. When the lotus is in full bloom, the air is full of fragrance, a mixture of the smell of the yeast and the lotus flowers. The tranquil water of the lake, the red and green touches here and there, all shine under the sun.

Three Pools mirroring the Moon shows an excellent place to enjoy the full moon. A few years ago, someone had a whim to confirm that the moon shines through the stone pagodas standing in the middle of the lake. As it happens, in the bright

moonlight – with the shaky shadows of the pagoda and the glistening reflection of the water – the dim surroundings themselves lead the visitor to associations with Buddhism.

Autumn Moon on the Calm Lake: Admiring the moon on the lake is a common enough esthetic experience in relation to any inland water, but here autumn is the unique attraction. When the pure water and the clear moon are put together during this season on a vast expanse of water, how relaxed and happy the scene makes the viewer.

Two Peaks piercing the Clouds: This is the only mountain scene in the Ten Views series. There are two hills by West Lake, North Hill and South Hill. On their tops two ancient pagodas were built in the Southern Song dynasty. They collapsed during the Qing dynasty. Of course, the peaks are still there, the clouds and the rain are still there, and it is still worth a visit.

Listening to Orioles singing in Willows: This is a spot by the lake with excellent views. There used to be an imperial garden named the Ju Jing Garden, which wound alongside the lake toward Qiantang Gate, with willows waving all the way. Just as a poet wrote, "Willows outside Yongjin Gate, In three days comes the green shade. Carry a twig to show, The Spring would never wait for you."

Viewing Fish at Flowery Harbor: At the time of the Southern Song dynasty, Lu Garden was an ideal place to appreciate unusual flowers and fish. In the past, there used to be a brook named Flowery Harbor here, flowing from the nearby Hua-jia Hill (Flower House Hill) into the lake. Now it's hard for us to find any trace of the brook.

Sunset at Thunder Peak Pagoda: This scene acquired its name from Xizhao Hill (Sunset Hill) on the southern bank of the lake, only a slight elevation of the land in reality. The Emperor Wu Yue built a pagoda for his favorite concubine here and bestowed on it the title of "Thunder Peak Pagoda." At sunset, the pagoda creates a silhouette against the dusk, adding a sense of desolation to the delicate lake scene.

Late Bell at Nanping Hill refers to the tolling of the bell and the poetic atmosphere of Jingsi Temple on the northern foot of Nanping Hill. The title first appeared in the paintings of Zhang Zeduan, a famous artist of the Song Dynasty. It was perhaps the earliest of the Ten Views, and therefore is a well-known title.

The series is not just concerned with the natural scenery. When you recite the Ten Views titles in a leisurely way, or take a walk along any of the settings for the Ten Views, you cannot but feel the culture. All the year round you touch and you feel, from deep down calmness, the poetic rhythm and elegance as well as the cultural beauty accumulated here, generation after generation.

Summer: Lotus in a Breeze at Qu Courtyard (above)

Winter: Remnant of Melting Snow at Broken Bridge (below)

Takelamagan Desert (Xinjiang)

The sound of the camel bell in the desert

The Takelamagan Desert is situated in the center of the Talimu basin of Xinjiang Uygur Autonomous Region (left)

Camel caravan in the Takelamagan Desert (above, right)

Ruins of ancient Milan city, in the Takelamagan Desert (above, center)

Situated in the center of the Talimu basin of Xinjiang Uygur Autonomous Region, the Takelamagan Desert covers an area of 130,347 square miles (337,600 square kilometers), and is about 625 miles (1000km) from east to west and about 250 miles (400km) from north to south. The desert, dubbed "a place of no return" or "the sea of death" by the local Uygur people, now ranks as the second largest in the world and has fostered lots of legends and wonderful sights.

Once upon a time, the local people longed for the melting snow from Mount Tianshan and Mount Kunlun to be used to irrigate the arid Talimu basin. A kind-hearted god, who had two treasures to hand – a golden ax and a golden key – was moved by the sincere wish of the locals and decided to give the ax to the Kazaks and the key to the Uygurs. Originally it was intended to have Mount Aertai cleft by the ax in order to draw its clean water out, and to open up the precious deposits of the Talimu basin by using the key. Unfortunately, the golden key was lost by Magesha, the god's youngest daughter, and the god was so furious that he locked her up in the Talimu basin. From then on, the basin's center became the Takelamagan Desert, and it has remained so til this day.

A desert is usually both enchanting and awesome. On the one hand, it can create a magnificent scene, as in a beautiful sunset. On the other hand, people may be frightened by the fact that a village can be buried under sand dunes overnight, and thus disappear with the wind. For travelers, choosing desert means choosing a challenge, and at the same time it also entails enjoying victory and devoting effort to a cause. It has nothing to do

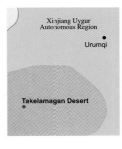

Xinjiang Uygur
Autonomous Region

Urumqi

Takelamagan Desert

LOCATION
Situated in the center of the Talimu basin, Xinjiang Uygur Autonomous Region, and covering an area of 130,347 square miles (337,600 square kilometers). It is about 625 miles (1000km) from east to west and about 250 miles (400km) from north to south.

CLIMATE
The golden season for crossing the Takelamagan Desert is during the 20 days or so between late October and mid-November, as the leaves of the Populus diversifolia in the Talimu basin turn to gold. Visitors will gain a rich and colorful personal experience by walking along the picturesque Hetian River at this time.

OF SPECIAL INTEREST
Large moving dunes may be as high as 984 ft (300m), and there are complex and varied types of dunes, some shaped like giant dragons resting on the sand.

MAIN ATTRACTIONS
The Takelamagan boasts a magnificent history and culture based on the ancient Silk Road, which runs across the southern end. According to archeological data, there are a number of ancient sites deep in the desert that once enjoyed prosperity but are now forgotten or obscure.

with anything soft and gentle, and only when standing on the type of land that is part of it could you really appreciate its breadth and awesome features.

After all, desert has its own special way of expressing life – a river, a grove of *Populus diversifolia* trees perhaps. To the Takelamagan Desert, the Hetian River is its eyes and the *Populus diversifolia* trees its beard.

The Hetian River is the only river that has any life in the Takelamagan Desert. It originates on Mount Kunlun, winds down southward via the two towns of Hetian and Muyu, and then turns north into the depths of the Takelamagan, eventually vanishing into the boundless desert. All year round, the Hetian River looks like a river only when the snowfall from Mount Kunlun melts in summer. Sometimes it is affected by flooding even in such a dry area as the Takela-

magan. Nevertheless, the Hetian River will run dry as soon as summer slips by.

It is the Hetian River that makes it possible for explorers and backpackers to experience walking on foot through the whole of the Takelamagan. Prior to the construction of the cross-desert highway, 90 percent of the cross-journey had been performed along this very river.

The *Populus diversifolia* groves of Takelamagan, planted in its desert park, are about 50 miles (80km) away from Taixian county and located in the core area of Talimu's Populus Diversifolia Reserve. The park features a variety of colors: green trees, clear blue river, and clear blue sky – just like a colorful Chinese ink and wash painting. When fall comes, the color will vary from yellowish green at the beginning to golden yellow later on. Looking into the distance from high

ground, you will notice that the Talimu River is running tortuously nearby to form numerous branches, among which are some scattered lakes surrounded by the *Populus diversifolia* groves. They stretch out along the river and into the far horizon. The view is spectacular.

Desert land is characterized by impressiveness and fluctuation. As for the Takelamagan, though it does not have features that are as intriguing as Egypt's pyramids, nor as sweet as Tulufan's grapes, it indeed has a vast stretch of sand that blows dust in gentle strokes. Because of the loneliness and stimulation that come from standing on a place unmarked on the map, you can expect to be fascinated.

Three Gorges (in Sichuan, Chongqing, and Hubei)

Majestic gorges on the Yangtze River

As the saying goes, "Qutang Gorge is stately, while Wuxia is elegant and Xiling risky."

Since ancient times, the countryside around the Yangtze River Three Gorges has been known as "Four Hundred Li Art Gallery." Here is a continuous view of landscapes, impressive and ever changing, a combination of vigor and charm.

The Yangtze River Gorges start at Baidi city, Fengjie county in Chongqing, and extend 121 miles (193km), arrogantly extending to Nanjinguan, Yichang city, in Hubei province. During its course, it crosses the Wushan mountain range that runs from south to north and passes through numerous deep valleys with torrents sweeping down uncontrollably.

When traveling downstream by boat, with sheer precipices on both sides sliding by and roaring water like galloping horses under their feet, travelers may experience some fear, but only the boatmen who have worked on the river for many years can fully understand the risk involved. A boatman's song that circulates around Xiling Gorge – which is characterized by roaring torrents and numerous reefs and shoals – goes like this:

"Terrible it is when the boat is traveling past Xiling George; Sweating all over with every tune, Courage called up with every tune."

When you hear this song, you realize the challenge involved in undertaking the Yangtze River voyage.

Of the Three Gorges, the Wuxia Gorge is the quietest section. It has 12 peaks, one of which is Shennu peak. On the north bank, a stone pillar stands high, with giant and lofty peaks gathering and acting as escorts all around, and clouds and mists veiling and unveiling the scene by day and night. This is the Shennu (Fairy Girl) peak. It is said that the Fairy Girl meets the king of Chu at Gaotang, and during that time there are clouds in the morning and rain in the evening. The story adds glamour to the mystery of the scenery. Three Gorges has three singular features: the Overhanging Tombs, the Plank Roads along the Cliffs, and the stone carvings. These are the essence of the culture of the Three Gorges.

The Plank Roads were built on the cliffs along the Qutang Gorge. There are two kinds of plank roads: wooden ones and stone ones. To construct the former, workmen fixed wooded pegs into the cliff, then laid wooden boards on them. For the latter, they dug roads directly along the cliffs. Many people sacrificed their lives to build the roads.

The Overhanging Tombs are said to have connections with the Ba people who used to live in the Three Gorges areas. They were descended from the Tibeto-Burman people. Coming from Hanshui and the upper streams of the Yellow River, moving continuously to the east and west of the Yangtze River and known for their strength and bravery, they played an active part in the history of this area during the sixteenth century BC. They planted paddy rice and wheat along both banks and they created a civilization as brilliant as that of the Yellow River. They disappeared into history, which is something of a mystery to anthropologists.

As well as the Ba, there was the Chu culture. Chu people practiced wizardry. The legend of the Wushan Fairy Girl was the natural development of this tradition. It seems to be the source of the mythological culture that features worship of maternity.

There are so many stories about the Yangtze River Gorges that have been passed down from generation to generation. An example is Qu Yuan, whose motherland was in the region of the Yangtze River. Wang Zhaojun, a famous beauty in the Han dynasty, once lived in the upper reaches of the Xiangxi River, at the west end of Xiling Gorge. A well on the northern bank of Qutang Gorge in Yufu county is called Baidi (White King) city, owing to the fact that white fog is forever rising from the well.

Rain is plentiful in this region. Clouds gather in the evening and it begins to rain in the dead of the night. The rain falls, pitter-pattering on the roofs, on the palm leaves, leaving sadness in the hearts of the poets. Li Shangying (Tang dynasty) once wrote, "Asked when to return, I can only say there is no certainty. Around Ba mountain area, the evening rains are overflowing the autumn ponds." There are many others, such as Li Bai and Du Fu, who left poetic stories behind them, too.

LOCATION
The Yangtze River Three Gorges is the general term for Qutang Gorge, Wuxia Gorge, and Xiling Gorge. It starts in the west at Baidi city, in Fengjie county of Chongqing province, and extends 6 miles (10km) to Nanjinguan, Yichang City in Hubei province. People usually refer it to it as the Big Three Gorges.

CLIMATE
There is a moist subtropical climate, obviously influenced by the topographical features. The annual average temperature is 65 °F (18.4 °C), coldest in January when the average temperature is 44.78 °F (7.10 °C) and hottest in July, with an average temperature of 84.74°F (29.30°C).

OF SPECIAL INTEREST
The Yangtze River Three Gorges is the most attractive section of the landscape gallery along the Yangtze River.

MAIN ATTRACTIONS
Besides the Three Gorges, Ghost City in Fengdu and the so-called Small Three Gorges are also worth a visit.

The Qutang Gorge (left)

The elegant Wushan Mountain in the clouds (below, center)

The Quyuan Temple at Zigui (below, right)

Hailuo Gully in Mount Gongga (Sichuan)

A landscape filled with many wonders

Hailuo Gully is an official scenic zone. The zone straddles Luding, Kangding, and Jiulong, the three counties of Ganzi Tibetan Autonomous Prefecture, and covers an area of 3,860 square miles (10,000 square kilometers). It consists of scenic places around Mount Gongga such as Hailuo Gully, Muge Lake, the Wuxu Sea, the southern slopes of Mount Gongga, and so on.

In Mount Gongga there are over ten alpine lakes, clear and pristine, at the foot of glaciers or deep in the forests. In the scenic zone a primitive ecological environment with diverse species of flora have been preserved – 4880 distinct species have been identified. Over 20 fauna species are subject to first, second, or third level state protection. Besides this natural diversity, the temples of Tibetan Buddhism such as Gongga Temple and Tagong Temple open to the rich and extraordinary customs and culture of the Tibetan and Yi people.

Hailuo Gully is defined by three major features. First, there are the best views of the snow-capped peaks of Mount Gongga afforded at the Hailuo Gully, particularly the Golden peak and the Silver peak, both dazzling in the sunlight. Second, most of the glaciers in the world are located at a relatively higher altitude, but Hailuo Gully is known for its glaciers at relatively low altitudes – the lowest among glaciers of the same latitude. The lowest glacier in Hailuo Gully is only 9350 ft (2850m) above sea level and extends 4 miles (6km) into the virgin forests, demonstrating that it is possible for glaciers and forests to coexist here. The cascading glaciers turn the serene gully into a crystal palace with huge ice caves and precipitous ice bridges. The third feature of Haihuo Gully is that hot springs with a temperature as high as 194°F (90°C) keep bubbling up from this world of ice and snow. Visitors can take a bath in a hot spring amid glaciers or swim in a pool of hot spring water.

Hailuo Gully also accommodates an icefall, 3543 ft (1080m) high and 3610 ft (1100m) wide. It is the largest in China and peerless in the world. It is ten times as big as the famous Huangguoshu Falls. When an avalanche occurs, ice and snow roll down, thundering and overwhelming. Glacier movements result in glacier arches and faults, and there are various grotesque ice forms to be seen – such as ice pagodas, bridges, mushrooms, city gates, and so on. Hailuo Gully provides different and equally splendid views on sunny days and in moonlit nights.

On the way to Hailuo Gully, visitors can make a brief trip to Mount Paoma (Running Horses) in the outskirts of Kangding county. Here, every year, the festival of Yufou (Bathing the Buddha) is observed on April 8th of the lunar calendar which, according to legend, is the birthday of Sakyamuni, the founder of Buddhism. During the festival, horsemen of all ethnic groups gather for activities like horse racing. It is an exciting and impressive event that will be appreciated fully by visitors.

LOCATION
Mount Gongga is located in Luding, Kangding, and Jiulong, the three counties of Ganzi Tibetan Autonomous Prefecture.

CLIMATE
The climatic conditions of the Tropic, Temperate, and Frigid Zones prevail. They are influenced by monsoons that come in from the ocean along the river gullies. Rainfall is abundant, and it is often cloudy and foggy. Weather conditions vary rapidly.

OF SPECIAL INTEREST
This area boasts undulating mountains with snow-capped peaks, and there are a number of rare flora and fauna species as well as precious herbs.

MAIN ATTRACTIONS
Glaciers, Muge Lake, Wuxu Sea, Renzhong Sea, Bawang Sea, Mount Paoma, Gongga Temple, Tagong Temple, and so on.

The main ice peak of Hailuo Gully on Mount Gongga (center)

The virgin forests of Hailuo Gully, Mount Gongga (above, right)

The hot spring of No. 2 campsite of the scenic zone of Mount Gongga's Hailuo Gully (below, right)

Kanas Nature Reserve (Xinjiang)

A magical place with extraordinary beauty

Russia
Altay Mountains
Kanas Nature Reserve
Xinjiang Uygur Autonomous Region

Western China has, for ages, possessed a powerful mystique. From the biography of Faxian to The Journey to the West by the monk Xuan Zhuang, the quest to learn more about the west has never been quenched. The west recalls to us such familiar terms as the 36 mysterious kingdoms, the ancient Silk Road, the girls of the vanished ancient city of Loulan, Luobupo Lake, and so on. We cannot help feeling excited by the unique landscape of the west, featuring desolate deserts and ironclad troops on horseback. However, the remoteness and wilderness are only partially true of the west in its real sense. The other side of the west is gentle and graceful with oases, as is evidenced by Kanas Lake.

Kanas means "the lake in the valleys" in Mongolian. The surface of the lake is 4396 ft (1340m) above sea level and the deepest place in the lake reaches 618 ft (188.5m). The whole Kanas Nature Reserve covers an area of 2158 square miles (5588 square kilometers).

The scenery around the lake is quite extraordinary, featuring undulating ice-capped peaks, lush forests, luxuriant grasslands, flowers in bright colors, and butterflies flapping around. Kanas, the only Palaearctic Euro-Siberian wildlife region in China, abounds in precious tree species such as Siberian larch, Korean pine, dragon spruce, firs, and birches. Many of the flora and fauna species found here are the only ones in Xinjiang or even in the whole country. With forests linking up with grasslands – crisscrossing rivers, lakes, ravines, and gullies – the natural reserve offers not only a feast for the eyes but also great historical and cultural value for sightseeing, nature preservation, and scientific research.

In Kanas Country Villa, there are luxuriant grasslands and a bridge that extends to the heart of the lake. Standing on the bridge, visitors can marvel at the view around the lake and the morning mist shrouding the mountains in foggy grandeur. Visitors can also enjoy fishing along the railings or take a cruise on the lake.

On the way from the county seat of Burqin to Kanas lies the Crouching Dragon Bay. It is also known as Guodi Lake (meaning lake in the shape of the bottom of a pan). Dense forests, blooming flowers, and meadows in lush green can be found around the lake. A huge rock sits in the middle of a stream that flows into the lake, giving rise to waves that lap against it, with foam drifting and swirling. A log bridge spans the east and west ends of the lake near the lake's outlet. To the north of the bridge is the lake, as limpid as a mirror, while to the south the surging Kanas River roars on its way down its course.

Along the Kanas River and two thirds of a mile (1 km) north of Crouching Dragon Bay is Blue Moon Bay, among the valleys. Like a prismatic gem in the Kanas River, the water in Blue Moon Bay changes along with the Kanas Lake. It is said that bare footprints were left in the lake by Chang'e in her legendary flight to the moon. Blue Moon Bay, graceful and tranquil, is an emblem of the Kanas Nature Reserve.

The Tuwa tribe is an ancient ethnic group that has lived near Kanas Lake for almost four hundred years, subsisting mainly by herding and hunting. Brave and strong, the Tuwa people are talented in riding horses, skiing, singing, and dancing. Their traditional way of living and customs have been preserved. Their log houses are scattered all over, forming several villages with small bridges across the gurgling streams. Cooking smoke arises and the aroma of milk wine permeates the air. The ancient Tuwa villages remain as mysterious as Kanas Lake.

In Kanas, visitors are not only enchanted by the natural landscape – composed of serene river valleys, rich fauna species, luxuriant grasslands, the dense and lush Taiga Forest, mysterious alpine lakes, and grand glaciers – but are also exposed to the ancient and unique customs of the Tuwa tribe who hold dear the belief that humans are an integral part of nature. Undoubtedly, Kanas is a precious gift of nature to mankind.

LOCATION
Kanas is located to the north of Burqin county of Xinjiang, 94 miles (150km) away from the town center. Kanas Lake is an alpine lake deep in the forests of the Altay Mountains.

CLIMATE
There is a fairly long winter, lasting seven months, and a warm spring and fall, but there is effectively no summer. July is the hottest month, with an average temperature of 60.6°F (15.9°C). The annual average temperature is 31.64°F (-0.2°C).

OF SPECIAL INTEREST
Kanas is a state-level nature reserve and a state geological park. It is China's only extension of the Siberian Taiga Forest and the place of origin of the biggest tributary of the Ertix River, part of the river system of the Arctic Ocean.

MAIN ATTRACTIONS
Kanas Lake, Kanas Country Villa, Crouching Dragon Bay, Moon Bay, and villages of the Tuwa tribe.

The enchanting scenery of fall at Kanas Lake (left)

Kazakh herdsmen living in Kanas (below, right)

Hukou Falls (Shanxi)

The Yellow River rushes down from the Sky

The Hukou Falls (center)

The Yellow River in force at Hukou Falls (above, right)

The impressive scenery of the river course at Hukou Falls, like a stone trough (below, right)

" Do you not see the Yellow River come from the sky?" This is the first line of the lyrical poem by Li Bai (701–762 AD), a great Chinese poet of the Tang dynasty, who could not have written it without having been to the falls at Hukou Mountain. The Yellow River, known as the mother river of the Chinese nation, has remained the symbol of Chinese civilization and the national spirit.

The waterfalls at Hukou are cited as one of the national scenic areas. Going southward across the Central Shanxi Plain and passing through high mountains to Jixian county, you will find the Yellow River at the juncture of Shanxi and Shaanxi provinces. The Grand Shanxi–Shaanxi Gorge is the natural passage changing the Yellow River's east–west flow direction to a south–north one, which is a rare situation since almost all rivers in China flow eastward. The Yellow River, with its more than four thousand tributaries, originates in the plateau at Qinghai, and runs all the way across Sichuan province, Gansu province, and Ningxia Hui Autonomous Region down to Hekou town in Inner Mongolia. Blocked by Lvliang Mountain, the river turns abruptly to the south, roaring through the Grand Gorge into Hukou, where – owing to the sudden narrowing of the watercourse from over 884 ft (300m) to only 164 ft (50m) – it rushes 98 ft (30m) down below.

Legend has it that the formation of the falls is thanks to Yu the Great, who managed to tame the Yellow River from causing floods, by opening up the course at Hukou, Mengmen, and Longmen, and diverting the water to tributaries. That gave rise to a lot of traditional stories

about Yu the Great, in whose honor many temples and shrines were set up.

Having seen the spectacular scene of the falls at Hukou, you will be aware of their remote antiquity, perhaps while cherishing lofty aspirations and becoming broad minded and in harmony with the great Yellow River, which Li Bai tells us comes from the sky.

Invitation to wine

Do you not see the Yellow River come from the sky
Rushing into the sea and ne'er come back?
Do you not see the mirrors bright in chambers high
Grieve o'er your snow-white hair though once it was silk-black?

When hopes are won, oh! Drink your fill in high delight.
And never leave your wine-cup empty in moonlight!
Heaven has made us talents, we're not made in vain.
A thousand gold coins spent, more will turn up again.
Kill a cow, cook a sheep and let us merry be.
And drink three hundred cupfuls of wine in high glee!
Dear friends of mine,
Cheer up, cheer up!
I invite you to wine.
Do not put down your cup!
I will sing you're a song, please hear,
O hear! Lend me a willing ear!
What difference will rare and costly dishes make?
I only want to get drunk and never to wake.

How many great men were forgotten through the ages?
But great drinkers are more famous than sober sages.
The Prince of Poets feast'd in his palace at will,
Drank wine at ten thousand a cask and laughed his fill.
A host should not complain of money he is shot,
To drink with you I will sell things of any sort.
My fur coat worth a thousand coins of gold
And my flower dappled horse may be sold
To buy good wine that we may drown the woes age old.

LOCATION
Hukou Falls are situated at the junction of Shanxi and Shaanxi provinces, about 138 miles (220km) from Yan'an

CLIMATE
Shanxin has cold winters and hot summers. The best time to visit is from April to October. You need to be careful about windy and dusty weather and avoid becoming sunburnt.

OF SPECIAL INTEREST
Hukou Falls, the greatest waterfall in the Yellow River, are second only to Huangguoshu Falls in Guizhou province.

MAIN ATTRACTIONS
The roaring of the Yellow River at Hukou, and local customs and conditions.

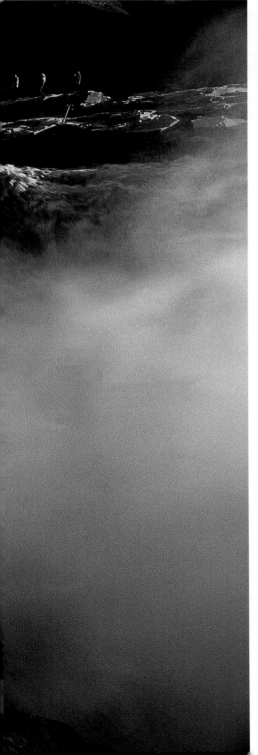

The Golden Stone Beach (Liaoning)

A huge collection of rare and precious stones

Extending 5 miles (8km) on the eastern peninsula at Dalian and surrounded by the sea on three sides, the Golden Beach Stone bears witness to a major part of the earth's long geological evolution history, from 700 million to 300 million years ago.

This is praised as the most important site for rare stones in China, and in the Stone Hall here you can see nearly a thousand specimens of over two hundred varieties, among them Langhua stone, Boshanwen stone, and Kunlun Caiyue stone, which are the most valued kinds in the country.

Each stone on the beach is more precious than gold since it is the only one of its kind across the land and is rarely seen in the rest of the world as well. Geologists claim that each one will never be produced again.

These unusual stones seem to "bloom" and "sing," in that they show up in a variety of colors and give off sounds as the tidal waves come and go. Known as the garden of grotesque stones, this beach features an extensive area of pink and yellow stones. They look like golden roses in full bloom, row upon row of them. The pink stones are actually piled up fossils of seaweed that flourished 700 million years ago.

Covering an area of more than 10,765 square feet (1000 square meters) and made up of over a hundred huge and unique rocks, the Rose Stone Garden turns into a riot of flowers against the blue sea when the waves approach.

Discovered in 1996, the Golden Stone Garden extends for more than 107,640 square feet (10,000 square meters). Every stone looks golden, especially in sunshine.

One unique type of stone to be seen here is called a Guilie (turtle-splitting) stone because its pattern looks like the cracks on a turtle shell, combined with a lattice effect. On its outer surface this stone is patterned in green, while inside it is red. Praised as the best of the golden stones, it is even said to be the most outstanding stone in the world – after making a tour of inspection in this area, many eminent geologists have come to agree that the biggest and most beautiful examples of Guilie stone are displayed on the Golden Stone Beach in Dalian. They have claimed that it is a treasure not only in China, but also throughout the whole world.

On the beach there are nearly a hundred scenic places that are the result of geological processes that took place millions of years ago. They feature the sea-eroded coast, with caves and pillars revealing a huge variety of bizarre forms. For instance, one rock looks like an elephant drinking water, while another seems to represent the flying roc of *The Arabian Nights*.

There are a number of other amusing animal representations. One rock is just like a tiger scrambling for food, a second seems to be a monkey watching the sea, and yet another a dinosaur swallowing the sea. Everything to be seen on the beach is vivid and exciting. There are estimated to be more than three hundred dramatic rock formations to be seen here.

Situated east of the town of Dalian, covering an area of about 1,400,000 square feet (130,000 square meters), the Golden Stone Park also is known as the Stone Forest of the Sea, the Natural Geological Museum, the Fixed Animal World, and the Magic Sculpture Garden.

LOCATION
The Stone Beach is located on the shores of the Yellow Sea, 31 miles (50km) from Dalian.

CLIMATE
It is neither too cold in winter nor too hot in summer here. There is an annual average temperature of about 50°F (10°C) with four seasons.

OF SPECIAL INTEREST
The best summer resort in the northeast, this area includes the eastern peninsula, the western peninsula, the valley between them, and the swimming beach. The Stone Hall is the biggest home for the rare stones to be seen here, and is known today as the Garden of Precious Stones.

MAIN ATTRACTIONS
The Rare Stone Hall, the Golden Stone Park, the Jinshi Waxworks of World-famous Figures, the Flower World, and the swimming beach.

The Golden Stone Beach in Dalian, which has witnessed the long history of the geological evolution of the earth from 700 million years ago. (left)

The best beach for a vacation in northern China, the Golden Stone Beach is on a peninsula surrounded by the sea on three sides. (below, right)

Huashan Mountain (Shaanxi)

Where legend, romance, and cliffs meet

LOCATION
With an altitude of 7220ft (2200m), Huashan Mountain is situated at Huayin, 75 miles (120km) east of Xi'an in Shaanxi province.

CLIMATE
It is rainy here, and less foggy in spring. Summer has a pleasant temperature with good visibility, so you may enjoy the sunrises and the cascades in the valley, which are bathed in a sea of clouds. Autumn is the best season for climbing and offers the finest view of the red maple trees. Snow-capped in winter, the mountain is truly a fairyland. The recommended time for touring is from April to October.

OF SPECIAL INTEREST
The passage to the peak is serpentine and for most of the way it is sandwiched between steep cliffs.

MAIN ATTRACTIONS
Yuquan Temple, Qinkeping, Qianchiz-huang, Baichi Gorge, Canglong Ridge, Princess Peak, and Xiyue Temple.

The west peak of Huashan Mountain, sometimes called the world's most breathtaking place (right)

The outstanding natural scenery of Huashan Mountain (below, left)

50

Huashan Mountain is renowned for its steep cliffs. The route to the north leading to its peak zigzags for as many as 7.5 miles (12km), with crags to the east, west, and south. This is the source of the old saying: "There has been only one path to Huashan Mountain since ancient times."

The mountain boasts five major peaks, in its center, and to the east, west, south, and west. Its well-known historical sites include the Yuquan Temple, the Zhenwu Monastery, and the Jintian Palace.

The east peak, named the Sunrise peak Since from there climbers may view spectacular sunrises, has three caves which house the statue of Master Chen Tuan. Outside one of the caves you will find the Pond of Honeydew. Nearby stands an isolated summit on which there is an iron-tiled pavilion and an iron-cast chess-board. The legend goes that this is the very place where Zhao Kuangyin, the first emperor of the Northern Song dynasty (960–1127 AD), played chess with Chen Tuan, the master. They had a bet that meant that the winner would be the owner of the mountain, and it was taken by Chen, who beat Zhao in three games consecutively. Therefore, the pavilion is called the Pavilion of Chess Gambling.

Climbing southward from the north peak along the perilous route there, you will find a steep ridge, the Canglong Ridge, which is only 2 ft (0.6m) wide but extends for a considerable distance. The ridge is sandwiched between fathomless cliffs and is the only crossing point to the opposite side.

It is hair raising to make your way along this narrow path. It is said that Han Yu, a well-known man of letters of the Tang dynasty, trembled and regretted following the ridge when he looked down at the deep valley below. He thought that he would never get back safely. Indeed, he was so terror struck that he burst into tears and finally wrote his last words, which were thrown down into the abyss. Later, the rock on which the writer once shivered with fear became known as the Place of Han Yu Throwing his Last Message.

The north peak, which is a little lower than the other peaks and in a strong defensive position, is surrounded by steep cliffs in the three directions and is the gateway to the rest of the summits. There is only one ridge leading to the south. On this peak stands the Zhenwu Monastery, which looks over an amazing view. The monastery has its own unique architectural style.

The middle peak, also called the Princess peak, has its own story related to a princess of the time of King Qin Mugong in the Period of Spring and Autumn (770–476 BC). A young man, Xiao Shi by name, was expert at the long flute. One day his excellent flute playing gave rise the princess's admiration, and she traveled a long way from her home to live with the musician in the mountain, giving up her royal status and huge wealth.

The west peak is the most spectacular and breathtaking one, and on its top stands a huge lotus-shape stone in front of the Green Cloud Palace. This is where the events of the legend of Chen Xiang rescuing his Mother by splitting the Mountain took place. Nowadays, a crack can be seen in the huge stone, which looks as if it were chopped apart by an ax. Nearby there is an ax-shape rock, with which little Chen Xiang opened up the passage in the legend. The northwest side of the west peak gives way to an awesomely steep vertical cliff.

Xiyue Temple is where the god of Huashan Mountain is said to be enshrined. Built during the reign of Emperor Wudi in the Han dynasty (206 BC–220 AD), the temple became a sacred place where later emperors held ritual ceremonies. Facing south, its front gate is opposite Huashan Mountain. The temple is constructed in a magnificently ornate style. From its Five-phoenix Tower you may enjoy a panoramic view of the famous five peaks.

Many more stories and legends add their mysterious atmosphere to Huashan Mountain. It was so inaccessible that even the emperor was powerless if a subject refused to pay tax to him, as indicated in an old Chinese saying: "The emperor fails to exert any influence on Huashan Mountain, which is too high and perilous."

Huangguoshu Waterfall (Guizhou)

Presenting different views from vantage points

LOCATION
Huangguoshu Waterfall is located in Huangguoshu, in Zhenning Bouyei and Miao Nationalities Autonomous County, 28 miles (45km) southwest of Anshun city in Guizhou province. It is 94 miles (150km) from Guiyang, the capital of the province.

CLIMATE
The area has a subtropical climate, with a clear temperature contrast between the four seasons, but no extremes of cold in winter nor of heat in summer. There is plentiful rainfall.

OF SPECIAL INTEREST
There are dozens of waterfalls above and under ground, and the gorgeous Tianxing Garden to be seen.

MAIN ATTRACTIONS
Waterfall cluster, Water Curtain Cave, Tianxing Bridge Stone Forest, Tianxing Cave, and many more.

As the legend goes, Huangguoshu Waterfall pours down directly from the Milky Way in the highest heavens.

The story is that while falling, the main part of the Milky Way becomes the major waterfall, the splashing parts are turned to a cluster of small waterfalls, and the stars falling together are changed into glittering stones, ponds, grasslands and trees, bridges and caves.

In Zhenning Bouyei and Miao Nationalities Autonomous County, 28 miles (45km) southwest of Anshun, the Baishui River rushes furiously all the way to Huangguoshu and suddenly breaks, creating this wonderful sight. Down the Rhinoceros Pool from high above, with thunderous roars that can be heard far away – as if the Yangtze River were truly being poured down from heaven – nature offers a masterpiece to the visitor. Huangguoshu Waterfall is traditionally compared to a white dragon. It dashes out from its heavenly palace, down to a deep pool resembling a rhinoceros that is leisurely enjoying its view of the moon. When the dragon runs into the rhinoceros, the latter becomes so angry that it stirs the water of the pool completely upside down and produces terrible howls. It offers kaleidoscopic views, causing confusion and fascination.

The original name of Huangguoshu Waterfall was Baishuiquan Waterfall. It has acquired its present name from the yellow fruit called the *huangguo* that grows here in abundance. With regard to geological features, this is typical karst topography.

A mountain building phase of ten thousand years ago created the rupture in the rocks that accounts for the local configuration. Presented here is a main fall that is 243 ft (74m) high and 266 ft (81m) wide, with dozens of other falls scattered around, some visible and others invisible. It is rare, both here in China and elsewhere in the world, to see such a concentrated cluster of waterfalls in one area. The falls have a plentiful supply of water all through the year, the average fall being 35,100 cubic feet (1000 cubic meters) per second at a speed of 56 ft (17m) per second. You can feel the tremendous momentum even from a distance. Even when you are as far as half a mile (1000m) away, and separated from the falls by the river and the forest, you are affected by it. As soon as you enter the gateway to the scenery, you hear the deafening roar, like continuous thunder. You will certainly feel excited, for you know that after taking a turn around the hill at the front and behind the thick forest, you will immediately begin to experience the wonders ahead of you. Here is revealed the power of nature that works wonders throughout the universe, and that for long ages people have worshiped and marveled at. The surrounding air is so damp that it seems as if water is coming out of your hands, and you find that cool water beads are unexpectedly hanging down from your hair and your eyebrows.

Xu Xiake, a famous traveler of the Ming dynasty, once offered a splendid description of Huangguoshu Waterfall: "A giant cloth is flying down with stones like lotus leaves covering three caves, like curtains of silk and satin, splashing pearls and jade, glistening in a torrent of foam."

Huangguoshu Waterfall comprises three main scenic features: the waterfalls themselves, the Water Curtain

Cave, and the Rhinoceros Pool. Every summer when the river floods, the abundant water crashes down with a sound like hordes of troops and horses marching forward, and the sound flows out to the surrounding area.

Then there is the extensive Water Curtain Cave, which seems to hide itself behind the waterfalls, with drapes of anonymous creeping and climbing plants hanging down over its entrance. Inside the cave, you can watch the waterfall sweeping down and you become aware of the dangers. The Water Curtain Cave is a limestone structure, and it lends great charm to the scene. Still another marvel is the Rhinoceros Pool. Here there are in fact two pools. The one on the left is 57 ft (17.5m) deep, and the one on the right is 50 ft (15.2m) deep. The snow-white water of the falls dashes down to the bottom of the two deep green pools, then rises up again angrily, scampering out through the deep valley like a multitude of silver snakes.

After coming out from the Water Curtain Cave and passing by the Rhinoceros Pool, you climb up the mountain slopes opposite and the mountain ranges and the fog-veiled green forests are before you, and the scale of your surroundings opens up your mind. On a fine day in summer, you can see rainbows appearing through the mist.

Rainbow over Huangguoshu Waterfull, Guizhou province (below, left)

The Longgong scenic area (above, right)

Huangguoshu Waterfall, like the Milky Way pouring down directly from the highest heavens (below, right)

Mapang Yumco (Tibet)
Forever invincible jade lake

LOCATION
Mapang Yumco is located within Burang county in Ngari district, at the foot of Kangdese peak, and has an area of more than 154 square miles (400 square kilometers).

CLIMATE
Ngari district is located in the west of Tibet, at an average elevation of 14,764 ft (4500m) above sea level. The weather in this rugged natural environment is variable.

OF SPECIAL INTEREST
Mapang Yumco is one of the highest freshwater lakes in the world.

MAIN ATTRACTIONS
Pilgrims come to take a ritual walk round the holy lake, traveling clockwise. The perimeter of the holy lake is about 38 miles (60km), and this takes two days to complete.

Mapang Yumco is the name of a holy lake. It is at an elevation of 14,435 ft (4400m), and is one of the highest freshwater lakes in the world.

Mapang Yumco is located within Burang County, Ngari District, at the foot of Kangdese peak (Mansarovar), with an area of 154 square miles (400 square kilometers).

In the Tibetan language, "Mapang Yumco" means "forever invincible jade lake." The title can be traced back to the time of a famous religious war which happened near the lake in the eleventh century. The result was that the Gagyu Sect of Tibetan Buddhism defeated paganism decisively. The title of the lake reflects their overwhelming victory.

The vast, tranquil, and transparent lake is now deemed a holy lake by devotees of several of the world's religions, and it is one of the most renowned lakes in Asia. In many ancient Buddhist sutras the lake was referred to as "King of the Holy Lakes." And according to the earlier Bon religion, Mapang Yumco is the palace of a holy dragon that

has a man's body and the head of either a snake or a horse. In many ancient murals, the lake is depicted as a fairy maiden with a girl's head and a fish's tail.

Mapang Yumco is encircled by snowy mountains on three sides. The mountains are precipitous, craggy, and dazzlingly white, while the water of the lake is so blue. The reason for the color is the unfathomable depth of the water. Some say it is as much as 253 ft (77m) deep. The snowy mountains around are just like white jade, setting off the beauty of the lake. The water is absolutely still, without any sound of wind whistling and not even tiny waves on the surface. The unique surroundings and stately atmosphere leave a lasting impression.

In Indian mythology, Mapang Yumco Lake was conceived in the mind by the great god Brahma. His son needed a lake to bathe in after adopting asceticism in the divine mountains. Usually followers of Hinduism would bathe in the lake during their ritual worship. Tibetans make a similar walk round the lake, but differ from the Hindus

in that they prostrate themselves instead of bathing.

It is said that the water in this lake can remove the five sufferings of the human mind. These are greed, madness, anger, laziness, and envy. It can remove dirt from the body, too. Bathing in the lake can clean a person's body and soul, build up their health, remove annoyance, and prolong life. A lot of followers of Buddha, come here to worship and bathe some time during summer and fall every year. After bathing, they often take some "holy water" back with them to give to their friends as a gift.

According to the monk Xuan Zhuang of the Tang dynasty, in his *Journey to the West* – written after he made his pilgrimage to India to find the Buddhist sutras – this lake is the abode of the immortals, and is associated with the fairy mother goddess. It has four bathing places, with Lotus Bathing Gate in the east, Sweet Bathing Gate in the south, Dirt Removal Gate in the west, and Belief Bathing Gate in the north. It has consistently been held by Buddhist pilgrims that taking the op-

Mapang Yumco, the holy lake (below, left)

The Chuguogongba Pagoda (top, right)

An old Tibetan man standing beside Mapang Yumco Lake, watching the sun rising in the east (center, right)

Mani Piles beside Mapang Yumco Lake (below, right)

portunity to bathe in this lake brings great fortune in life. Buddhists believe that Mapang Yumco is the nectar bestowed to human beings by the great god Chakrasamvara, and that it can cleanse our bodies as well as removing all kinds of vexation, annoyance, and improper thoughts from our souls. Drinking the water of the lake can get rid of numerous diseases and keep our bodies healthy. If pilgrims make the ritual walk around this lake, they obtain boundless benefits.

Besides its unusual significance for pilgrims, Mapang Yumco – the King of all the Holy Lakes – is such an outstanding scenic place that no-one can pass by without being affected. Even though they may not pay attention to the fascinating myths and legends associated with it, on account of its rare and pure beauty travelers will effectively prostrate themselves before it and may even feel it appropriate to worship it after their long and arduous journey.

Zhada clay forest (Tibet)

A creative work made by wind and water

Tibet Autonomous Region

Zhada Clay Forest

LOCATION
Zhada Clay Forest is located in Zhada county in Ngari prefecture, on the west of the Tibet Autonomous Region.

CLIMATE
The annual average temperature of Ngari is 66°F (19°C). At more than 16,405ft (5000m) above sea level, the temperature here varies greatly from day and night.

OF SPECIAL INTEREST
Zhada Clay Forest features unique landforms with straight, steep, and majestic clay pillars in various shapes.

MAIN ATTRACTIONS
Zhada Clay Forest, Tholing Monastery, the ruins of the Guge kingdom, and more.

The splendid effects of the sun in Zhada county of the Ngari prefecture have become legendary. In the myriad rays of the sun the famous clay forest is particularly stunning. Endowed with life and vigor by glowing clouds at sunset, the clay pillars in their different shapes shine against the highland in a fascinating light.

Under the influence of mountain-forming movements in ancient times, the clay forest was formed when sediments deposited by lakes and rivers were exposed to erosion by water. Standing straight, steep, and majestic, these clay "trees" are in various fascinating shapes, some much taller than oth-

ers. The clay forest of Zhada appears magical and gorgeous, made by the inspired and delicate touch of nature.

If you climb over the Kangdese Mountains, you will be struck dumb with amazement by the sight of the clay forest in its unparalleled magnificence. It looks splendid when seen from afar and exquisite on closer scrutiny.

Clay pillars are scattered everywhere on the slopes around the county seat of Zhada. You can take a walk from the town to the clay forest, and will find that you are offered scenes similar to those of the Great Canyon. The clay forest in Maoci Valley is considered the most

spectacular of all. The castle-like clay pillars cover a huge area.

It is no wonder that people resorted to legends for an interpretation of what they could see here. A long time ago, it is said, there used to be a vast ocean where present-day Zhada stands. Under the blue sky, there was nothing but wind and water. Gradually, the clay forest began to emerge from under the sea. Though this is only a legend, it contains some elements of the truth. According to scientific research, in the area where the clay forest now stands there used to be a lake which was approaching 200 square miles (500 square kilometers) in area. The mountain-forming movements that

created the Himalayas resulted in an uplifting of the lake's basin and a reduction in the water level. The clay forest was formed by the effects of erosion, which scoured and sculpted the clay from the basin into all manner of shapes of different heights.

Erosion continued for tens of thousands of years, adding more delicate details to the clay pillars – as if they were touched by a stroke of genius.

Rainbow over Zhada Clay Forest (above, left)

Zhada Clay Forest under magical light (above, right)

Everything is still in Zhada Clay Forest, except souls floating in sunlight, along with clouds (center, right)

The magnificent scenery of Zhada Clay Forest (below, right)

Qiantang Tide (Zhejiang)

A natural water wonder of the world

Jiangsu Province

Anhui Province

Qiantang

Hangzhou

Zhejiang Province

Jiangxi Province

Fujian Province

LOCATION
On the southern border of Hangzhou Jiaxin Plain, 75 miles (120km) west of Shanghai, and 38 miles (60km) east of Hangzhou.

CLIMATE
There is a northern subtropical and moist climate. It is temperate, with a clear contrast among the seasons. The annual temperature average is 60.6 °F (15.9 °C).

OF SPECIAL INTEREST
August 18th of the lunar calendar is the best time to watch the famous tide.

MAIN ATTRACTIONS
Watching Tide Park in Yanguan township, Haining, Chanshan Dam-watching Tide Pavilion, the Big Dent, and the Dragon Head of Babao.

It is said that watching the Qiantang Tide began in the Tang dynasty and was in vogue in the Song dynasty. In the centuries that followed, it became a custom. Every year on August 10th of the lunar calendar, people hold ceremonies of various kinds to honor the god of the tide, pray for peace, and set forth their hopes for a better future.

A good place to watch Qiantang Tide is at Yanguan township in Haining county, Jiaxing city. Though this is just a small place, here tourists can appreciate the Thread Tide, the Clashing Tide, and the Returning Tide. It is said that the returning tide swells up to 39 ft (12m) high.

It is nearly one thousand years since people set up the Zhenhai Pagoda in Yanguan township. They did so in the hope of suppressing the tide god.

The ancient Qiantang River flowed into the sea at Guanshan, now in Fuyang county. At that time the tide was not as great as it is now. The Yangtze River flows down from the north, carrying mud and sand all the way from its upper streams. These are deposited at the river's estuary and form sandbars. The waves of the sea are now held up by the sandbars, but they continue to be pushed forward by the waves that are behind them. In this way the head of the waves swells up, forming a great tide. Under the effects of the phases of the moon, the tide runs in a even more dramatic way, arriving near Yanguan with its head sometimes more than 10 ft (3m) high.

The Qiantang River has two big recurrent tides. At these times the magnificent surges of the water last for three to five days. The big tide usually appears in the first two or

three days after the first or the fifteenth day of the lunar calendar.

Fall is the season that produces the biggest tide. The maritime climate, the influence of oceanic currents, and the high rainfall and typhoons at this time of the year make the tide fiercer than ever.

When the tide reaches you, you can imagine that you see hordes of troops and horses charging forward and galloping, sweeping over the raised banks, splashing in all directions. It is as if fireworks are exploding in the sky. The roaring and turbulent waves, full of power and grandeur – like a giant wall towering over you – make a deep impression that never fully fades away over the following years.

On August 18th every year, there is sure to be a big tide. Tourists swarm to Yanguan township to experience the excitement. The most

renowned places for watching Qiantang Tide are Changshan Dam, the Big Dent, the Dragon Head of Babao, and Xiaoshan.

A pavilion for watching the tide is set up on the Changsha Dam, where you can see the tidal bore approaching. The Big Dent is the place to watch the soul-stirring "Crossing Tide," which is caused by the sand of the riverbed here. At the Dragon Head of Babao, there is a reef protruding from the sea wall, and you can stand here to watch the "Furious Billows," terrifying and stormy, seeming to shake heaven and earth. In Xiaoshan, you can experience the Thread Tide, the imposing Returning Tide, the Boat-challenging Tide, the Tide between Tides, and the fierce Tide from the Rear. Tide Watching Park is a good place to watch the evening tide. It presents a different view, but the grandeur and astonishment is the same. In the supreme stillness and tranquility of night, you can hear the roar, as if numerous horses are running and rolling.

Beside playing its part in the Qiantang Tide, the sea wall is also an important component of the Qiantang Tide culture. In ancient

times, for those living along the river the Qiantang Tide was a disaster that ruined their crops and their houses. People tried to ward off the threat, but the gigantic force of the tide made it nearly impossible to control it. Local people devised various ways to contain it in their struggle against the Qiantang Tide. One impressive creation was the Fish Scale Sea Wall. It was unprecedented anywhere else in the world. People placed piles 16 ft (5m) long in the bank to form a foundation. The walls, which at the bottom have a width of 13 ft (4m) and the top 5ft (1.4m), were made with stone bars, each laid upon another to form from 18 to 23 layers. They were glued together with a mixture of glutinous steamed rice and lime. Finally, they were locked with iron buckles. The Qiantang Tide Sea Wall, extending along the river and winding like the Great Wall, has been a spectacular sight ever since.

The sea wall on the northern bank of Qiantang River is a great feat of architectural engineering of ancient China. It enjoys equal popularity with the Great Wall, and it is listed as one of four great ancient

constructions, offering to the world an outstanding example of the ingenuity of early people.

The Tide Watching Site in Yanguan township of Haining county. It is best to watch Qiantang Tide around the mid-autumn festival every year. (above)

The Anta Pagoda at the Tide Watching Site in Yanguan township of Haining county (below)

Crescent Moon Spring (Gansu)

A bright pearl and a crescent moon in the desert

LOCATION
Located on the northern side of the ringing sand hills, 3 miles (5km) south of Dunhuang city in Gansu province.

CLIMATE
There is a temperate and continental climate, with an annual average temperature of 48.7°F (9.3°C). Rainfull is poor, and there is a big temperature difference between night and day.

OF SPECIAL INTEREST
The area is renowned for its desert wonders.

MAIN ATTRACTIONS
Ringing Sand Hill sliding, camel riding, parachute jumping, and so on.

Crescent Moon Spring is located on the northern slope of Ringing Sand Hill (Mingsha Hill), 3 miles (5 km) south of Dunhuang city in Gansu province. It is 984 ft (300m) long from east to west, 164 ft (50m) wide from south to north, and 16 ft (5m) deep. It has the appearance of a crescent moon, hence the name of the spring. Crescent Moon Spring used to be a section of the Danghe River. Owing to a change in its course, a bend of the river gradually became a separate pool.

On its north and south sides are the tall sand hills, each named Ringing Sand Hill. The hills have not ac-quired this name because they can produce sounds on their own. It is because when people slide down the sand hills, the sliding action makes a ringing sound. Because of the special configuration of the sand hills and the unique topography around, the wind – when blowing down the low-lying land – forms exceptional air currents as they bring the sand along and sweep by the spring. The spring is constantly supplemented by the undercurrent of the Danghe River, and therefore the spring water maintains a dynamic balance. As a result of all this, over the past thousand years the spring has brimmed over with water and coe-xisted with the sand hills. It never dries up, even in long droughts, and it never overflows in rainy days either. The water is forever limpid and bluish. People have given this area the name of Limpid Crescent Moon Spring at Dawn.

An ancient poet once wrote, "In the shape of a crescent moon, You offer a mirror to us. The wind can never bring sand to you, A tranquil life accompanies us forever." Through the ages, tourists have been fascinated by the beauty of Crescent Moon Spring.

It is said that a long, long time ago, the area around Dunhuang was the Great Gobi Desert. Then there

were no ringing sand hills – and no Crescent Moon Spring either.

One year there was a prolonged drought. All the crops and all the plants withered and died. People were terribly thirsty, and they cried and cried. When the beautiful and kind-hearted White Cloud Fairy Maiden was passing by, she heard their heart-rending cries. She felt pity for the sufferings of the people, and her uncontrollable tears rolled down from heaven as she went by. They at once became limpid springs which rescued the people from their disaster. The people felt deeply grateful to her and they built a temple to worship the White Cloud Fairy Maiden. This aroused the anger of the Big Sand Immortal in the Divine Sand Temple. He used his magic power to throw down the sand piles, with the intention of burying the spring in them. But the White Cloud Fairy Maiden, with the help of the moon, which she borrowed from the moon goddess, deter-

mined to fight against the Big Sand Immortal. The day when all this happened was the fifth day of the Chinese calendar, when the crescent moon shone in the sky in favor of the White Cloud Fairy Maiden, who converted herself into a cool and transparent pool from which the people could drink and irrigate the land. The Big Sand Immortal used more witchcraft in order to vanquish his opponent. When she discovered this, the moon goddess became very angry. She denounced the Big Sand Immortal as being impertinent and bullying. With a gentle stroke of the wide sleeve of her gown, she produced a gale, sending the drifting sand up to the hill's top. The Big Sand Immortal roared at this like thunder, which caused the ringing of the sand hills.

People that come to Crescent Moon Spring nowadays want to witness the wonder of a crescent moon encircled by hills of sand.

The spring water, so cool, so limpid, and so sweet, has been lying quietly in the embrace of the sand hills for thousands of years. Though there has been frequent harassment by the fierce wind and ominous sand, the bluish spring is still there, and the murmuring water is still there. It is just like the eyes of a rare beauty, lucid, charming, and passionate – or the lips of a maiden, so mysterious, so soft, and so seductive – or more likely a slice of Hami melon, jade green, crystal, and sweet.

By the Crescent Moon Spring, the poplar trees stand gracefully, and the weeping willows dance with the

wind. There you can smell the fragrant flowers of the narrow-leaved oleaster, and see the swaying groves of reed and the hovering wild birds. What a poetic and picturesque landscape this is. On the southern bank of the spring are the Goddess Temple, the Dragon Emperor's Palace, the forefathers' Cave of Chinese Medicine, the Jade Spring Building, and the Thunder's Echo Temple.

The Crescent Moon Spring abounds in fish. They are called Iron Back fish, and they are said to cure some intractable diseases. There is also a species of grass called Seven Star grass. It is said that if someone eats the fish and the grass, they will live for ever. The Crescent Moon Spring is therefore also a medicinal spring.

The marvelous scenery of Crescent Moon Spring and Ringing Sand Hill (Mingsha Hill) (below, left)

Sand-skiing at Ringing Sand Hill (Mingsha Hill) (above, right)

Camel caravan at Ringing Sand Hill (Mingsha Hill) (below, right)

Yuanyang terraced fields (Yunnan)

Symphony of man and nature

LOCATION
The area occupied by these peoples is in Honghe Hani and the Yi Minorities Autonomous City, Yunnan province.

CLIMATE
Most of the Honghe areas belong to the subtropical plateau monsoon climate, with annual average temperature of 59-72.7°F (15-22.6°C). Yuanyang is foggy. In February the average temperature is 51.8°F (11°C) and there is an average of 14 rainy days.

OF SPECIAL INTEREST
The terraced fields in Yuanyang covering more than 329 acres (133 hectares) present a vast outlook, graceful and powerful.

MAIN ATTRACTIONS
T oggy mountainous city, Bada, Duoyishu, Longshuba, and the rural landscape of Jinzhuzhai.

Yuanyang is located in Yunnan province, and it is the central area of the Hani minority terraced fields. In the flat land of the river at an altitude of 472 ft (144m) to 1970 ft (600m), the Tai people live. The valley areas from 1970 ft (600m) to 3280 ft (1000m) are inhabited mainly by the Zhuang. The lower mountainous areas from 3280 ft (1000m) to 4595 ft (1400m) are for the Yi. The upper mountainous areas from 4595 ft (1400m) to 6560 ft (2000m) are the place to see the Hani people, and the areas above 6560 ft (2000m) are for Miao and Yao. The Han people usually live in townships or along the roads.

The upper mountain areas where the Hani people live have a temperate climate and plentiful rainfall, with an annual average temperature of 59°F (15°C) – very suitable for rice

growing. Since the Sui dynasty and Tang dynasty, the ancestors of the Hani came here to reclaim terraces on which to grow rice. In the past 1200 years, the Hani have made painstaking efforts and brought their great wisdom and bravery into full play, reclaiming the horizontal terraced fields that were arranged layer after layer up to the top of the mountain. They have also dug thousands of irrigation canals and ditches which are just like silver girdles encircling the mountains.

The Hani made plans according to the topographical features, with immediate adjustments to suit the surrounding conditions. Wherever there was a big piece of land and the slope was gentle, they made large fields, but on the small strips and steep slopes, the terraces shrank to a very small size. Usually bigger ones have the area of an average field, while small ones are as tiny as a dustpan. Sometimes on a single slope there are hundreds, even thousands, of terrace pieces, together comprising a versatile and ever changing symphony.

When approaching the terraces, it seems as if there is nothing blocking your field of vision. So beautiful, so impressive – every piece of land seems to be filled with water, and every piece of land filled with water is like a mirror. Some are high and some low, some big and some small. In every mirror you can see the blue sky, the white clouds, the sunshine, the inverted reflection of trees, the color of flowers, and the silhouettes of birds. It's as if all the colors of a season are reflected.

Those hundreds and thousands of fields, one by one, look like a giant printed cloth pieced together with odds and ends of colored materials in the hands of a clever woman, or like a magical jigsaw.

At sunrise, all the landscapes are plated with a thin layer of gold. The sun with divides the terraced fields

into two parts. Some are halfway up the mountains, reflecting the rosy dawn. Others hide in mountains covered with winding clouds and mists. The two parts are harmonious and beautiful. A sea of clouds, lingering, often seems not to want to leave, eastward or westward, upward or downward, taking forms of infinite and ever changing variety. As you look, a sound comes to you, very distant, and very near, very grand, and very minute – as if the silkworms are chewing the mulberry leaves, or the wild horses are galloping in the wildness. The terraced fields are witness to the brave struggle of human beings against nature, as well as the conditions they have created in order to survive.

This is not a historic site such as the Great Wall, the Forbidden City, Qinshihuang Mausoleum, the Pyra-

mids in Egypt, or the Taj Mahal – they have already lost their functions. Nor is it merely a natural sight like Taishan Mountain, Huangshan Mountain, or Niagara Falls. It is a great creation by the Hani people during their long relationship with the Ailao mountainous areas, representing the integrity of nature and humans when working in harmony and in compensation – a product of culture and nature in an artistic combination and crystallization.

Yuanyang terraced fields, a symphony of the art of nature and an eyecatching wonder (above)

Hani women in Yuanyang (below, right)

Yuanyang rural fair, showing the minorities' character and style (below, left)

Dragon Ridge Terraced Fields (Guangxi)

Rising and falling as if on a Dragon Ridge

In the area of Heping township, in the southeastern part of Long Sheng county, Guangxi province, there is a range of magnificent terraced fields, the highest 2887 ft (880m) above sea level and the lowest 1247 ft (380m). They wind from the foot of the mountain to the top, a perpendicular difference of 1805 ft (550m). This area is known as "The World's Best Terraced Fields."

Dragon Ridge Terraced Fields spread over a large area between the general elevations of 984 ft (300m) and 3609 ft (1100m). They have a variety of gradients, generally between 26 and 35 degrees, but the steepest slopes are up to 50 degrees. Although there are terraced fields to be seen all over the southern part of the country, such intense concentration as may be seen here is particularly rare. From the precipitous valleys to the white clouds that encircle the mountain tops, by the dense forests and by the steep precipices – wherever there is earth – there are the terraced fields to be found. They seem to rise and fall as if part of an attempt to put a ladder up to the heavens.

The reclamation of the land to make the terraced fields began in the Yuan dynasty, and was completed in the early Qing dynasty. The efforts of the farmers to increase the amount of land available lasted for a period of more than six hundred years. Those ancestors who toiled on the mountain slopes could never have imagined what it would become. Their great achievements embody the strong will, the intelligence, and the strength of mankind.

The terraced fields present spectacular views all through the year. When spring comes, the terraced fields are full of water and look like silver necklaces hanging between the mountains. Summer presents a joyous picture, with green waves of plants swelling and pouring from heaven. During fall, entire mountains become golden towers, promising a good harvest. And in winter they offer a crystallized world of white ribbons circling the peaks, winding and overlapping. It is said that the best time of year to appreciate the Dragon Ridge Terraced Fields is at some point in spring or in mid-fall. During the busy spring plowing season, you can see the thin clouds moving slowly between the hanging fields, the peasants in brightly colored clothes at work, and the cattle feeding in the mirror-like green fields. It is interesting that in the expansive world of the terraced fields, the biggest individual fields are of very little account by themselves, and most of the fields are fit only for one or two rows of plants.

The scenery of Seven Stars accompanying the Moon refers to the seven highest points of the terraced land, while Nine Dragon and Five Tigers are the terraced ridges soaring to the sky. They are at their most spectacular when they are full of water and in spring, when the peasants transplant the rice seedlings.

Here, you can appreciate the original, authentic, and refined local arts – such as the Dragon Ridge Copper Drum Dance, the Master Dance, and the Shoulder Pole Dance – and taste the fragrant Dragon Ridge tea and wine,

and other local delights. The ancient and primitive Zhuang construction methods remain unchanged. The Zhuang people set up their houses along the mountains and they keep the surroundings clean. The lifestyle here is easy and simple. Push open the back window, and see a girl combing her long hair on the veranda, women carrying babies in their arms, old men walking slowly with hoes on their shoulders, and grandmothers ever embroidering at the front doors. You cannot but be aware of the intoxicating simplicity of life here.

The Yao are usually related to the Red Yao, mainly living around the Heping township area. Women of the Red Yao maintain the tradition of having their hair long. Lingering on the terraced fields, sometimes you will catch sight of a woman with her hair hanging down to her feet. And once a Guinness World Record was created here by 60 women who all had 4 ft 7 in (1.4m) long hair!

Standing on the viewing platform, which overlooks the beautifully as well as convolutedly curving terraced fields, you can spot the display of the Red Yao women's long hair. What a pleasant experience to have!

LOCATION
Dragon Ridge Terraced Fields are located in Ping'an village at Ping township in Longsheng county, 14 miles (22.5km) from Longsheng and 64 miles (103km) from Guilin city.

CLIMATE
Dragon Ridge has a moderate and humid climate. Owing to the fact that the terraced fields are located at a high elevation, between 980 ft (300m) and 3600 ft (1100m), there is a big temperature difference between night and day.

OF SPECIAL INTEREST
The landscape varies with the four seasons. In spring, summer, and fall, it is a series of color engravings. In winter, it is a stark woodcut in black and white.

MAIN ATTRACTIONS
The Zhuang and Yao live here. You will be able to appreciate their special clothes and individual dances, as well as their ancient folk songs.

Spring plowing in the Dragon Ridge Terraced Fields (left)

Dragon Ridge Terraced Fields in Ping'an village, Guangxi (below, left)

Dragon Ridge Terraced Fields after irrigation in April (below, right)

Limestone forest at Lunan (Yunnan)

The fantastic stone forest

LOCATION
The Limestone Forest is situated in the Lunan Yi Minority Autonomous County, about 63 miles (100km) from Kunming, the capital city.

CLIMATE
Featuring the continental monsoon pattern, the Limestone Forest is not overhot in summer, nor is it very cold in winter. Every season is pleasant for sightseeing.

OF SPECIAL INTEREST
Lunan is the most typical area of karst in China. It boasts a stone forest of about 150 square miles (400 square kilometers), unusual in the world in terms of its area and attraction for tourists.

MAIN ATTRACTIONS
The Liziqing Stone Forest, the ancient Stone Forest, the Dadieshui Cave, the Changhu Lake, and Yuehu Lake.

Covering an area of 150 square miles (400 square kilometers), the stone forest at Lunan in Yunnan province is made up of diverse forms of stalactites and stalagmites. In limestone country, it is common for mysterious rivers and fathomless karst caves to be hidden under the surface rocks. What is more, many huge gray rocks stand high, reaching toward the sky, with other rocks in groups creating scenic points and some standing alone. On sunny days, they become deep silver in appearance, while on wet days they look deep blue, sometimes appearing to form an extensive forest in the distance.

Sheer stones and wooded precipices are visible too, all products of the wonder of nature.

The Liziqing Stone Forest is the main attraction in this area, and comprises the Major Part, the Minor Part, and the Outer Part. Here you can see such Chinese characters carved in the stone as "In the Depth of the Cloud,"

"Monolithic Summit," and "Numerous Peaks contending for Magnificence."

In one place you will come across a huge stone spanning two crags high in the sky. Elbowing your way through the narrow passage, you squeeze into a stone "building" where a stone bed, a stone pillow, a stone chess table, and a stone tea table come into your sight. What a quiet and elegant world this is! Suppose you could stay overnight, listening to the natural melodies here.

Stepping out of the stone "building," you stand on a huge meadow surrounded by tremendous stones, some of which are as high as 130 ft (40m). Perched on the narrow and long Jianfengchi Lake is the Yixian Spring with its permanently gurgling water. The spring overlooks manifold reflections of the blue sky, the white clouds, and the huge stones in the clear water.

Lying on a point more than 98 ft (30m) above Jianfengchi Lake, the Lotus peak has a mammoth stone on its top, forming a lotus blossom with an array of

spreading "petals." From the peak you may catch sight of endless abysses and valleys extending in the far distance. On the way you will also find stones that are grouped into different interesting configurations. Some look like frolicking mandarin ducks in the water. Some are like two lambs tending each other. Some appear like an elephant standing on top of a hill. Some show up as a phoenix spreading its wings. What is even more enticing is that you may hear music as you strike the bizarre stones on your way. The harder you hit them, the better the music.

Every stone and peak is a masterpiece, and they are put together to create a marvelous labyrinth. All the stone passages, corridors, doors, caves, and bridges crisscross one another, making a complicated network inside which you may roam. You will be delighted with the many fantastic views and reluctant to leave.

The Outer Part is a plain that is planted with dense trees and bushes. There are many, many stones. The Minor Part, also on the plain, is dotted with numerous trees, including peach, plum, apricot, and camellia. On your way you

will come across clusters of buds, and even veritable bouquets of flowers from time to time.

There is a popular saying here, that you may not ever again be surprised by the wonders of the karst after you come back from a tour to the Limestone Forest at Lunan in Yunnan province.

A view of the Limestone Forest in Yunan (above)

A Sani girl in the Limestone Forest (below, left)

Craggy stones (below, center)

Scene in the bizarre limestone forest (below, right)

Russia
Diversiform-leaved
Poplar in Alashan League
Inner Mongolia
Autonomous Region
Gansu
Province

Poplar trees in the Erjian League (Inner Mongolia)

A symbol of eternal love in Inner Mongolia

LOCATION
The diversiform-leaved poplar forest is situated in the Alashan League in the Inner Mongolian Autonomous Region.

CLIMATE
This area often experiences drastic temperature changes between day and night. It is usually dry all through the year. Tourists should take precautions against travel sickness, sunburn, the sometimes icy climate, and storms. It is recommended that tourists bring warm coats and sun cream with them. October is the best season to enjoy the splendid trees.

OF SPECIAL INTEREST
Since ancient times the Erjina League has been known as the place where the northern Silk Road and the ancient road of Longcheng merged. It boasts the unique local customs of the Mongolians and enchanting natural scenery as well.

MAIN ATTRACTIONS
The golden diversiform-leaf poplar forest in autumn, the Gujuyan Ruins, and the spectacular desert.

There is a big desert in northwest China. A kind of poplar tree, energetic and impressive, grows vigorously in the harsh environment of the barren sand.

If you want to find a way to express eternal love, the *Populus diversifolia* that grows in Inner Mongolia is perhaps the right thing. Regarded as the oldest poplar of its kind on earth and a living fossil, the tree has everlasting vigor, for it lives for as long as one thousand years, after which it may stand for another one thousand years – and it may not decay for one thousand years more. The local people often tell tourists, very proudly, "When you tour the Alashan League and wonder at the grandeur of the oasis, please come to enjoy the magnificence of the diversiform-leaf poplar in our home town."

As the home of this poplar and the largest league of the Inner Mongolia Autonomous Region, the Alashan League boasts its own distinctive views, enchanting desert scenery, and lots of unique historical sites.

It is very important to choose the right time to visit this area. For instance, the Gobi is usually less windy during the month of October,

which is the best time to see the extensive golden-leaf poplar forests that grow on the wavy sand hillocks. The blue sky and the dense yellow foliage work together to present a spectacular natural picture.

On the banks of the Ruoshui River at Dalaihubu town, the seat of the government of the prefecture, the golden-leaved poplars and the pink willows paint the desert so wonderfully. What is more, the best view of the trees is from the eight bridges that cross the dried-up river bed, for the forest presents a world of golden color at different distances. There are many variations in color that make the view all the more more enchanting.

One miracle of the diversiform-leaf poplar – and the reason for its name – is that it has three shapes of leaf: poplar, willow, and maple. For this reason, it is also called the three-leaved tree, and it is unique and impressive with its beautiful trunk, its golden color, and its splendid branches.

The tree is magnificent and its grandeur is enhanced because it is often covered with extensive foliage. The largest trunk ever recorded for this type of tree had a cir-

cumference of more than 20 ft (6m). And its expansive shade may extend as far as 720 square feet (200 square kilometers). Let us make a comparison so that you may gain an idea of how huge the area shaded by the tree may be. If an adult camel were allowed to stand below the tree, they would be in proportion to a lamb standing alongside an elephant.

Nowadays, the diversiform-leaved poplar is very rarely encountered.

It is a matter of concern to find that the forest of *Populus diversifolia* is on the verge of extinction owing to global climatic changes and a local irrigation project. Its territory is shrinking noticeably year by year. A large number of poplars have disappeared. You may be shocked by the sight of the dried stumps that extend into the distance.

The poplar forest when the leaves are green (below, left)

The golden leaves of the poplar forest in fall (above, right)

View of the poplar forest in the desert (above, far right)

A golden corridor in the poplar forest (below, right)

The Forbidden City (Beijing)

Where 24 emperors of the Ming and Qing lived

A view of the Wumen Gate under the pristine snow (above, left)

Sunset at the Watchtower (above, right)

A distant view of the Forbidden City (center, right)

The golden throne in the Hall of Supreme Harmony (below, right)

Located in the center of Beijing, the former Imperial Palace, known to foreigners as the Forbidden City, is the largest and best preserved palace in the world. Construction of the palace began in 1406 during the reign of Yong Le – the third emperor of the Ming dynasty, whose capital was Nanjing. In the early 15th century, however, Yong Le or Zhu Di, who was garrisoning Beijing, usurped the throne from his nephew and made Beijing the capital. Its construction was completed in 1420. A total of 24 emperors of the Ming and Qing dynasties lived here over a period of about five hundred years. The entire palace area, rectangular in

shape and 7,750,080 square feet (720,000 square meters) in size, is surrounded by walls 33 ft (10m) high and a moat 171 ft (52m) wide. Originally extended to 1,829,900 square feet (170,000 square meters), the existing ensemble now covers only 1,614,600 square feet (150,000 square meters).

In this grand palace complex, the high walls, heavy doors, and thick windows cut off the imperial family from the ordinary people, and kept imperial secrets closely guarded. Among the fascinating artifacts are the knobs and "animal-head knockers" on the doors. The knobs look shiny against their ver-

milion background. Each door has a total of 81 knobs arranged in nine horizontal rows and nine vertical rows. The number nine – the biggest single odd number – is regarded in ancient Chinese philosophy as the maximum *yang* number, representing the masculine or positive principle in nature, and since it is believed to be supreme it is therefore reserved for emperors only. The horizontal and vertical rows of knobs must be arranged according to the imperial hierarchy. In addition to 81 knobs (9 X 9) for the emperor, there are 49 knobs for the prince's residence and other official buildings, while there are 35

knobs for the crown prince's residence or for that of a marquis or below. Violators of this rule were severely punished. The only exception in the Forbidden City is the East Flowery Gate, which has 72 (8 X 9) knobs on it. The story behind this is that the gate, also known as the Ghost Gate, is where several emperors lay in state before their funeral service. The ancient Chinese believed that odd numbers and the living belonged to *yang* while even numbers and the dead belonged to *yin*.

The emperors of the Ming and Qing dynasties lived in the Palace of Heavenly Purity. The Emperors Shunzhi and Kangxi lived in its Western Warm Chamber. After Emperor Yongzheng's reign ended, he moved to the rear hall of the Hall of Mental Cultivation. The rear hall contains five main rooms, the cen-

tral one used as an audience chamber, and the eastern and western ones functioning as bedrooms. Out of fear Yongzheng did not allow anyone to sleep beside him, because one former emperor had been strangled by a concubine and a palace maid.

The Summer Palace (Beijing)
No. 1 Imperial Garden under the sun

Lotus in the breeze at the Garden of Harmonious Interests (above, left)

Distant view of Longevity Hill (above, right)

Suzhou Street, imitating the style of the gardens in the south (below, right)

The Summer Palace, locally known as Yiheyuan – meaning Garden of Nurtured Harmony – comprises Kunming Lake and Wanshou (Longevity) Hill. The garden was first made in 1750 in celebration of the 60th birthday of Emperor Qianlong's mother. The next year Qianlong named it Qingyiyuan, or Garden of Clear Ripples.

When he was 40 years old, the country being prosperous and the people living in peace and harmony, Qianlong decided to have his own place for relaxation and the expression of his aspirations. His choice was the Summer Palace, adorned with views of the hill and the lake, halls, pavilions, towers, corridors, bridges, temples, and a marble boat. They were all harmoniously situated and the entire garden became a beautiful scenic place in the picturesque Jiangnan region.

It was destroyed by fire in 1860, and rebuilt in 1888, occupying 717 acres (290 hectares), with over three thousand varied types of building. It became ever more splendid and impressive in terms of the variety of scenes, the harmonious unity of the past and the present, and the scale, history, and system of horticulture. It continues to rank among the greatest imperial and royal gardens of the world.

In spring, peach blossoms bloom along the western causeway spanning Kunming Lake and the ancient arched bridges shine brilliantly at sunset. Though the lake is not as pretty as the West Lake in Hangzhou, it features wild ducks swimming about and small fish that appear to find it fun to hold hooks in their mouths. Angling in the rain here would be a delight.

Inner Mongolia
Autonomous Region

Hebei Province Liaoning Province

The Summer Palace

Beijing ●

Bohai Sea

LOCATION
The palace is located in the northwestern suburbs of Beijing.

CLIMATE
The area enjoys hot summers, cold winters, and a mild spring and fall (the golden season). The best months are May, September, and October, but in spring it may be dusty.

OF SPECIAL INTEREST
The Summer Palace was the summer resort for the imperial family of the Qing dynasty and has China's largest and best preserved classical garden. It is on the World Heritage List.

MAIN ATTRACTIONS
Hall of Benevolence and Longevity Hall, Garden of Virtue and Harmony, Garden of Harmonious Interests, Long Corridor, Cloud-dispelling Hall, Buddhist Incense Tower, Suzhou Street, Longevity Hill, Seventeen-arch Bridge, and Jade Belt Bridge.

In summer there are lotus scenes around the Jade Belt Bridge, which looks like a rainbow spanning the water. Playing chess in the shade of willow trees or singing to the accompaniment of a Chinese zither on the lakeside are activities that brings immense pleasure.

In fall, the six bridges appear as still as silk. Autumnal charms are displayed in these golden months. With the winter approaching however, wild geese fly over the lake southward, the lotuses begin to wither, and no more flowers come after the chrysanthemums – it is a scene that might put poets in a reflective or even a melancholy mood.

Winter snow makes Kunming Lake more attractive again. The winter scene is no longer the one described by ancient Chinese poets as

bleak, dreary, and lonely. Sweeping snow, sipping tea, skiing about, or enjoying the distant view from the Buddhist Incense Tower are popular activities.

In all seasons, Longevity Hill remains imposing and impressive. The marble Seventeen-arch Bridge spanning the blue-green waters of the lake, modeled on Lugou Bridge (Marco Polo Bridge), has 544 balusters along its entire 490 ft (150m) length, all of which are topped by carved lions, each in a different pose.

This palace was thought to be an ideal resort for the members of the emperor's family in the Qing dynasty. They were able to enjoy the picturesque scenery in the direction of the Yangts River in Beijing.

In modern times several films on the Opium War have brought the

Summer Palace to the screen. More and more westerners have come to know and love this renowned imperial garden.

Ming Tombs (Beijing)

Ming Tombs depicting the whole Ming dynasty

Inner Mongolia Autonomous Region

Hebei Province / Liaoning Province

Ming Tombs

Beijing•

Bohai Sea

Here is a personal reminiscence: "Being a native of Beijing, I am fascinated by its past and its present. I still remember how immersed I was in old folktales as a little boy. Strangely enough, aware as I am that people live only in the present, I still can't help recalling things past. Alas! How many days have passed between then and now."

Near Tianshou (Longevity) Mountain, 25 miles (40km) north of the Desheng Gate, lies a large piece of tranquil, secluded wooded land – a blessed spot in terms of feng shui – with red walls, yellow tiles, and white bridges. It is the actual site of the tombs dedicated to

13 of the 16 emperors of the Ming dynasty, hence its name, the Ming Tombs. These tombs stand in a line at the foot of the mountain, with the Changling Tomb for Zhu Di, the third Ming emperor, at the center.

The first emperor of the Ming, Zhu Yuanzhang, was buried in Nanjing, where he had his capital. The burial place for the second Ming emperor is as yet unknown. And the seventh Ming emperor was dethroned and buried in an ordinary tomb near the Fragrant Hill.

Of all the 13 Ming tombs here, the Changling Tomb and the Dingling Tomb are already well-known tourist attractions.

A few others, such as the Zhaoling and the Xianling, have also been fully restored. Buried in the Yongling was the famous Ming emperor Zhu Houcong, who reigned for 45 years and died at the age of 59.

In the Qingling tomb, however, rested the emperor of the Ming dynasty who had the shortest reign, Zhu Changluo. During his one-month-long reign, he indulged in sensual pleasures while enduring a series of notorious court cases. He died as a result of these events.

The last Ming emperor was Zhu Youjian, who under the pressure of an uprising of the peasants, hanged himself in despair at the age of 34. Unlike his predecessors, he was buried in the Siling Tomb, the smallest known tomb of any emperor of his dynasty and far away from the imperial cemetery, in Tianshou Mountain.

It is true to say that the Ming tombs lie on the ground, while the history that is related to them is buried in the ground.

LOCATION
The Ming Tombs are located at the southern foot of Tianshou Mountain in Changping county, Beijing.

CLIMATE
There are hot summers and cold winters, and the spring (which tends to be dusty) and fall are mild. May, September, and October are the best months to visit.

OF SPECIAL INTEREST
The Ming Tombs are on the World Heritage List. The tombs were constructed over a period of two hundred years beginning in 1409, when the first one was built. They are the last resting places of 13 emperors, 23 empresses, a high-ranking imperial concubine, and dozens of human sacrifices. The best-known tombs are the Changling Tomb and the Dingling Tomb.

MAIN ATTRACTIONS
Changling and Dingling Tombs, Zhaoling, and the Sacred Way.

The Ming Gate Tower in Tailing Tomb (left)

Jingling Tomb (above, right)

The underground palace of Changling Tomb (below, right)

Eastern and Western Tombs of the Qing dynasty (Hebei)

The last Imperial Tombs

The Sacred Way in the Eastern Qing Tombs (below, left)

The stone sculpture offering protection against evil forces and the memorial archway in the tomb of Emperor Yongzheng (center, right)

Tombs for the emperor's concubines (below, right)

The Qing dynasty, the last feudal reign in Chinese history, had ten emperors enthroned in the Forbidden City. Unlike Puyi, the last emperor, the other nine emperors were buried separately in the Eastern and Western Tombs located in Hebei province, the largest imperial mausoleum in China.

The Eastern Qing Tombs that housed emperors, empresses, and concubines is the largest and the most complete one of its kind in China. There are five tombs here: Xiaoling for Emperor Shunzhi, Jingling for Emperor Kangxi, Yuling for Emperor Qianlong, Dingling for Emperor Xianfeng, and Huiling for Emperor Tongzhi. There are also three tombs of empresses, five tombs of concubines, and 372 other constructions of various types. All of these combine to make the Eastern Tombs the largest complex of ancient architecture preserved in China.

The Eastern Tombs not only have a unique layout, but also display a host of construction types, which vary in architectural complexity. The stele pavilion, erected on the southern tip of Xiaoling, is 10876 ft (3315m) wide, the widest of its kind in China. Winding through the Eastern Tombs and linking all the scattered constructions, the "soul path" (or the "sacred way") runs for over nine miles (15km) and is the longest such route in China. In the Qing dynasty a total of twelve tombs were built for its emperors. According to the standardized layout, in front of the tomb of every deceased emperor stood a gravestone recording his feats and merits. In front of the Jingling of Emperor Kangxi, who ruled for 61 years, twin gravestones were housed in the Pavilion of Feats and Merits, the first of its kind constructed in the history of the Qing dynasty. Of the tombs of the Qing dynasty in northeast China and in the Eastern and Western Tombs, ten were for imperial concubines, among which those in Jingling in the Eastern Tombs are the most impressive. The interior decoration of the tomb for Empress

Dowager Cixi is of such a high architectural standard that it defies comparison in China. Also impressive is the underground palace of Yuling for Emperor Qianlong: visitors cannot help marveling at its elaborate carvings.

The Western Tombs housed four emperors, namely Yongzhen, Jiaqing, Daoguan, and Guangxu. They also included three tombs for empresses and seven tombs for princes, princesses, and concubines. There were more than a thousand palaces, covering a total area of over 5,382,000 square feet (500,000 square meters). Why Emperor Yongzhen chose to set up the separate burial ground known as the Western Tombs still remains a mystery. One of the many possible explanations offered is that he found, after sending his experts to do a thorough study, that the eastern imperial burial grounds had no more places ideal in terms of geomancy for housing emperors.

Another story is that Emperor Yongzhen, having usurped his father's throne, couldn't bear the thought of being buried next to his father and therefore found an excuse to institute a new burial ground.

The construction of the Western Tombs began in the eighth year under Emperor Yongzhen, and they were completed two years after Emperor Qianlong came to power. Built according to the standards designated by the imperial courts of the Qing dynasty, the general layout of the Western Tombs was identical to that of the Eastern Tombs, every tomb being completed with a tower-like building, a sacred kitchen, outhouses, a Gate of Eminent Favors, side halls, and so on. Tailing, built for Emperor Yongzhen – the construction of which spanned the seven years from 1730 to 1737 – was the first tomb in the Western Qing group. Tailing and Taidongling (Eastern Tailing) are located at the center of the Western Qing Tombs,

with Changling and Changxiling (Western Changling) for Emperor Jiaqing and his empress to their west. Further to the west are Muling and Mudongling (Eastern Muling) for Emperor Daoguang and his empress. The layout of the Western Tombs is roughly the same, following the example of Tailing, except that of Emperor Daoguang's Mudongling (Eastern Dongling). The originality of this tomb is a result of its being a co-burial ground for the empress and the concubines. The emperor and the empress are not buried together, nor are the empress and the concubines buried in separate tombs. Chongling for Emperor Guangxu, three miles (5km) east of Tailing, is the last imperial tomb built in China.

In 2000, the Eastern and Western Tombs of the Qing dynasty in Hebei province were inscribed on the World Heritage List by UNESCO as "Imperial Tombs of the Ming and Qing dynasties."

LOCATION
The Eastern Qing Tombs are located in Malanyu in Zunhua county, Hebei province, while the Western Qing Tombs are situated at the foot of Mount Yongning in Yi county, Hebei province. Both are imperial tombs for the Qing dynasty.

CLIMATE
Located on the east coast of China, Hebei province is under the influence of the continental monsoon climate of the North Temperate Zone with four distinct seasons and an annual average temperature ranging from –33°F to 58°F (1°C–14.2°C).

OF SPECIAL INTEREST
The Qing dynasty was the last feudal dynasty in China. Nine emperors of the Qing dynasty are buried in the Eastern and Western Tombs, forming the largest complex of imperial tombs.

MAIN ATTRACTIONS
Xiaoling, Jingling, Yuling, Dingling, and Huiling in the Eastern Qing Tombs. Tailing, Changling, Muling, Chongling, three tombs for empresses, three tombs for concubines, and four tombs for princes and princesses in the Western Qing Tombs.

Xi'an (Shaanxi)

An ancient capital witnessing 13 dynasties

There is one ancient city in China that can be called a living history book, recording as it does the numerous exploits and the vicissitudes of the Chinese nation. It is Xi'an, one of seven ancient capitals in the country.

China means "a country in the center" in Chinese, and its central point falls in Xi'an, which is reflected in the old saying "Emperors have set up their empires in Qinzhong since the ancient times." (Qinzhong is the area around Xi'an.)

Xi'an has a fairly long history. The Lantian who lived here in the Old Stone Age turned over the first page in the history of human civilization as early as over one million years ago. Then, about six to seven thousand years ago, the ancestors of the modern state set up the primitive village that is called Banpo by archeologists. It is regarded as a model of the Chinese matriarchal community during its most flourishing period.

Emperor Qinshihuang (Ying Zheng), the first Chinese emperor, had his mausoleum built in Xi'an, which served as the capital city for 13 dynasties spanning 1140 years – ranging from the Xizhou (1046–771 BC) and its society based on slavery to the other 12 dynasties of the feudal society (up to the Tang, the last one). From 1057 to 904 BC it was the political, economic, and cultural center of the country. Like Athens, Cairo, and Rome, Xi'an is one of the most famous ancient capital cities in the world.

The first emperor of the Chinese feudal system, Ying Zheng, reunited the country in 221 BC, and established the Qin – the first feudal centralized dynasty – in Xianyang (today's Xi'an). Then he began to work on the construction of the Efang Palace, a masterpiece in the history of Chinese architecture. Moreover, the emperor ordered the building of a large-scale mausoleum for himself. Among the total of nearly

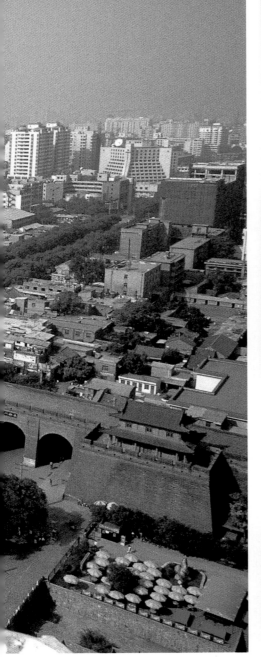

LOCATION
Xi'an is situated in the middle of the Guanzhong Plain in the Yellow River area. In the vicinity is Qinling Mountain to the south, which borders the Wei-he River to the north.

CLIMATE
At Xi'an the climate is of the monsoon type, with four seasons and mild temperatures for most of the time.

OF SPECIAL INTEREST
Xi'an is the ancient capital city of China and has links with more dynasties than anywhere else in the country.

MAIN ATTRACTIONS
Banpo village ruins, Emperor Huangdi's mausoleum, the Stele Forest, and the ancient city wall.

one hundred emperors' tombs in the country, Ying Zheng's mausoleum comes in first in terms of its grand scale and rich burial reserves. The terracotta warriors dug from the mausoleum look like the troops of the Qin, which may indicate their great military strength and incomparable fighting spirit. You can imagine how mighty and powerful Ying Zheng must have been when he led his troops across the land, conquering one kingdom after another before the reunification of China.

A good many of the earthshaking events in China's history took place in Xi'an – Jing Ke's attempt to assassinate Ying Zheng, Xiang Yu's burning of the Efang Palace, and the Hongmen dinner among them.

Xi'an society was at its peak in the Tang dynasty (618–907 AD), when it became the greatest metropolis in the world, with a population of over one million. This is indicated by the saying: "As there is Rome in the east, so there is Xi'an in the west." Many of the most mighty emperors left valuable historical sites after them. The Zhao mausoleum of Li Shiming, the second emperor, is the largest one among the 18 emperors' tombs of the Tang. The Qian mausoleum, where Emperor Gaozong and Empress Wu Zetian were buried together, is the most complete and magnificent tomb of that period, and of particular interest because it was, unusually, constructed for two rulers.

In addition, Huaqingchi, the construction of which was begun by the Xizhou and continued down to the Tang, is a renowned imperial garden and winter resort, with splendid palaces and pavilions as well. In Huaqingch, the imperial bathing pool is where Emperor Xuanzong and his mistress Yang Yuhuan played out their romance in full. Bai Juyi, the well-known poet of the Tang, described their love story in one long poem. Some of the lines go as follows: "In spring the emperor bathes with Yang in Huaqingchi, where Yang's fine skin is nourished with spa water. So delicate and tender is Yang, for she gains new favor from him."

Emperor Qin's terracotta warriors and horses (Shaanxi)

The eighth Wonder of the World

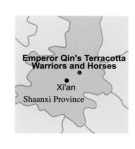

It is truly breathtaking to visit the museum of the terracotta warriors and horses – the majestic buried sculpture legion of Qin Shi Huang (259–210 BC), the first emperor of the Qin – who annexed the six other ducal states to his own and unified China, founding the Qin dynasty.

It is said that before the time of the Qin emperors in China, the custom was to bury boys and girls alive with the dead emperor in order to ensure service for him in his afterlife. Instead, Qin Shi Huang had a magnificent tomb built to house not only his remains but eight thousand clay warriors, horses, and battle chariots intended to serve his needs.

The terracotta warriors and horses were buried 16 ft (5m) down in what are now designated Pit No. 1, Pit No. 2, and Pit No. 3. Pit No. 1, the biggest one, is 755 ft (230m) long and 203 ft (62m) wide, covering an area of 153,495 square feet (14,260 square meters). It contains about six thousand clay warriors 6–6 ft 6 in (1.8–1.97m) tall. These armorclad warriors, holding bronze weapons, were arrayed in a practical formation, poised for battle. The first three rows facing east, with 70 warriors in each, total 210 and constitute the vanguard. Following up are 38 columns of infantrymen with horse-drawn chariots, forming the principal force. Flanking it are two rows of warriors, 180 in each, facing south and north respectively. Besides, there are 32 life-size clay horses in groups of four, drawing the chariots.

The L-shape Pit No. 2 is about 79,900 square feet (26,000 square meters) in area, and contains over a thousand clay warriors (including figures of charioteers, cavalrymen, and infantrymen), five hundred horses drawing chariots, and cavalry horses known as commandos. Pit No. 3, containing clay horses and chariots as well as 64 warriors, is concave in shape with an area of 1900 square feet (520 square meters). It seems to be a headquarters for the troops of Pits Nos. 1 and 2.

No one can fail to be impressed by the amazing workmanship achieved by the Chinese two thousand years ago. Of all the eight thousand underground imperial guards, no two guards are alike in facial expression and posture. Their weights vary from 220 to 660 pounds (100 to 300 kilograms).

Two sets of large painted bronze chariots and horses are known as the "crown of bronze." The chariots are each drawn by four horses connected with a single shaft and placed one above the other vertically. The front chariot (chariot No. 1) is called a "high chariot" and protects the back one, named the "security chariot," which is used by the emperor. These are 10 ft 3 in (3.18m) long and 3 ft 6 in (1.06m) high, both featuring dragons and phoenixes, along with cloud patterns and various geometrical patterns. All these fully display exquisite craftsmanship and superb techniques such as casting, welding, riveting, mounting, embossing, and carving.

The bronze weapons unearthed in the pits include swords, spears, halberds, crossbows, and arrow heads. Though buried two thousand years ago, they are still shiny and sharp, which shows the level of metallurgical expertise at that time. It is no surprise that Jacques Chirac, the French president, has commended the terracotta warriors and horses as the eighth wonder of the world.

LOCATION
The mausoleum of the first Qin emperor is located about 4 miles (6km) east of Lintong county, and some 19 miles (30km) east of Xi'an. It is a mile (1.5km) east of the mausoleum of Emperor Qin Shi Huang.

CLIMATE
The local area enjoys an inland climate. The best seasons to visit are spring, summer, and fall.

OF SPECIAL INTEREST
Qing Shi Huang's buried sculpture legion is on the World Heritage List on account of its great historical importance.

MAIN ATTRACTIONS
Pits Nos. 1, 2, and 3, and the bronze chariots and horses.

Pit No. 1 of Emperor Qin's terracotta warriors and horses (left)

A terracotta warrior and a terracotta horse, in situ in Pit No. 2 (below, right)

A colorful terracotta warrior, still buried in Pit No. 2 (below, far right)

Luoyang (Henan)

An ancient capital over one thousand years old

The White Horse Temple, the first temple built by the government after Buddhism spread to China (above, left)

The Guanlin in Luoyang (above, right)

The ancient part of Luoyang city (below, right)

Luoyang was named after the Luohe River – the city is situated on the northern side of the river. As the national capital of a total of 13 dynasties, Luoyang enjoys a history of up to five thousand years, and served as capital for as long as 1529 years. The city ranks as the earliest capital in China, representing the most dynasties and being the longest lasting of all of China's ancient capitals. And the royal magnificence of Luoyang is probably unmatched, apart from Xi'an and Beijing, across the nation.

Crossing the Luohe River Bridge during the twilight at dusk in early fall, you will come across "Luopu in

Autumn Breeze," one of the eight famous scenic places in Luoyang. In this season the breezes bring welcome alleviation of the summer's heat. With the shade of poplar and willow groves on both banks and the long bridge spanning the river, the Luohe River is indeed a poetic place. More than a thousand years ago, the poet Cao Zhi of the Three Kingdoms Period (220–280 AD) once stood here, close to the river. He was in a state of melancholy as he gazed at his lover, who was in the distance. Four distinguished poets of the Tang dynasty (618–907 AD) – Wang Bo, Yang Jiong, Lu Zhaolin, and Luo

Binwang – dubbed the Four Outstanding Poets of the Early Tang – also had the experience of wandering about this area, and were unwilling to leave it. Today the river remains as wide and misty as ever, and yet Luoyang no longer retains its splendor.

Contrary to the popular misconception, there no longer remain quaint old buildings in Luoyang city, and even eye-catching high-rise structures are scarce. Zhongzhou Road, the straight and broad street crossing the city proper, connects history and reality and seems to be the only thing that has kept up Luoyang's royal atmosphere. The clas-

sical implications of Luoyang need to be gradually discovered and subtly tasted. Its whole history has been deposited into the luxuriant peony flowers, onto the dilapidated old walls, and under the thousand-year-old flowing rivers.

It used to be said in the past that Luoyang was bound to be the first battleground in the event of war. As the springboard to central China, Luoyang really was a place full of trouble in history. The alternating dynasties and countless wars rendered the former capital liable to being plagued by massacre and bloodshed, rather than being regarded as a symbol of peace. On the other hand, a rich and glorious heritage of culture has been handed down in Luoyang by history – such as the Longmen Grottoes (on the World Cultural Heritage List) and the White Horse Temple (consid-

ered to be the birthplace of China Buddhism), and so on. It also encompasses the ruins of five ancient capitals, of the following dynasties: Xia, Shang, Zhou, Eastern Han and Wei, and Sui and Tang – all of which are located around the Luohe River. As vestiges of the Chinese forefathers, one by one they all relate in silence the stories linked to their respective dynasties.

Luoyang's peonies are renowned for their large blossoms, bright color, and gorgeous appearance. When they are in full bloom, it seems that every house in the city is in the shade of these beauties. There are lots of legends about Luoyang's peonies. One of them is concerned with Tang's Wu Zetian who, according to the story, had strains of fine peonies brought to Luoyang from Changan, then the capital of the Tang (now Xi'an). Obviously Wu

had a strong liking for Luoyang. Otherwise she – China's only ruling empress of ancient times – would not have selected Luoyang to be the Tang's new capital. The White Horse Temple is another site with links to Wu. Situated 7.5 miles (12km) east of Luoyang city, the temple has Mount Mang as a backdrop to the north, and faces the Luohe River to the south. It is generally recognized as the birthplace and origin of Chinese Buddhism. The White Horse Temple had its heyday in the Tang dynasty, during which, in order to strengthen her throne, Wu adopted a religious policy of "Respecting Buddhism while Repressing Taoism." Meanwhile, Xue Huaiyi, the chief monk of the White Horse Temple, was believed to be her lover, and in the year 685 Wu ordered a full renovation of the temple. Thereafter it became very grand and splendid, and the community of monks there were said to have become three thousand strong. Its prosperity may be illustrated by the following detail. Owing to the long distance between the main building of the monastery and its gate, closing the gate in the evening was carried out by riding there on horseback.

Nowadays, after ascending Mount Mang in the setting sun, you should look beyond at the darkening dusk. You may get a hint of Luoyang's former magnificence and beauty. The glory of its past however soon fades further and further away from you.

LOCATION
Situated in the west of Henan province, with neighboring Zhengzhou city to the east and Sanmenxia city to the west.

CLIMATE
In a transitional area ranging from a southern mild temperate zone to a north subtropical type, with four distinctive seasons and a pleasant climate.

OF SPECIAL INTEREST
A tourist resort offering a combination of Chinese history, culture, and natural sights.

MAIN ATTRACTIONS
Luopu Park, Mount Mang, Luoyang Museum of Ancient Tombs, the Royal City Park, and the White Horse Temple.

Kaifeng (Henan)
A thousand-year-old dream

Kaifeng is a city familiar to anyone who knows something of China's history. Now most people come to Kaifeng to explore the past prosperity of the Northern Song dynasty (960–1127 AD). Perhaps they are there to consider what is shown in a famous painting of that period by Zhang Zeduan, titled "Riverside Scenes of Pure Brightness." Despite having been the ancient capital for seven dynasties in history, Kaifeng is a city where modern visitors can find hardly any trace of its history. Only two items of antiquity, an old house wall and an iron pagoda, are reminders of its past. Except for some buildings in Longting district which were constructed in either the Ming dynasty (1368–1644 AD) or the Qing dynasty (1644–1911), most of the present buildings in the sightseeing area are contemporary imitations. What used to be the flourishing city of Kaifeng has been long since buried under heavy layers of loess, and even its ruins have disappeared from sight.

Kaifeng began its history as the capital of the Wei kingdom. In order to avoid invasion by the Qin as part of its expansion toward central China, Wei's King Hui decided in 364 BC to transfer the capital to Kaifeng, and renamed it Daliang. However, Wei did not remain a powerful state for long, and Daliang came under siege in 225 BC by Qin's troops, led by General Wang Fen. As the city's defenses proved hard to break through, the Qin's troops drew water from the rivers of neighbors to pour into the city. The result was that Daliang, a capital city with a 140-year history,

was ruined in an instant. From then on, Kaifeng never seemed to rid itself of the tragedy, even during the Northern Song, its most glorious and proud period. Walking about the beautiful city today, you cannot help feeling nostalgia for its past, and awareness of its historical ups and downs.

Through the efforts of the local people, Kaifeng is now reshaping its character and confidence as an ancient capital. Located on the west bank of the Longting Lake, the Garden of Riverside Scenes of Pure Brightness is a large theme park set up according to the blueprint of the renowned painting by the Song's Zhang Zeduan. Visitors can catch a glimpse of the municipal conditions and customs of the Song's capital more than a thousand years ago. The park offers a wide range of performances, including Song style music, ancient dancing, acrobatics, puppet shows, folk arts, and so on. Traditional opera is also performed to tell some of the well-known stories of events that occurred here in the Song dynasty. Longting Park is the largest historical site of its kind in Kaifeng city.

Upon reaching the main road of Longting, you can see two lakes, one on each side: Yangjia Lake is on the left and Panjia Lake on the right. It is said that Yangjia's water is clear while Panjia's is muddy, but the fact is that the two lakes are connected to each other. This area is the site of the ruins of the imperial palaces of the Song and the Jin dynasty (1115–1234 AD), and of King Zhou's residence of the Ming dynasty (1368–1644). A total of nine emperors of the Northern Song played out the tragicomedy of their

empire here at Kaifeng during the period between 960 and 1127. On going up to the higher parts of Longting, there is a bird's-eye view of Kaifeng. Of the historical events that took place around the city at the time of the Song, particularly notewortly is the humiliating moment when the Song's last two emperors were taken as prisoners of war by the invading Jin's army in 1127.

The visitor may leave Longting for another scenic place, Song's Street, in which all the buildings are rigorously designed and constructed according to the Song's architectural standard, and reproduce the former prosperity of the ancient capital that was unmatched in wealth and beauty in its heyday. On Song's Street, there lies a storied building called Fanlou, in which the Song's famous geisha Li Shishi once lived. Song's Emperor Huizong (Zhao Jie), despite being an ineffectual political leader, was a genuine master of the arts. The romance between Zhao Jie and Li Shishi has generated popular legends and tales that have circulated widely among later generations.

The only proof of Kaifeng's historical prosperity is an iron pagoda standing downtown. It was founded in 1094, measures 179 ft (54.66m) high, and has 13 stories. It is an octagonal glazed pagoda built in imitation of a wooden structure, and was decorated by covering the outer surface with a variety of bricks made in 28 shapes and fixed in a mosaic style. In addition, it has also been embellished with colored glazed and carved bricks bearing images of Buddha. Maybe the pagoda's builders were hopeful that they would be blessed by Buddha, and that there would therefore be stability and unity in their country. Unfortunately, even Buddha was unable to prevent the empire from crumbling. With the passage of a thousand years, today what remains is nothing but the Song's shadow, revealing a hint of Kaifeng's past glory.

LOCATION
Situated in the east of Henan province, 38 miles (60km) from Zhengzhou city.

CLIMATE
The area is in Central China, where cold fronts and warm fronts frequently encounter each other, and there is a distinctive monsoon climate.

OF SPECIAL INTEREST
The town itself is a historical museum as the capital of the Song, one of China's eight ancient capitals.

MAIN ATTRACTIONS
Garden of Riverside Scenes of Pure Brightness, Longting Park, and Song's Street.

Garden of Riverside Scenes of Pure Brightness (left)

Kaifeng Iron Pagoda (below, left)

The Yanqingguan Temple in Kaifeng (below, right)

Chengde (Hebei)

Best known as the Imperial Resort

The imperial mountain resort of Chengde went into construction in 1703 and was completed in 1792, during the reign of Emperor Kangxi when the Qing dynasty reached its heyday. Some 156 miles (250km) from Beijing, the resort covers an area of 60.75 million square feet (5.64 million square meters), twice that of the Summer Palace and eight times that of Beihai Park in Beijing.

The mountain resort consists of two main sections: the palace and the scenic part. The palace section is actually a group of "office buildings" for the Qing emperors. Though, in accordance with tradition, the imperial palace is situated in the innermost position, its architecture – featuring the simplicity of a residential compound in north China – is austere and unadorned, using only gray bricks and tiles rather than glazed ones. Therefore, the architectural style is in sharp contrast to that of the magnificent Forbidden City. The main hall, which takes its name from *nanamu*, the fine-grained fragrant rare hardwood of which it is built, is where Qing emperors handled state affairs, held ceremonies, and re-ceived foreign envoys and the nobility of China's various ethnic groups.

Behind the Nanmu Hall is the rear part of the palace building, housing the imperial bedchambers for empresses and concubines, from which numerous anecdotes about the dynasty come. The Western Warm Pavilion is the imperial chamber, and also a place where historic events took place. Emperor Xianfeng once signed the Convention of Peking here, and recognized the validity of the Sino–Russian Treaty of Aigun, resulting in heavy losses of China's territory and sovereignty. In addition, the Empress Dowager Cixi plotted the coup d'é-tat of 1861, starting her reign behind curtains.

Beyond the palace is the section that possesses characteristics of the scenery of both north and south China. As the biggest existing classical park in China, it boasts 90 pavilions, 29 causeway bridges, 25 stone inscriptions, 70-odd groups of rockery, and 120 or so groups of architectural buildings – palaces, towers, halls, temples, pavilions, terraces, and pagodas. Among them the "72 sights of the mountain resort" are the most famous: 36 sights with Emperor Kangxi's four-Chinese-character inscriptions and 36 sights with Emperor Qianlong's three-Chinese-character inscriptions.

The Qing emperors, of nomadic origin, had their own peculiar way of having fun. The most arresting picture displayed in the palace section is *Autumn Hunting*, drawn by the Qing folk artist Xing Long E, which shows the grand scene of Emperor Qianlong hunting at the Mulan Ground two hundred years ago. Today, this imperial hunting ground is included in the tour itinerary.

LOCATION
The mountain resort and its outlying temples are located in the north of Chengde, Hebei province.

CLIMATE
There are cool summers with ample rainfall, and very seldom excessive heat. April to October is the best time to enjoy this resort.

OF SPECIAL INTEREST
The imperial resort is on the World Heritage List, and is famed as China's largest existing classical imperial garden and imperial summer resort, and is where the Qing emperors enjoyed their leisure while handling state affairs.

MAIN ATTRACTIONS
Lizheng (Beauty and Righteousness) Gate, Danbo Jingcheng (Simplicity and Sincerity) Hall, Sizhi (Four Knowledge) Study, Yanbo Zhishuang (Refreshed by Mists and Waves) Hall, Hall for Moon and River (Yuese Jiangsheng), Jehol Spring, and Wenjin Pavilion.

The Golden Hill in Chengde imperial mountain resort (left)

The Xuguangge Tower at Pule Temple (above, left)

The Yanyulou Tower (Tower of Mist and Rain) at Chengde imperial mountain resort (below, left)

Nanjing (Jiansu)

An old city of six dynasties

Dr Sun Yat-sen's
mausoleum, Nanjing
(above, left)

The Neixu Garden at
the residence of the
former president of
the Republic of China
(above, right)

The sacred way of
the Ming mausoleum
(below, right)

As the ancient capital for a total of six dynasties and the birthplace of the Republic of China (1912–1949), Nanjing reminds people of such characteristics as classic simplicity, profundity, vicissitudes, and grand style. Though located in Jiangnan (south of the lower reaches of the Yangtze River), Nanjing is a city embracing a temperament that features harmonious coexistence between the Yangtze River's culture and the Yellow River's culture. This ancient city blends a variety of styles from both southern and northern China in terms of culture, custom, diet, and even its dialect, each of which can be easily appreciated.

From the perspective of geographical location, the urban area of Nanjing is mixed with the local nat-ural scenery to form a landscape fig-uratively compared in history to "Coiling Dragon and Crouching Tiger," a figure of speech in ancient China indicating a forbidding place with strategic importance, and sometimes exclusively relating to Nanjing. And today there are two main streets in the city that are named after such a comparison: one is called "Coiling Dragon Street" (eastern city) and the other is called "Crouching Tiger Street" (western city). The whole city is surrounded with hills and lakes and crossed by winding rivers. These include Mount Zijin, Mount Qixia, Mount Niushou, and Mount Qingliang, as well as Xuanwu Lake, Mochou Lake, and the Qinhuai River. Today's Yangtze River is no longer what was a "natural moat" in history. Nanjing still has its ancient city wall with dark gray bricks and shadows from the surrounding trees. And the city well, which has undergone much damage and renovation in the past, is somehow a reminder of what took place here in the past.

The so-called classic simplicity and profundity, as shown by the lo-cal people in their mentality and spirit, has perhaps been caused by the proximity of Mount Zijin, a hill close to the bustle of a modern big city and a place of historic interest and cultural value. The Ming mau-soleum, the royal tombs of emper-ors of the Ming dynasty (1368–1644 AD), is included on the World Cul-tural Heritage List, and the Sun Yat-Sen* mausoleum is regarded as a model of Chinese architectural history. Upon arriving at the gate of

LOCATION
Situated in the lower reaches of the Yangtze River, and capital of Jiangsu province.

CLIMATE
There are four distinct seasons in the year. It is sultry in summer, and the area is dubbed one of the "Heating Stoves" in China.

OF SPECIAL INTEREST
A long history and rich cultural heritage; 6000 years of civilization and 2400 years of civic history.

MAIN ATTRACTIONS
Sun Yat-sun mausoleum, the Ming mausoleum, the site of the residence of the former president of the Republic of China, Mount Zijin, and the Fuzi Temple.

Sun's tomb, you will see four Chinese characters, "Tian Xia Wei Gong" (quoted from what Sun used to say, this means "governing for the people") inscribed on a board hung high in front of the tomb. The effect is as if this great man were looking down over the ancient city in his lofty spirit, while standing on the top of Mount Zijin.

All through the year, there is something attractive to see on Mount Zijin. At the time between late winter and early spring, groves of plum trees, planted at the foot of the hill, are as rosy as the evening clouds while in full bloom. Near the Linggu Temple in late fall, ginkgo and maple trees shine in golden yellow and brilliant purple respectively. On certain warm sunny days, looking up from the Zixia Lake halfway up the hill, you feel as if a giant and colorful palette has been tipped to pour down everything into the pool of the blue waters below.

In contrast with the brightness and openness of Mount Zijin, the Qinhuai River, with all of its ancient beauties, represents the female disposition of the Jiangnan culture, and both the Qinhuai River and the Fuzi Temple have a more material and secular feeling. Even if many ancient beauties did live here during the six dynasties and contributed to its culture, even if many poems were created by numerous ancient poets, and even if the blood and tears of the people of a conquered nation were expressed by the ancient poets, history itself has always been advancing under the impetus of the time. To a large extent, Nanjing is a city fit for living, and it enjoys a good urban layout and orderly society, while the living pace here is relatively unhurried. Whenever there is a fine day, the locals go to fly kites on the square in front of the Ming Palace Museum, and meanwhile middle-age and elderly people do their physical exercises in Hanzhongmen Square. Occasionally in the street, you may come across some locals speaking at a high pitch and laughing frankly and openly. Nanjing has its unique style and features that reveal its cultural heritage, the modern economy of a civilized city, and splendid natural scenery.

* Sun Yat-sen (1866–1925): a modern Chinese revolutionary leader and statesman, he was the first president of the Republic of China following the overthrow of the Qing dynasty in 1912.

Hangzhou (Zhejiang)
Onetime capital of the Southern Song dynasty

The Drum Tower of Hangzhou, which was named Chaotianmen Gate when first built in the Wu and Yue kingdoms. In the Southern Song dynasty, the Imperial Street passed through here to Hangzhou city. (above, left)

The front gate of Yue Fei's temple (above, right)

The eight-diagram field, which is said to have been plowed at the time of the emperors of the Southern Song dynasty about eight hundred years ago. Eight kinds of differently colored plants used to be grown in the field in order to make the eight diagrams. (center, right)

The temple of King Qian Liu, a fine example of an ancestral temple (below, right)

There's a popular road name that may be found in almost every big city in China: Zhongshan Road. No matter which Zhongshan Road you are on, you'll get a sense of the city's identily, its people, and its history. Hangzhou is no exception.

The Zhongshan Road in Hangzhou is the main urban street, about 4 miles (7km) long, crossing the whole city from north to south. Eight hundred years ago, it was officially named "Imperial Street," and also called "Heavenly Street" by local civilians.

To the south of Hangzhou city is the famous Phoenix Hill, which is historically significant. Early in the Sui dynasty, the hill was chosen as the seat of the city's government. And later it was made the capital seat of Wuyue kingdom in the Period of Five Dynasties and Ten Kingdoms (907–960 AD). When the Southern Song dynasty established its capital here, the city was dramatically expanded and renovated into a heavenly palace, officially called Lin'an, which means "temporary peace." Most of the capital was burnt down in the invasion by the Mongols under Kublai Khan.

Today, some ruins of imperial stone tablets can still be seen among the rocks of the hill, reminding us of the onetime prosperity of the city, of its majestic royal palace, of its mighty imperial army, and of the most luxurious and extravagant life of the emperor. But now, all the glory and splendor have gone with the wind, leaving almost nothing of the grandeur of long ago. However, the imperial spirit is still lingering at the tranquil hill.

The imperial palace offered everything one could wish for, even including a man-made "small West Lake." But occasionally the emperor liked to go out to visit the authentic West Lake or to offer sacrifices to the gods in the Jingling Palace west of the city. As a result, the "Imperial Street" was built, starting from Hening Gate (the present Phoenix Hill Gate) at the north end of the Imper-

LOCATION
Hangzhou lies close to China's southeast coast and is on the south wing of the Yangzte River delta.

CLIMATE
Hangzhou features a favorable climate and four distinct seasons. The weather is generally warm and humid. Every March, spring comes and a variety of flowers are in bloom. And in September and October, you can enjoy the clear sky and fresh air of fall, another golden season.

OF SPECIAL INTEREST
As a city of historical and cultural importance, Hangzhou is not only the birthplace of Liangzhu culture, but was also the capital of the kingdom of Wuyue (907–979 AD) under the Five Dynasties (907–960) and then the national capital of the Southern Song dynasty (1127–1279). On account of this, it has been cited as one of the seven most important ancient capitals in China.

MAIN ATTRACTIONS
Phoenix Hill, Dumb Tower, sites of imperial ancestral temples, and Southern Song Imperial Kiln Museum.

ial Palace and leading to Tianshui Bridge in the north of the city. Built with stones and sand, the street was so well designed that it was still dry enough to travel along on rainy days.

In the first month of every season, the emperor, with his numerous guards of honor, would pass down the Imperial Street toward Jingling Palace. At that moment, all the shops had to be closed and all the civilians were ordered not to make any noise. The only sound was the rumbling of the wheels of the imperial carts on the stones. What a magnificent scene that must have been!

As the Imperial Street was specially renovated for the emperor, there was no civilian residence along the street, only shops and stores. All the civilians had to reside in *Fang* and *Xiang* (lanes and alleys) behind those buildings. All the *Fang*, intersecting with the *Xiang*,

were laid out in proper order on the two sides of the Imperial Street. At present, Hangzhou boasts more than seven hundred lanes, about two fifths of which were named early in the Song dynasty, and most of them have kept their names till now. Traveling from south to north along the street, one will occasionally come across those old lane names, such as "White Horse Temple Lane." To read these names is to read the city's history.

Now, near the middle of Zhongshan Road, the Drum Tower, also known as Chaotian Gate, is located. It is the only surviving city gate of ancient Hangzhou. During the Southern Song dynasty, the gate served as the boundary separating the Imperial Palace from the civilian residences. Outside the gate was the hustle and bustle of the marketplaces of the common people. A bit further to the north was the All Peace Bridge where the famous Xia

Wa Zi (another name was Bei Wa), the biggest entertainment place in Hangzhou at that time, was located. There were more than a dozen theaters, in which many performers were constantly singing, performing plays, telling stories, and playing all kinds of musical instruments until midnight. Now the area attracts thousands of tourists every day.

At that time, the West Lake was known as a Xiao Jin Guo, which means "a most luxurious place." And Hangzhou city, with its large population and prosperous commerce, flourished as the biggest urban concentration in the world. No wonder the Venetian explorer Marco Polo described it in his *Travels* as "the city of heaven" and "the finest and most splendid city in the world."

The imperial tombs of the Western Xia regime (Ningxia)

The romance of the Xia regime

Yinchuan
The Imperial Tombs of the
Western Xia Regime
Ningxia Hui
Autonomous Region
Gansu
Province

LOCATION
The imperial tombs of
the Western Xia regime
are located in the
western suburbs of
Yinchuan and at the
eastern base of Helan
Mountain. It is 22 miles
(35km) from the city
proper.

CLIMATE
Yinchuan has an arid
temperate climate with
four seasons. It is dry,
windy, and sandy, with
May to October the
best months.

OF SPECIAL INTEREST
The imperial tombs
of the dynasties of the
Western Xia regime are
the important remains
of the Western Xia
culture. The whole
area, 6 miles (10km)
from north to south
and 2.5 miles (4km)
from east to west,
comprises eight ceme-
teries and seventy or
so subordinate tombs.

MAIN ATTRACTIONS
The site of the tombs
of King Li Yuan Hao,
the tombs of King Li's
grandfather and father,
a museum, and an art
gallery.

In the mysterious, vast, but distant northwest still stands an age-old barren mountain called Helan, which brings back memories of battles of past dynasties. Its description can be found in many ancient poems.

Helan Mountain opens like a history book. Rock paintings on the mountain reveal the ancient scripts of the ancient Western Xia kingdom, which disappeared overnight. As early as the eleventh century, a kingdom was founded here with today's Yinchuan, the capital of Ningxia Hui Autonomous Region, as its capital. It lasted for more than 190 years. Located near the Yellow Mountain on the east, the Yumen Pass on the west, the strategic Xiaoguan Pass on the south, and the vast desert on the north, the kingdom was inhabited by those who worshiped Helan Mountain as their god. Wearing sheepskin cloaks, they were said to drink liquor in human skulls, wipe their foreheads with the blood of their slaughtered enemies, and open up territories with their horses' hoofs. The regime suddenly disappeared and people have not been able to find anything except a few dozen tombs that reflect the past glory of the kingdom. The heads of the heroes seemed to become the rocks of Helan Mountain, no longer visible to us.

Stories about the kings of the Western Xia regime (1038–1227 AD) have already passed into legend. The founding king killed his brother-in-law and took his wife as his new queen; her enchanting beauty prevented him from killing any more people and from running state affairs as well. He was eventually beheaded by his son and daughter-in law.

Helan Mountain can be thought provoking. The view from the top, of imperial tombs and the open desert, is the only place in which the kings' legendary stories and philosophical reflections are available.

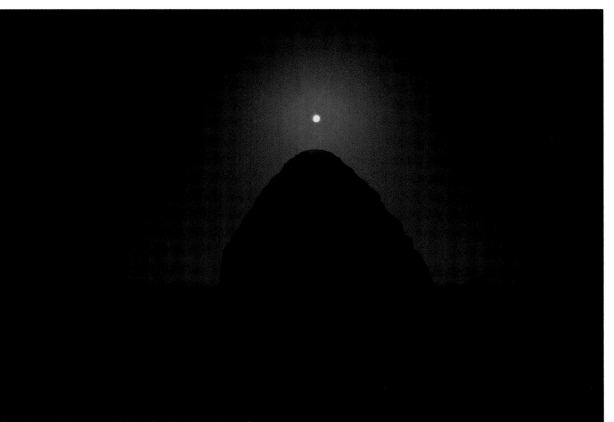

**The tomb of Li Yuan-
hao, an emperor of the
Western Xia regime
(above, right)**

**The sunset in tomb
T93, which is called
the "Eastern Pyramid."
(below, left)**

The ruins of walls of the tombs (below, right)

A stone sculpture of a strong man unearthed in the tomb (below, far right)

Site of the former
Jingjiang Palace
(above, left)

Dr Sun Yat-sen's
memorial monument
in Jingjiang Palace,
Guilin (below, right)

The Jidifang city gate
of the former Jingjiang
Imperial City, Guilin
(above, right)

The former headquar-
ters of the Northern
Expedition in Jingjiang
Palace (below, right)

Jingjiang Palace (Guangxi)
A dynasty receding far into obsurity in the southwest

The history of Guilin dates back 30,000 years, when its earliest people lived in caves. As civilization was put in place, the first emperor of the Qin dynasty built a canal that transformed the mountains into accessible roads. The civilization of central China began to form along the Li River and blended itself with the indigenous Baiyue culture, giving rise to a unique culture that incorporated the natural landscape and has lasted until today. Guilin is one of the first 24 famous ancient historic and cultural cities to be acclaimed as such by the State Council of China. The Jingjiang Palace in Guilin epitomizes the history and culture of the Ming dynasty.

Jingjiang Palace, also called the Imperial City of Guilin, has been put under key state-level protection as a cultural heritage site. It was built in 1372, the fifth year under the rule of Emperor Hongwu in the Ming dynasty, and was followed by the construction of the city walls in 1393, the twenty-sixth year under Emperor Hongwu. With a history of over 630 years, it was built even earlier than the Forbidden Palace in Beijing.

The Imperial City measures 1829 ft (557.5m) long from the south to the north and 1102 ft (336m) wide from the east to the west, covering an area of 2,012,870 square feet (187,000 square meters). It has a city wall 26 ft (7.92m) high and 18 ft (5.5m) wide. The city wall was connected by four gates named Duanli, Guangzhi, Tiren, and Zunyi.

On the left of the city gates there are ancestral temples and on the right, temples for worship. A stately architectural complex was formed with Chengyun Gate, Chengyun Hall, living chambers, and the royal garden built around a central axis. All were surrounded by various halls, mansions, pavilions, and terraces. Specifically, the halls were called Baoshan, Zunle, and Rixin; pavilions were named Qingyue, Xiyang, Wangjiang, and Gongxiu; and other structures include Lingxu Terrace, Zhonghe Mansion, Yansheng Chamber, Kexin Veranda, and Xiuxuan Residence.

LOCATION
Jingjiang Palace is located in the city center of Guilin, Guangxi province.

CLIMATE
The climate is moderate and comfortable, with an annual average temperature of 66°F (19°C). There are mild winters and summers. It rarely snows and it is green all year around.

OF SPECIAL INTEREST
This is the best preserved and oldest palace in China of a vassal king of the Ming dynasty.

MAIN ATTRACTIONS
Jingjiang Imperial City, Duxiu peak, imperial mausoleum, the museum of Jingjiang Imperial Palace.

The Crescent Pond in the royal garden is big enough for boating. Duxiu peak (Solitary Beauty peak) stands gracefully in the Imperial City with Xuanwu Pavilion, Guanyin Hall, Sanguan Temple, and Sanshen Temple on top of the peak and the three other structures of Leshan, Tanqi, and Zhanyun that provide a view into the far distance.

In 1650, the seventh year under the rule of Emperor Shunzhi of the Qing dynasty, Commander Kong Youde – who used to fight for the Ming dynasty and later surrendered to the Qing troops – captured Guilin and was granted the title of King of Dingnan, on account of which Jingjiang Palace was renamed Dingnan Palace. In 1652, the ninth year of Emperor Shunzhi, Li Dingguo, at the head of a peasant revolt, seized Guilin and the defeated Kong Youde committed suicide by setting himself on fire. Jingjiang Palace, having survived over 280 years, was burnt to ashes, leaving behind only the city

wall, city gates, Chengyun Gate, the foundations of the Chengyun Hall with its carved railings, and the marble steps.

Towering in the Imperial City, Duxiu peak thrusts high up in the sky and is known as the Sky-supporting Pillar in the South on account of its steep slopes and the majestic atmosphere it generates. Here you can find inscribed a famous line from a poem written by Wang Zhenggong in the Song dynasty: "Guilin's landscape is unparalleled under heaven."

Jingjiang Palace is the best preserved and the oldest palace of a vassal king in China. Prior to the construction of the palace, at the foot of Duxiu peak there stood the Learning Hall of the Tang dynasty, which was turned into Tieniu Temple during the Song dynasty. It was renamed Dayuan Temple during the Yuan dynasty and later changed to Wanshou Hall. In 1657, the fourteenth year of Emperor Shunzhi and after Jingjiang Palace was leveled to ground, Gong Hall was built on this place. Here, in 1921, Sun Yat-sen, in his Northern Expedition, stationed his troops. During the first few years of the Republic of China, this place accommodated successively the No. 2 Normal School, Model Elementary School, No. 3 High School, and the School of First Industry. In the winter of 1925, the fourteenth year of the Republic of China, it was transformed into Zhongshan (Yat-sen) Park. In 1937 it became the site for office buildings of the Guangxi provincial government, and was then entirely destroyed during the anti-Japanese war and later rebuilt. At present, this is where the Guanxi Normal University is situated.

In the museum of Jingjiang Palace in the ancient Imperial City, exhibition halls focusing on the three themes of "privileges of the imperial family," "life of the imperial family," and "imperial palace in vicissitudes of time" display the ebbs and flows of how the imperial palace of the Ming dynasty was transformed into Gong Hall in the Qing dynasty, government office buildings in the Republic of China, and schools and a university in modern times.

Duxiu peak stands majestic amidst the changing buildings. The carved railings and marble steps in front of Chengyun Hall, the remaining pieces of the Jingjiang Palace, are reminiscent of the glorious past as embodied in the lines written by Emperor Guangxu of the Qing dynasty in the annals of Guilin: "The peak stands as an indifferent witness to the thousands of permutations the imperial family has gone through."

Qinhuangdao (Hebei)

Where lyrics are left beside the East China Sea

Qinhuangdao was named after the first emperor of the Qin dynasty and has become well known all over the world owing to prominent historical figures who have visited the place.

The legend goes that Qinhuangdao acquired its name from being the lodging place of the first emperor of the Qin dynasty when he was on his travels. Some evidence of that was revealed by a recent archeological discovery: the relics of the supposed lodging palace used by the emperor, with an area of 1,076,400 square feet (100,000 square meters), were excavated in Beidaihe. The first emperor of the Qin dynasty, having accomplished the feat of unifying all

the kingdoms into one country, made several trips out of Xianyang, the capital, toward the east. He was fascinated by the east, with its mystical sea, towering mountains, legendary paradise, and promised panacea of immortality that he thought would greatly boost his ruling power. The emperor sent two teams to make discoveries by exploring the seas but neither of them managed to return. The sea, however, was still there, luring generations of emperors.

Among them there was Emperor Wu of the Han dynasty, an emperor with ambition and vision. He went even further than the first emperor of the Qin dynasty in his belief in

occultists and supernatural power. Out of his fancy for the sea, he built platforms in the hopes of getting in touch with supernatural powers. One of the platforms, known simply as the Platform of Emperor Wu of the Han dynasty, was excavated in 1992 on top of the Zhonglian peak in Beidaihe, and that was followed by many other similar discoveries. However powerful and glorious these emperors were, they lacked the ability to conquer the vast ocean.

In 1046 BC, when Emperor Wu dethroned Zhou, the last emperor of the Shang dynasty, and established the Zhou dynasty, two men of virtue in this place, Boyi and Shuqi,

were defiant about accepting the new ruler. They decided they would rather live on wild grass than eat any food provided by the new government. In the end they starved to death, and their story – as well as their virtue of being loyal – passed down through the generations. When the Period of Warring States arrived, Zhou Yan, a great thinker, climbed onto a stone in the Bohai Sea and preached his theory of *yin* and *yang*, attracting a great number of followers.

There is a famous line that referred to "ascending the stone in the east to view the vast sea." Several hundred years after this, it was Cao Cao who ascended the stone on his way back to the south after his northern expedition to Liaodong. Inspired by the overwhelming sea, he wrote his famous essay, "Observing the Sea." Following suit, Emperor Li Shimin of the Tang dynasty, Emperor Kangxi, and Qianlong of

the Qing dynasty all left in Qinghuangdao poems or essays in memory of their eastward journeys to the sea.

Shanhai Pass is a signature scenic spot in Qinhuangdao. The Great Wall stretches eastward, over the mountains, until it dips into the Bohai Sea, integrating the inland landscape of yellow soil with the landscape of the blue sea, Shanhai Pass at the exact place where the Great Wall meets the sea. Known as the Yu Pass in ancient times and an imposing military stronghold, the Shanhai Pass was strategically situated in the narrow space that comprised a route between the mountains and the sea. Built in 1381 by Xuda, a commander in the Ming dynasty, it acquired its name from being constructed to link the mountains and the sea and was known as the First Pass under Heaven.

The section of the Great Wall in Qinghuangdao offers an impressive

and beautiful landscape that integrates mountains, sea, passes, and ancient towns – hence it is a highlight of the Great Wall of the Ming dynasty. Standing high on the Great Wall, there is a panoramic view of both the mountains and the sea, looking into the glorious past and setting yourself free from all that most engages you.

After reading the history, contemplating the sea, and climbing the Great Wall, it is time to go to the beach. With fine sands and gentle waves, Beidaihe is an ideal summer resort that offers a good view of the sea. The ocean, vast and misty, blends into the horizon in the far distance.

LOCATION
Qinhuangdao is located on the northeast of Hebei province, with Bohai Sea on the south and Mount Yanshan on the north.

CLIMATE
In the warm temperate zone, with a semi-humid monsoon climate that has four seasons: a relatively long winter and a short spring, summer, and fall.

OF SPECIAL INTEREST
This is a seaside resort with a landscape of both mountains and sea.

MAIN ATTRACTIONS
Beidaihe, Shanhai Pass, Golden Beach, Jieshi Mountain, Mengjiangnu Temple, and Laolongtou (Old Dragon's Head)

Qufu (Shandong)
Home of Confucius and cornerstone of oriental culture

Dacheng Hall in the Confucius Temple in Qufu (below, left)

Qufu's Cemetery of Confucius Families (above, right)

The Wanren Palace wall in Qufu (below, right)

The dragon poles in the Dacheng Hall of the Confucius Temple (center, right)

"The several thousand year old rites come from eastern Shandong while millions of people bow to the king without a crown."

As is indicated in these lines, a sage makes a holy city. Qufu, is world famous in honor of Confucius, one of the world's greatest philosophers.

Qufu is the home town of Confucius, the founder of Confucianism. In the past two thousand years Confucianism has gradually become the traditional orthodox philosophy in China. And it has exerted a far-reaching influence on east Asia and southeast Asia, becoming the cornerstone of Oriental culture.

In Qufu there are the Confucius Mansions, the Confucius Temple, and the Cemetery of Confucius Families, which are regarded as the essential places in which to remember Confucius and study Confu-

cianism in history. They are treasure houses in terms of their rich cultural connotations, long history, abundant cultural relics, and large scale. Thanks to its important position in both Chinese history and oriental culture, Qufu has a claim to be regarded as one of the three most famous sacred cities of the world.

The largest site at which to remember Confucius, the Confucius Temple, is majestic with regard to its architecture and area. It was in 478 BC, one year after the death of Confucius, that a decree was issued to expand his former residence so that it would become a temple. Emperors of the following dynasties conferred more and more titles on Confucius and also added more and more to the temple. Then Emperor Yongzheng of the Qing dynasty ordered a restoration of the temple around 1725. As a result, the temple

became very much as it looks today in scale.

The Confucius Temple is composed of nine compound courtyards with the central axis running from south to north, supplemented by three divisions to the left, in the middle, and on the right. The temple measures 2070 ft (630m) long and 460 ft (140m) wide, and it contains more than 460 palaces, halls, altars, and pavilions, along with 54 arched gateways and 13 imperial stele pavilions. In the Shengji Palace, the Shisan Stele Pavilion, and the Dacheng Palace a large number of carved steles of different dynasties are stored. Also, the temple has the largest collection of steles of the Han dynasty (206 BC – 220 AD) and is the second largest storage place of steles from just after the Stele Forest of Xi'an throughout the country.

The Dacheng Palace is the main palace and the core section of the Confucius Temple. Made up of five halls, it was called the Wenxuanwang Palace in the Tang dynasty. Then, in 1022, the palace was expanded to seven halls. Emperor Huizong ordered that it should be called the Dacheng Palace in 1104, under the inspiration of the classical works of the philosopher Mencius. Later, in 1724, Emperor Yongzheng had the building renovated. Consequently, the temple was reconstructed with overlapped eaves and carved and painted beams, and was decorated with golden dragons and other intricate patterns. Three Chinese characters expressing the word *dachengdian* (the name of the palace), handwritten by Emperor Yongzheng, were engraved using gold powder on the huge plaque that was hung on the main front. The Dacheng Palace stands 81 ft 4 in (24.8m) high, 150 ft (45.69m) long, and 81 ft 6 in (24.85m) wide on a 7 ft (2.1m) high foundation. That makes it the highest architectural feature of the Confucius Temple.

Situated in the center of the passage in front of the Dacheng Palace, the Xingtan Terrace is said to be the very place where Confucius presented his famous lecture. Beside the terrace stands an ancient tree, which is said to have been planted by the master. Encircled by a red balustrade, the terrace has two layers of eaves made of yellow tiles in double half arches. The pavilion is adorned with fine carvings and dragons covered with gold. An imperial stele engraved with three Chinese characters representing *xingtanzan* (which means an ode to the Xingtan Terrace) and handwritten by Emperor Qianlong in the Qing dynasty is erected nearby. In addition, in front of the pavilion there is a stone incense burner one foot (1m) high that dates from the Jin dynasty (1115–1234 AD).

The Confucius Mansion is a gigantic compound structure, where the generations that followed Confucius lived. It is the third largest residential mansion, coming just after the imperial residential palaces of the Ming and Qing dynasties.

Located in the north of Qufu, the Cemetery of Confucius Families is the exclusive burial ground for Confucius and his relations. Since his time, the Han dynasty emperors carried out a series of 13 renovations and expansions to the cemetery. Nowadays, covering an area of 0.77 square miles (2 square kilometers), with a circumference of 3.5 miles (5.6km) of forest wall which stands over 10 ft (3m) tall and 3 ft (1m) thick, it is the family burial ground with the longest duration and the largest such area in the world.

LOCATION
Qufu is situated in the southwest of Shandong, 84 miles (135km) north of Jinan, the capital city.

CLIMATE
With plentiful rainfall overall, Qufu has a drought in spring and fall and a great amount of rain in summer. It is dry and cold in winter, but there is some snow.

OF SPECIAL INTEREST
As the birthplace of Confucius - the great thinker, educator, statesman, and founder of Confucianism in ancient China - Qufu boasts a long history, a rich reserve of cultural relics, a galaxy of celebrities, and a picturesque landscape.

MAIN ATTRACTIONS
The Confucius Temple, the Confucius Mansion, and the Cemetery of Confucius Families

Zhengzhou (Henan)
Traveling in time

LOCATION
Zhengzhou is located in the center of China and is the capital city of Henan province.

CLIMATE
There are a four distinct seasons. The annual average temperature is 57.7°F (14.3ºC). Spring and fall are the best seasons in which to visit.

OF SPECIAL INTEREST
This is one of China's eight ancient capitals and is considered the cradle of the Chinese civilization.

MAIN ATTRACTIONS
Henan Museum, Relics of Shangcheng, and Erqi Square.

Of China's eight ancient capitals, four are in Henan province.

The relics of Shangcheng in downtown Zhengzhou show where the earliest and biggest capital city of the Shang dynasty used to be. It is also the first capital city in China's history that had a definite boundary. With an area of 9.7 square miles (25 square kilometers), the capital was encircled by a city wall and accommodated an imperial palace, handicraft workshops, cellars to store sacrificial items, bronze musical instruments for ceremonies, defense facilities, a water supply, and a disposal and storage system. The melody played by the giant bells (an ancient musical instrument made up of 16 bells) leaves you imagining you can see the grand banquets hosted by Emperor Shang at which his ministers would eat from ancient vessels (typically with two loop handles and three or four legs) to the music created by the instrumentalists striking the bells.

The long history of Zhengzhou reaches far beyond this. The civilization of Zhengzhou dates as far back as eight thousand years ago. Evidence for this comes from archeological studies carried out in the home town of Xuanyuan, an alternative name for Huangdi (the Yellow Emperor, who was regarded as the first great ruler of China) and the Peiligang culture. Zhengzhou was made the capital during the time of the kingdom of Guan in the Xia, Shang, and Zhou dynasties, and continued in the kingdom of Zheng during the Period of Spring and Autumn, and the kingdom of Han during the Period of Warring States. Back in that remote period of history, this piece of land was referred to as Zhongzhou or Central China. It was not only physically the center of China, but also the center of the politics, economy, and culture of the time. It was densely populated and became the cradle of the Chinese civilization.

There are quite a few places of historic interest in Zhengzhou.

A good understanding of its history and an in-depth insight into the ebbs and flows it has experienced are afforded by the Henan Museum. On exhibition there are items created by the ancestors of China that were buried under the earth for thousands of years before they were excavated and washed clean. The messages they bring are about to reveal more about the country's history.

Henan Museum is a modern museum of history and art, covering an area of more than 1,076,400 square feet (100,000 square meters) and with 839,052 square feet (78,000 square meters) of floor space. The main building of the structure looks overwhelming and strikes awe in the beholder. It is inspired by the relics of the observatory constructed by Guo Shoujing, an astronomer of the Yuan dynasty. The slopes on the main building are covered with white nails, decorations customarily used in bronze utensils – precious cultural relics of Central China. The blue windows on the roof and the glass belt running from the top to the bottom to let in sunlight represent the Huang He (Yellow River) roaring with tremendous momentum and also the well-established and longstanding civilization of Central China. The museum boasts a collection of 130,000 articles. Many of them are at the top of collection lists both at home and abroad. When you take a walk inside the museum, you will find yourself in a sacred shrine of art.

Erqi Pagoda is not as old as Zhengzhou. It is neither taller nor more grandiose than the modern skyscrapers standing row upon row in downtown Zhengzhou. However, the pagoda is, without doubt, the symbol of the city. A trip to Zhengzhou would not be considered complete if Erqi Pagoda were excluded. The pagoda, glittering with lights, provides an amazing view at night. Businesses flourish on the streets around it. This twin structure is actually two pagodas, originally built in memory of two martyrs who sacrificed their lives for the rights and freedom of people in the 1920s. It now stands as a symbol of Zhengzhou's urban culture and a witness to Zhengzhou's history.

Night scene at Henan Museum (below, right)

A view of Zhengzhou, a green city (above, left)

Erqi Pagoda in Zhengzhou (above, right)

Yili (Much)

Much further on the road to the West

The following story took place over two thousand years ago: One day in 138 BC, the city gate of Chang'an was opened wide for a team of over a hundred civil and military officials led by Zhang Qian, who was sent by the emperor on an epic journey to the west. Heading for Yili, a town in the remote west, Zhang Qian aimed to pay friendly calls on behalf of the emperor to kingdoms in the west. His party was confronted by desolate country with blinding sand storms and deserts that seemed to sprawl for thousands of miles. Apart from braving the unfriendly nature of the landscape, they suffered raids by the Xiongnu, a nomadic people. The peaceful diplomatic visit turned out to be a failure. However, the determination of Emperor Wu of the Han dynasty to bolster Han power in the west was not defeated. Twenty years later, Zhang Qian made a second trip at the emperor's request and, against all the odds, he reached the Yili River. As he trudging westward to Yili, he could not have imagined that his successful endeavor would be only the first of countless journeys that would be undertaken by generations to come, and which finally gave birth to the famous Silk Road.

In fact, people of great perseverance made pioneering journeys long before Zhang Qian. In the fifth century BC, the Sai tribe, a nomadic people, drove cattle along the Hexi corridor to the riverbanks of Yili. They could not resist the temptation of Yili's fertile and beautiful land and made it their home. Dayue people and Wusun people, offspring of the Sai, began to migrate to the west, escaping the slavery imposed by the Xiongnu. The Wusun people

LOCATION
Yili is located in the Yili Valley on the western ranges of Mount Tianshan, Xinjiang. It shares borders with Kazakhstan to the north and west, and with Mongolia to the northeast.

CLIMATE
There is a moderate climate, with plentiful rainfall and sunshine. The best seasons to visit are summer and fall.

OF SPECIAL INTEREST
Yili is characterized by a mixed culture of the east and the west, with a unique ethnically diverse society and a spectacular landscape. It is known as the Jiangnan of the west (Jiangnan refers to the to the south of the Yangtze River).

MAIN ATTRACTIONS
Guozigou (Fruit Valley), Jingyuan Temple, the ancient city of Huiyuan, Museum of Lin Zexu, Sayram Lake, and so on.

in particular, the forefathers of the Kazakhs, established the Wusun kingdom in Yili, the most powerful one of all the 36 kingdoms in the west.

In 1764, with a view to forging a defensive frontier, the Qing dynasty dispatched to Yili over four thousand Xibe (or Sibo) people from the northeast. Theirs was doomed to be an arduous journey. Bidding farewell to their homeland, the Xibe people, after one year and five months, finally made it to the beautiful Yili River, and the area became their second homeland. Now two hundred or so years later, on April 18th, people gather beside the Yili River and sing and dance in the traditional way of the Xibe people, and pay tribute to the ancestors who made Yili their home and to the beautiful Yili as well.

Guozigou (Fruit Valley) in Yili is a passage of strategic importance through the Yili valleys. This is where merchants traveled to the prairie, and where Genghis Khan made his way to the Black Sea. In 1218 AD, when Genghis Khan led his troops on a westward expedition, he found the Fruit Valley so perilous that he commissioned his men to construct a broad and smooth road through the valley.

When China lost the Opium War in 1841, Lin Zexu – a strong advocate against drugs who fought fearlessly against the British invaders – was removed and banished to Yili. In the face of the harsh conditions of the west, he proved himself to be a man of strong convictions and integrity. During his two years in Yili, he devoted himself to developing water conservancy and irrigation projects for the benefit of the people there.

The ancient city of Huiyuan was in Yili, the most important of the nine cities built during the reign of Emperor Qianlong. Huiyuan has been well preserved. A panoramic view is afforded by the bell tower inside the city.

In 1876, tsarist Russia invaded Yili. Zuo Zongtang, governor of Gan and Shan at the time, led his troops on a westward expedition. Unlike his predecessors, he was so determined to recover Yili that he ordered his men to carry an empty coffin for him all the way into the west, showing he would struggle to the end.

The footprints of our ancestors, firm and unyielding, have covered the ground all over Yili, an oasis in the depth of deserts as well as being on the ancient Silk Road.

Pingyao (Shanxi)
Financial center of the Ming and Qing Dynasties

A distant view of the North Gate Tower of Pingyao (above, left)

Panorama of ancient Pingyao city (above, right)

The mansion house of a wealthy Pingyao family (below, left)

A view of ancient Pingyao city, showing Ming and Qing Street (below, right)

This is how we see the ancient town of Pingyao on TV: elegant buildings enclosed by imposing high walls with gray bricks and tiles, simple and poetic in white snow. As you step into this ancient town, get ready to be carried away by the profundity of time and history.

Initially built during the reign of King Xuan of the Western Zhou dynasty (827–782 BC), when General Yin Jifu stationed his army here, Pingyao is an ancient town of rich cultural legacy with a history of over 2800 years. Having weathered the vicissitudes of time, Pingyao remains intact as the best-preserved

example of ancient towns of the Ming and Qing dynasties in China. Pingyao as we it see today looks much the same as when it was expanded in 1370 – the third year of Emperor Hongwu of the Ming dynasty – with streets, *yamun* (government offices in ancient China), shops, and residential compounds, all maintaining the original architectural features of the Ming dynasty.

At the center of Pingyao is a city wall of brick and stone that was built when King Xuan of the Western Zhou dynasty ruled and expanded during the reign of Emperor Hongwu of the Ming dynasty.

The city wall, square in shape, measures 33 ft (10m) high and 20,200 ft (6157m) long. Paved with brick and stone, it allows two carriages to run side by side. Defensive structures on the wall include watchtowers, battlements, and so on. Legend has it that the three thousand battlements and 72 towers represent the 3000 disciples and 72 men of virtue who were the early followers of Confucius. Enclosed lookout towers were built symmetrically, with two on each side of the East and West Gates of the city wall. On the southeastern part of the city wall, there stands the Kuixing Tower, a small but tall and graceful octagonal building 79 ft

LOCATION
Pingyao is located
56 miles (90km) south
of Taiyuan in Shanxi
province.

CLIMATE
Typical of the
continental monsoon
climate with a cold
and dry winter,
in which there is a great
temperature fluctuation.
The area has a rainy
summer, and a short
spring and fall.

OF SPECIAL INTEREST
Pingyao is considered
the best preserved
prototype of an ancient
town of the Ming
and Qing dynasties.

MAIN ATTRACTIONS
Ancient city wall,
courtyard residences,
Ri Sheng Chang, South
Avenue in the ancient
town, and Dacheng Hall
of the Wenmiao Temple.

(24m) high covered with a roof of colored glaze. The ancient city boasts a number of historical buildings, such as the Great Hall of Zhengguo Temple, an ancient structure built of wood in the period of the Five dynasties, and the Dacheng Hall of the Wenmiao Temple – built in the Jin dynasty. Apart from a host of historical and cultural relics, Pingyao also boasts several courtyard residences, another unique feature of this ancient town. Most of the 3797 traditional courtyard residences that have been well preserved to date are still in use, encapsulating a prosperous Pingyao at its prime time in history.

What makes Pingyao more extraordinary is its role as a financial center in ancient China. During the Qing dynasty, Pingyao was known as Little Beijing (Beijing in miniature). A large number of banks of considerable size were opened along the West Street of Pingyao, which was widely acknowledged as the most important financial street of the Qing dynasty. The eight banks, led by the Ri Sheng Chang Money Exchange, expanded their banking businesses to 45 residential cities. Among them, Ri Sheng Chang, the provincial forerunner of banks of all types, was capable of handling financial business worth 1 million to 38 million *liang* (a traditional Chinese unit of money) annually. Its business, as well as its fame, expanded to the rest of the world, as evidenced by its presence in San Francisco and New York in the United States. A glimpse into the courtyards where those banks used to be will leave visitors overwhelmed with wonder, with roofs and high walls in multiple layers. Banknotes of various types and in different colors are on exhibition. This is the place where the professional and networked mechanism of money exchange in ancient China gradually took shape, replacing the burdensome transportation of silver. Right on this "Wall Street" – not as well known as its counterpart in the United States – banks like Ri Sheng Chang and Bai Chuan Hui were busy handling savings and granting loans to boost commercial exchange.

The ancient town of Pingyao was admitted to the World Cultural Heritage List by UNESCO in 1997.

Chengdu (Sichuan)
A land of abundance

LOCATION
Chengdu is situated in central Sichuan province, of which it is the capital.

CLIMATE
A subtropical moist monsoon climate, with four distinct seasons each year. The summers are not intensely hot and the winters escape extreme cold.

OF SPECIAL INTEREST
The city is representative of the Shuhan culture of ancient China.

MAIN ATTRACTIONS
Wuhou Memorial Temple, Du Fu's Caotang, the Qingyang Palace, and Dujiangyan.

Dujiangyan Weir, located in the west of Dujiangyan city, Sichuan. Part of the oldest irrigation works known in the world, Dujiangyan Weir is famous for channeling water without a dam. (below, right)

Gudashengci Temple in Chengdu (below, left)

A giant panda (above, right)

A scene from a Sichuan opera, which is an important feature of local Sichuan culture (above, right)

For ordinary people, the city of Chengdu is mostly linked to what is depicted in a Chinese classic historical novel entitled "The Three Kingdoms." As capital of the Shuhan kingdom in the Three Kingdoms Period (220–280 AD), Chengdu was the place where historical figures such as Liu Bei and Zhege Liang in the Three Kingdoms Period wrote their famous chapters long ago. The Yangtze River has been running eastward ever since.

However, Chengdu enjoys a much longer history than this, dating over 2400 years ago. As early as around the middle of the fifth century BC, the Kaiming dynasty of the ancient Shu kingdom transferred its capital to Chengdu. The Shu kingdom was then defeated and its territory (what is now Sichuan province) was annexed by the Qin kingdom (later the Qin dynasty of 221–207 BC) in 316 BC. The city was later rebuilt by Qin's General Sima Cuo in 311 BC. During the Han dynasty (206 BC – 220 AD), Chengdu became one of the five most significant cities across the country, and afterward it was upgraded to become the national capital of Shuhan in the Three Kingdoms Period. Chengdu ranked as one of the four most distinguished cities of the nation in the Tang Dynasty (AD 618–907), and its prosperity as the economic and cultural hub of southwest China then is vividly described by Du Fu, a Tang poet. The city wall of Chengdu, which underwent reconstruction three times within the Kangxi years

of the Qing dynasty (1644–1911 AD), has a diameter of 7 miles (11km) encircling the city proper and a height of 33 ft (10m). The city consists of three components: Royal Town, Major Town, and Minor Town, each of which boasts a distinctive neighborhood system. Royal Town looks toward the south, and Major Town is located at an angle of 30 degrees from Royal Town. Minor Town has a system of streets rather like a fishing net. Stunned by what he had seen when he came here, Marco Polo praised Chengdu as a magnificent city.

Over the years, the sightseeing district in Chengdu has shaped up around the Huanhua Stream, which runs through many scenic spots such as Du Fu's Caotang (the old residence of Du Fu) and Wuhou's Temple (the memorial temple of

Zhuge Liang). Other well-known places include the Yong mausoleum (the royal tombs of Emperor Wang Jianzhi of the Qianshu kingdom in the Five Dynasties (907–960 AD) – as well as Dujiangyan, an ancient irrigation system on the World Cultural Heritage List.

The architecture of Chengdu's old city combines two sharply different styles: majesty in north China, and prettiness in south China, prompting Zuo Si, a man of letters in the Jing dynasty (265–420 AD), to regard it highly as a golden city with stone contours, both beautiful and lofty. The old city moat is surrounded by two winding rivers, which are spanned by attractive corridor bridges and arched stone bridges. The Golden River runs through the city proper, while the Royal River encircles the Royal

Town. There are rows upon rows of Siheyuan decorated with black tiles and white walls, and temples are scattered among them in classic elegance, as are verdant trees. Some outstanding buildings to note are the following: the Mingyuan Building in downtown Chengdu (a structure in the grand style), the Wangjiang Building in the southeast of the city (surrounded by groves of bamboo), Wuhou's Temple in the south (with dense cypress trees all round it), and the Caotang Monastery in the southwestern part (almost hidden by luxuriant nanmu trees) – as well as the Wenshu Courtyard, the Dachi Temple, and so forth.

Three different kinds of street systems derive from the coexistence of Major Town, Royal Town, and Minor Town, and constitute a striking feature of Chengdu's old city. Down the somewhat sloping terrain of the old city, Major Town's neighborhoods are based on a square-shape grid, similar to those seen in

China's most ancient capitals. Within Major Town, residential houses, government buildings, and schools are all to be found, and are encompassed by various shops. The result is a bustling area surrounding a serene interior. Royal Town is the political and cultural center of the city. With the official residence of King Shu of the Ming dynasty (1368–1644 AD) at its core, it has developed a street system running from north to south. Minor Town, a residential area full of lanes, is composed of neighborhoods arranged like a fishing net. Both ends of the each lane are connected with the business section, while between the lanes there are quiet and solitary courtyards. As for residential buildings in Chengdu, the vast majority of them are made of wood, modest in appearance, light in structure, and elegant in color.

More than two thousand years ago, the world famous Dujiangyan irrigation project was constructed by Li Bing, governor of Qin's Shu

district. Ever since then Chengdu has developed into "A Land of Abundance," promising its people a favorable climate and bumper harvests.

Dali (Yunan)

An ancient city immersed in culture and flowers

LOCATION
The town is situated in the central part of the Dali Bai Minority Autonomous Prefecture, in the northwest of Yunnan province.

CLIMATE
The city's climate follows the plateau monsoon pattern at the lower latitude. Cangshan Mountain and Erhai Lake work together to produce the obvious changes in climate. Whatever the time of year, it is pleasant enough to tour in this area.

OF SPECIAL INTEREST
The city is representative of the unique history, culture, and customs of the Bai people.

MAIN ATTRACTIONS
Cangshan Mountain, Erhai Lake, Three Pagodas at the Changsheng Temple, and the Butterfly Spring.

Three Pagodas at the Changsheng Temple (below, right)

A view of ancient Dali city (below, left)

The Butterfly Spring in Dali (above, right)

Renowned as the city of ancient literature, Dali has a long history of over 1200 years. Emperor Wudi of the West Han dynasty (206 BC – 25 AD) had annexed Dali and made it part of his territory, naming it Yeyu. Then the kingdom of Nanzhao in the Tang dynasty (618–907 AD) reconstructed the town from 764 onward and moved its capital here in 799. This comprises the original section of ancient Dali. It was the political, economic, and cultural center through the Tang and the Song (960–1279 AD), and continued right down to the Yuan (1206–1368) in this area. After this, the town was restructured into a square form in 1382, with gate towers built on the four sides, corner towers placed between the sides, and the Wuhua Building built in the center of the town.

At present, generally speaking, Dali is a replica of what could be seen in the Ming dynasty (1368–1644 AD) with regard to its architectural style. In the city some substantial sections of the Ming walls shed some light on its historical significance in the glow of sunset.

Dali serves us the best of the culture and local customs of the Bai people. The whole of the ancient city is built on the checkered network of the Qing (1616–1911 AD) and the Ming style, and is composed of 9 streets and 18 lanes. One street, which runs from north to south, is lined with blue-tiled, stone-built shops and eating houses selling marble products, batik, and souvenirs woven from straw. This kind of antique and elegant building typical of the Bai minority is found row upon row, extending from the west to the east.

Listed as one of the three unique things in the city, the stone-built wall that stands firmly against the rain and wind dates back as far as the Nanzhao architectural style in the Tang dynasty. The historical records show that some of the stone-built private houses of that time stood as high as 13 ft (4m), and the houses extended a long way from the center of the town. In Central China the main house in the courtyard is built to face south, but the main house of the Bai is built in an east–west direction. Therefore, the gate is usually found in the northeast of the courtyard, blocked by a screening wall on which one popular Chinese character, the one denoting happiness, is carved.

All the buildings are decorated with fine sculpture and paintings. Latticed doors, beams, and pillars are engraved with such symbolic patterns as curling straws, flying dragons, watchful bats, and jade rabbits. Some vivid and interesting compositions to be seen include the Golden Lion biting the Embroidered Ball and the Unicorn watching the Banana Tree. Bai sculptors of are expert at a kind of local engraving called "Hollowed Carving,"

made of three to four layers. Their sculptures – featuring mountains, rivers, figures, flowers, birds, insects, and fish – are lifelike and very impressive.

Poor or rich, the Bai have valued flowers since ancient times. As a result, every household boasts a garden of some size, where such precious plants as the Dali camellia, sweet osmanthus, and pomegranate are grown. Clusters of buds and thick foliage struggle over courtyard walls. They form a long lane adorned with overgrown blossoms, linking one house to another, creeping along the creeks from one street to the next. It is a really fascinating scene.

The group of three pagodas, situated about half a mile (1km) away in the north of Dali, is another historical attraction. Together with the Zhaozhou Bridge in Hebei province and the Wild Goose Pagoda in Xi'an, valued as examples of rare ancient architecture, this group is listed as a key cultural relic and is under the state-level protection of the State Council.

Lijiang (Yunnan)

An ancient town by a snow mountain, home to ancient Naxi music

LOCATION
Lijaing is located on the northwest of Yunnan province, on the southern tip of the Qinghai-Tibet Plateau, 7870 ft (2400m) above sea level.

CLIMATE
The area enjoys pleasant weather, with moderate temperatures in winter and summer.

OF SPECIAL INTEREST
The town has a unique culture and beautiful natural landscape, and was inscribed on the World Heritage List by UNESCO in 1997.

MAIN ATTRACTIONS
The ancient town of Lijiang, Jade Dragon Snow Mountain, Hutiao Gorge, Wenfeng Temple, Black Dragon Pool, and more besides.

A view of Lijiang, where jingling water flows beneath the bridges (above, right)

A distant view of the ancient town of Lijiang (below, left)

A Naxi inn in the ancient town of Lijiang (below, right)

Among all the historical and cultural ancient towns in China, Lijiang is the only one that has no city walls. This, as legend goes, has something to do with Mu, of the ruling clan of Lijiang in the Ming dynasty. It is said that as his family name was Mu, if city walls were to be built around his city, then the Chinese character of *mu* with a frame around it would take the place of another Chinese character, *kun*, which means "being besieged." It was considered inauspicious to encircle the city with a wall for this reason and as a result Lijiang remains without any. Mude, the chieftain of the Mu clan in the Ming dynasty, ruled with vision and open-mindedness. Though deep in the mountains on the southwest, he went beyond the mountains to the capital of the Ming dynasty, instead of isolating Lijiang from the outside world. He was so struck with awe and admiration by the majesty of the Forbidden Palace and the culture of Central China that, upon his return to Naxi, he began to promote actively the introduction of manufacturing technology, culture, and education from Central China. He made friends with celebrities from Central China and recruited people with ability in agriculture, mineral exploration, and handicrafts from Central China to Lijiang. Another priority on Mude's schedule was to commission the construction of a palace, which resulted in an imperial palace resembling the one he saw in Central China. Inscribed on the screen wall at the gate of the palace was a line by Xu Xiake, the great traveler of the Ming dynasty, extolling the palace: "the magnificence of this palace parallels the majesty of a king."

Lijiang does not have a big town center and visitors roaming in the city may come across friends and people with familiar faces everywhere. More often, however, visitors will encounter water. The water, originating from thawing snow from mountains and glaciers, has been here for ages. Water from the Black Dragon Pool at the foot of Mount Xiangshan, to the north of the town, flows down from three rivers. They split into nine channels and further subdivide into numerous smaller streams that thread through the whole town. The streams are not wide, just 6–10 ft (2–3m) across. Willow tree branches hang low on both sides of the rivers to caress the streams. Green trees shade the streams as well as the houses beside the water. This ancient town in high land, surprisingly, assumes similar features to those of villages south of the Yangtze River, which are said to have "water flowing through and willows waving in front of every household." Streams, carrying with them the heart and soul of the snowy mountains, wash the streets and lanes, and the residences, day and night, and lend a gentle touch to the daily life of the people in the town. It can be said that water is the soul of this ancient town.

Ever since the time when people rode on horseback, Sifang Street has been the town center where dozens of shops huddle around a square. All sorts of commodities from elsewhere are bought and sold here. From this small square that covers an area of about 4310 square feet (400 square meters), four main streets extend in four directions to reach the end of the town, crossed by a labyrinth of streets and lanes. Such a layout was said to be the product of designers of the Mu clan in the Ming dynasty, who were inspired by the shape of the seal that belonged to the Mu clan. The square is not only where people from outside gather, but also seems to be the place where the daily life of local residents begins. The square is like an open market, a social place.

Sifang Street has been paved with colored stones which came from the natural stone of the mountains around Lijiang. After being trampled thousands of times, their surface became clean and smooth and the stones became known as the Stones in Five Colors on account of the colors they reflect after being washed by rain. Most of the streets, like Sifang Street, were paved with

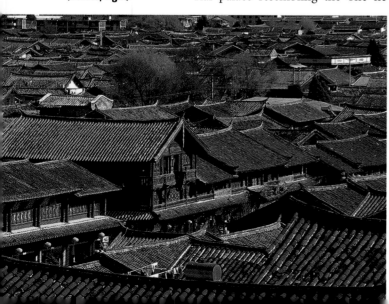

these stones, which protect against both dust and water. Just as it has taken hundreds of years to make the street, it has taken hundreds of years for the history and culture of the town to develop.

Naxi ancient music is considered to be a living artifact of Oriental music. An orchestra of old men play the magic Naxi music in a hall where a Dayan Naxi Ancient Music Concert is held every evening. The youngest musician among them is over 70 years old, while the oldest is 90. Every year some members of the band pass away, and their photos are hung high on the crossbeam above the stage. The souls of these old men remain in Naxi ancient music for those still alive to practice it in their remaining years. Walking out of their houses late in the afternoon

and making their way through the crowded town center to the stage, these old men are carried back by the tuneful melody of the ancient Naxi music to the best of times – or even further back to the history about which their fathers once told them.

Phoenix County (Hunan)

Where Dragon and Phoenix bring good fortune to people

It is the Phoenix Mountain that makes Phoenix county famous, and it is Shen Congwen that makes Phoenix county known to the outside world. Shen Congwen gained his reputation from his essay "The Border City," which in fact depicts Chadong township in Huayuan county, to the north of Phoenix county. In "The Border City" Shen Congwen said, "To enter Hunan from Sichuan, you can take the road in the east. When the road reaches Chadong, a mountainous township in the west of Hunan, you can see a stream, and by the stream a small white pagoda, and by the pagoda in a solitary house, there lived an old man, a girl and a yellow dog."

Tianwang Temple and the stage, one of the eight scenic places in Phoenix county in the past, were pulled down in the 1950s and restored in 1984. The houses, built on piles that support them from underneath, were also newly built then. The yachts by the bank were painted bright red. But Tuojiang, the river, remains there, the ancient city walls remain there, and the red stone slabs are there, too. In other words, the geographical layout remains untouched. People living there still follow the ancient way.

Tuojiang River passes by the border of the city. The water is pure and crystal clear. On the riverbed we can see the water plants clearly. Some fishing boats drift leisurely on the river, and fish hawks throw themselves into the water, leaving endless ripples on its surface. Away from the North Gate and along the Tuojiang River there are women scattered here and there by the bank, washing clothes and vegetables, rinsing dyed materials – as if some military commander had deployed them this way, with the utensils they need for their work in their hands, producing continual sounds as they continue with their tasks. Here the rhythm of life is before us. Passing the East Gate, we can see the Rainbow Bridge, which crosses the Tuojiang River and connects south and north. It was built during the Ming dynasty and has simply been changed into a road bridge. The bridge has three arches and two piers; it is quite big for a small town. Look ahead, and you will see the raised houses arranged row upon row by the banks, while in the distance the temple, the pagoda, and some small boats too, appear in the foggy air.

You can walk on the red stone slabs in the lanes and streets with native women moving leisurely beside you. They carry bamboo baskets filled with vegetables and commodities on their backs – sometimes the baskets hold their children. The baskets are woven from bamboo leaves and branches. They are one of the signs of the local way of life. Under foot, the red stone slabs become smooth and slippery, reflecting softly glowing lights. They are witnesses to the great changes in the history of this small town. The remote lanes are tranquil, with the wooden doors on both sides tightly closed in a mysterious way, rather like ancient books that have not been opened for a long time. They seem to be the most isolated area, the last stronghold that keeps away the outside world. They bring to mind clear reminiscences of a time that has long since passed away.

Along Tuojiang River, the raised houses by the city walls are open to tourists, and, door by door, visitors are welcomed wholeheartedly. Under the setting sun, from time to time you may catch sight of the curious eyes of local grannies and children. Now the tourists who have come to do some sightseeing become sightseeing objects themselves. Together with the green mountains behind, the elevated houses reflect inverted images in the water, so harmonious, so quietly elegant – you can get similar images from traditional Chinese poems and paintings. Through a back door, you can see the green water flowing past a house, and a girl cooking green vegetables at the stove. She becomes a silhouette with the frame of the door as a lens and the green banks of the river as the background. Maybe she is another Cui Cui, a character in Shen Congwen's works.

Shen Congwen said, "All are so tranquil. Everyone passes every day in the simplest way of solitude, of which no one can give an explana-

Houses supported by piles underneath, Fenghuang (above)

The beautiful scenery of Fenghuang county (below)

tion." Of course, Cui Cui is only one landscape, with a slight melancholy about it, among many others. He also said, "She may never return, yet maybe she returns tomorrow."

The phoenix is believed to appear in prosperous times in history. It doesn't matter whether she is transformed or not – all that matters is that she flies again.

Huizhou (Anhui)

Prosperity melting away

Shexian, in Anhui province, used to be in the territory of the old province of Huizhou. According to local historical records, it was home to the Neo-Confucianist Cheng-Zhu School of Principle, to the Xin'an school of painting, to the famous Huizhou ink and inkstone, and to the architectural school of Huizhou buildings. Traces of prosperity can be found everywhere in the old bridges, pagodas, streets, lanes, and workshops – and in the everyday life of the people, who still cling to ancient customs and lifestyles.

Shexian became an administrative region as early as in the Qin dynasty, but its prime time came in the Ming dynasty. Shexian was covered with mountains, thick forests, and infertile soil. The physical unfriendliness was compounded by a sharp rise of population begin-

ning in the twelfth century, when the amount of land available became insufficient to meet the demand for it. This led to an outflow of Huizhou people to make a living elsewhere. Savvy in doing business, Huizhou people became so successful that they earned themselves the title of "Huizhou Business Clans." They were deeply attached to their home areas, and as soon as they made enough money they returned with their fortune to Huizhou, where they constructed a number of distinctive buildings decorated with gold and silver among the woods and beside the lakes. Though the Huizhou Business Clans lost their prominence as time passed, the Huizhou buildings are still there, unveiling a glorious past.

Residences, ancestral temples, and memorial arches of the Ming

and Qing dynasties can be found almost everywhere in today's Shexian. Visitors will find themselves in the middle of an architectural museum of the Ming and Qing. Among these buildings, there are a great number of exquisitely built memorial arches, which are rarely seen in other parts of the country. Shexian became known as the "capital of memorial arches," with more than 250 memorial arches built in the Ming and Qing dynasties all over the county. With every arch telling its own story, they stand witness to Shexian's significance in history. The most well-known arches are the Stone Arch of Xuguo and the Memorial Arches of Tangyue clan.

The Stone Arch of Xuguo spans the street in the town center. Rectangular in shape, it was built on eight supports, four on the front and another four on the back. It was built with orig-

The Memorial Arches of the Tangyue clan (above, left)

The ancient Yuliang ferry in Shexian (above, right)

Evening mists at an ancient bridge (below, right)

LOCATION
Shexian is located in Huangshan city, Anhui province, 17 miles (27km) from the city of Huangshan proper.

CLIMATE
Conditions here are subtropical and humid, with a moderate temperature all the year round.

OF SPECIAL INTEREST
Shexian is a historical and cultural city renowned for Huizhou buildings constructed in the Ming and Qing dynasties and for the residents' traditional and simple way of life.

MAIN ATTRACTIONS
Doushan Street, Xuguo Stone Arch, and the memorial arches of Tangyue clan.

inal features rarely found in other arches. Xuguo, the owner of the arch and a native of Shexian, was a high-ranking official in the reigns of three emperors: Emperor Jiajing, Emperor Longqing, and Emperor Wanli of the Ming dynasty. In return for his contribution to the suppression of an upheaval in Yunnan, the emperor of the time granted him a month's leave. Upon returning to Shexian, Xuguo mobilized various resources to erect a stone arch in memory of the emperor's benevolence. To distinguish it from the arches that Shexian already had, he commissioned the construction of a huge eight-foot stone arch. This "Arc de Triomphe" of Xu's clan, with vivid patterns and elaborate decorations all over it, looks magnificent and stately. In most instances, memorial arches were built to commemorate loyalty, filial piety, righteousness, and chastity. Xuguo's arch is no exception. The carvings all over the arch were expressions of loyalty to the emperor, recognition of the owner's virtues, or an expression of the implication of peace in the world in general.

Located four miles (6 km) away from the town, the Memorial Arches of Tangyue were built by a Huizhou businessman clan during a period spanning more than four hundred years. This complex consists of seven arches. Though built at different times of the Ming and Qing dynasties and featuring different styles, they were well integrated and harmonious. During the Ming dynasty, an army that was carrying out an uprising kidnapped a father and son that were part of the Bao family in Tangyue village and asked for a ransom – without which they would kill one of the captives. The father and the son both wanted to be killed to save one another's life. The story spread, reaching the emperor, who then paid the Bao family the honor of allowing them to build an arch in recognition of the father's benevolence as well as the son's piety. This was the origin of the prestige of the Bao family. In the four hundred years that followed, the Bao family took up trading in salt. As they became prominent in the neighborhood, me-

morial arches were built one by one to honor their ancestors.

Doushan Street in Shexian is an ideal place for visitors who wish to get an idea of how common people lived in the Ming and Qing dynasties. Doushan Street displays a full array of things passed down from generations, from ancient carvings, wells, and buildings to memorial arches. With white walls and eaves shaped like a horse's head lining the road and indigo blue flagstones paving the way, the street is flanked by ancient buildings of various types, such as private residences, government offices, schools, and courtyards for wealthy business clans. Doushan Street truly reveals how people used to live and how they continue to live. As you step into these residences, you will find it easy to imagine what kind of people used to live here. In these ancient residences and courtyards, life flows on.

Suzhou (Jiangsu)
A dream in the past, at present, and in the future

The Wangshiyuan
Garden, Suzhou
(above, left)

A reception room
in the ancient town
(above, right)

As the only city in the world with its original urban site left unchanged for over 2500 years, Suzhou is renowned for its classical gardens, houses near small bridges, flowing rivers – and 2500-year-old neighborhoods. This is a landmark in the beautiful Jiangnan (south of the lower reaches of the Yangtze River), characterized by lush grass and small and exquisite bridges across running rivers. Owing to the many enticing expressions used to describe this place, like "Venice of the East" and "paradise on earth," and the compliments made about it by many of the poets of the past,

visitors usually come to this city with particular expectations. When they view the ornate boats and red-colored luxurious buildings, and listen to the chirp of the orioles, they will inevitably dream about Suzhou as it was in its past, as it is now, and how it will be in future.

Gardens are a must-see during a visit to Suzhou, and a hasty glimpse of them leaves simply an impression of some pavilions and terraces. It is easy enough to reproduce the buildings, yet the taste and character of Suzhou are incapable of being copied. There are currently scores of intact ancient gardens in

Suzhou, most of which are situated somewhere deep in the ancient neighborhoods or narrow lanes – and in some way reflect the jasmine, a favorite flower of the locals. The stretching branches and twigs of the jasmine in this city may be seen as tantamount to a crisscross network of streets and lanes, while the gardens themselves represent the jasmine flowers, concealed amid the green leaves. Lacking an impressive or famous style, Suzhou's gardens are secretive, making it impossible to guess how all encompassing and varied the atmosphere is inside the non-descript white walls. The fa-

mous names include Zhuoz-hengyuan, Liuyuan, Wangshiyuan, Canglangting, Shizi, Huanxiushanz-huang, and so on. The gardens are really a combination of garden and residence, and thus each is a mixed compound suitable for enjoying, visiting, and living. A wealth of cultural connotations can be appreciated almost everywhere in the gardens. In a sense, the gardens have been designed as mazes and made into urban forests by the ancients, displaying their striking features of either "concealment" or "obvious-ness" in a zigzag and roundabout way. You can get a sense of the wisdom that has resulted from both the space and the human life contained within them. Suzhou's gardens have been selected by UNESCO to be on the World Cultural Heritage List.

Suzhou boasts the beauty of both gardens and natural scenery, as well as cultural relics and historical sites across the city. Su Dongpo, a poet of the Northern Song dynasty (960–1127 AD), was quoted as saying that it would be a pity to leave Huqiu out of a visit to Suzhou. And a famous poem, about the Hanshan Temple on the outskirts of Suzhou by the poet Zhangji of the Tang dynasty (618–907 AD), is said to arouse readers to take account of the historical changes occurring around the city.

The ancient city of Suzhou is very small and it does not take much time to go around it. But if you turn into the maze-like and trance-in-ducing lanes, you are likely to go astray and find it difficult to discover your way out. However, it is those confusing old lanes that are the marrow of Suzhou city. A lot of the significant and quaint things have witnessed the passage of time, such as an old well in a courtyard, a worn-out house boundary tablet in a corner, and an arch above a gateway made with exquisitely engraved bricks in a compound of courtyards. Meanwhile the impression of the old houses, reflecting the town's history in its serenity, is so profound as to iron out the psychological wrinkles in people's minds. When you enter these old houses, you feel as if you have gone back to earlier times.

Maybe Suzhou is more than just a city. Perhaps it is a kind of spirit.

The city is compared by Yu Qiuyu, a contemporary Chinese writer, to the tranquil backyard of Chinese culture. Suzhou – with its culture upholding the principles of integri-ty, modesty, and elegance – distin-guishes itself as a place of seclusion for some of the significant people in history. Suzhou features a unique style: moderate, aloof from fame and wealth, introspective, content, and profoundly steeped in culture and the past. This is a style that must have provided its people with comfort and consolation throug-hout the ages.

This is Suzhou, a city without artifice and ostentation, but reveal-ing its own graceful style. The city has been accustomed to prosperity because of its long history, and what has been left for you to taste is the brilliance of the "Peaceful Time and Stable World."

LOCATION
Situated in Jiangsu province, adjacent to Shanghai in the east, to Zhejiang in the south, to the Taihu Lake in the west, and to the Yangtze River in the north.

CLIMATE
Mild and moist, with heavy precipitation in spring and fall.

OF SPECIAL INTEREST
The town boasts the best gardens in China, and the Zhuozhengyuan Garden and the Liuyuan Garden are among the Four Famous Gardens of China.

MAIN ATTRACTIONS
Zhuzhengyuan Garden, Liuyuan Garden, Shizilin Garden, Huqiu Temple, and Hanshan Temple.

Zhenyuan (Guizhou)

An important military town on the southern border for two thousand years

Guizhou Province

LOCATION
Zhenyuan is located in Miao and Dong Minorities Autonomous Prefecture, in the eastern part of Guizhou province.

CLIMATE
The climate is subtropical and moist, with an annual average temperature of 61.5°F (16.4°C). It is a temperate climate with clear temperature contrasts between the four seasons.

OF SPECIAL INTEREST
There are several different ethnic groups living around Zhenyuan, which leads to the great number of festivals held all through the year. Typical ones are Dong Minority Lovers' Day on March 3rd, Miao Minority King Ox Day of April 8th, Dong Minority Songs Party on July 7th, Tujia Minority Woodwind Instrument Festival of August 8th, and Miao Minority Harvest Festival on September 9th.

MAIN ATTRACTIONS
Qinglong Cave, Fu Family Residence, Wenbi Pagoda, Shiping Hill, and so on.

A view of the quiet and beautiful ancient town of Zhenyuan (above)

The entrance to Wanshou Temple in Zhenyuan (below, left)

The Kuixingge Tower in Zhenyuan (below, right)

This is a town that impresses because of its military connections, which are conveyed in its name. It is a town where you seem to hear the battle cry, the horses neighing, and the clash of weapons. It is a town that was set up for military purposes, and that developed and prospered alongside military activities.

Zhenyuan is located in the Miao and Dong Minorities Autonomous Prefecture, east of Guizhou. It used to be the territory of the ancient state of Shiluo. In the first year of Shaoding in the Song dynasty (1226 AD), it was named "Zhenyuan" by the emperor, meaning "a guarding post." That name has continued to be used for nearly eight hundred years.

In the early years of Hongwu in the Ming dynasty, the emperor launched several wars to suppress the remnant forces of the Yuan dynasty. Whenever they took a town, they left some unit of soldiers there, guarding it as well as farming the land for themselves. This famous "military farming" brought about the prosperity of the town. The emperor eventually set up four guard posts – namely Zhenyuanwei, Pingxiwei, Qingxiwei, and Pianqiaowei – and 120 fortresses around the town. Six thousand soldiers were

left to settle there, raising families, maintaining the defenses there, and finally dying there.

The military forces effectively controlled the southwestern highway and the upper stream of the Yuanjiang River, leading directly through Hunan and Yunnan provinces, to Laos, Burma, India, and so on. All this made the town the most important military post in the history of the southwest part of the country.

Ease of transportation brought unprecedented prosperity for the town. Once a place covered by the clouds of war, it has been transformed into a place where commerce flourishes, owing to its specific geographical location. There was a saying, "So many people in the streets, making pottery hawkers break their dishes and tung oil carriers spill their jars."

The delights of Zhenyuan county remain in the memory of many people.

The ancient and beautiful river, the Wuyang, flows from the west, like a jade band curving through the town; dividing it into two it forms a natural representation of the Eight Diagrams of ancient Chinese philosophy. Here there is a mixed landscape of hills, waters, and town, and the whole is praised by tourists as the Oriental Venice. Within the area of 1.16 square miles (3 square kilometers), eight official residences accredited by other provincial governments are maintained here; these serve Jiangxi, Fujian, Guangdong, Guangxi, Jiangnan, and so on. The four caves, eight ancestral halls, nine temples, twelve wharves, and the ancient city walls, streets, gates, highways, bridges, lanes, wells and streams, stages, and so on total about two hundred scenic places. In addition, there are other notable things to see, such as a remaining part of the southernmost section of the Great Wall, known as the Miao

Boundary Great Wall. Around the town, the lanes, stone bridges, and city walls are arranged in a unique way. The lanes zigzag around the hills, with high brick walls on both sides, emphasizing the quality of narrowness and mystery that is typical of the community. Zhenyuan in Guizhou is undoubtedly a town full of history. It was said that in the early 1950s, when Nehru, then the Indian premier, visited Beijing, he mentioned the Zhusheng Bridge and Qinglong Cave of Zhenyuan to the premier, Zhou Enlai.

Qinglong Cave is the biggest and most beautiful historic complex in

Zhenyuan county. It is one of the key sites for historic relics and is well known in China and further afield. It is connected to the town by Zhusheng Bridge. Standing on the end of the bridge, you can see the ancient site. All along the steep and narrow foot of the mountain, lofty buildings and pavilions are arranged row upon row, stretching into the far distance. A step up from the foot of Zhonghe Mountain is where the mountain gate leads to Qinglong Cave. There is Luzu Temple, Guanyin Temple, Zhongyuan Monastery, and the Saint's Palace to see. You will be close enough to appreciate the archi-tecture of the richly ornamented buildings. Its uniqueness lies in the fact that this used to be a place where Confucianism, Buddhism, and Daoism spread and rivaled one another, and yet coexisted. Because of this, it is renowned among the southeastern countries, including India, Burma, and Laos. The elegance, majesty, and uniqueness of Zhenyuan scenery contribute to its reknown: a famous city of history and culture.

Jingdezhen (Jiangxi)
A 1600-year-old capital of imperial porcelain

LOCATION
Jingdezhen is situated in the northeast of Jiangxi.

CLIMATE
There are four seasons, with ample sunshine and plentiful rainfall.

OF SPECIAL INTEREST
This is an ancient town, famous for its superb chinaware.

MAIN ATTRACTIONS
Jingdezhen Museum of Porcelain History, Chinaware Street, Hutian Ancient Porcelain Kiln Ruins, the Longzhuge Tower, and Gaolingshan Mountain.

Fine chinaware made in Jingdezhen; Jingdezhen was the center of China's ceramics industry for hundreds of years. (right)

Making the base, an early stage in the crafting of chinaware (below, right)

A view of a street in Jingdezhen (below, left)

Jingdezhen is an ancient town in Jiangxi known throughout the world for its superb porcelain.

As a matter of fact, *jingde* is *nianhao* (the period of the reign) of Emperor Zhenzong of the Song dynasty. *Jingde* refers to the time from 1004 to 1008 when the emperor ordered the town to make chinaware for the imperial family. Each imperial piece was then engraved with the four Chinese characters for *jingdenianzhi*, which means "made in the period of Jingde." After that the town was named Jingdezhen, and it is the only town in the country named after the period of a reign.

As early as the Nan dynasty (420–479 AD), local people started to make chinaware in the town. As a result, it has been a center of the porcelain industry in China since the Ming dynasty (1368–1644 AD) and the Qing dynasty (1616–1911). Its products are excellent in modeling, rich in variety, of high quality material, and unique in style. Therefore, they are traditionally highly praised in terms such as these: "as white as jade, as bright as a mirror, as thin as paper, and as sonorous as a bell ringing."

Near the town there are the ruins of the imperial kilns of the Ming and the Qing, which cover an area of 53,820 square feet (5000 square meters), roughly around that of Zhushan Mountain. Jingdezhen had been the imperial chinaware producer long before 1911, when the last emperor was dethroned. As a matter of fact, the im-

perial kilns system, which had lasted for as long as over six hundred years in the old feudal society, came to an end then.

Jingdezhen boasts the imperial kilns that have existed for the longest time, and that produced chinaware with the best workmanship in the country. Historically, the town had first-class craftsmen and the best materials, and thus turned out excellent chinaware of the highest technical quality. The central government put forward a decree that as more pieces were made than were needed, the quality was to be guaranteed absolutely. One regulation set out that only four out of a hundred pieces of chinaware could be accepted by the royal family. All the substandard samples must be piled up, destroyed, and buried within the confines of the imperial kilns. Consequently, the common people could have no access to the royal chinaware. They could never have expected that endless layers of crushed porcelain, hidden in the land, would become a treasure trove, the only evidence that shows the full picture of the production of goods at the Chinese imperial kilns and reveals a great deal of cultural information related to them.

Standing atop Zhushan Mountain, the Longzhuge Tower has been regarded as the symbol of Jingdezhen and the monumental architecture of the imperial kilns since ancient times. The tower is the treasure trove of a huge number of pieces of rare imperial chinaware, and its historical literature is

essential background material for research.

At present, some enormous dragon vases and rare imperial porcelain of the Ming dynasty, unearthed in Zhushan Mountain, are displayed in the Longzhuge Tower, which is also the home of a collection of chinaware fans from both home and abroad.

Hutian Ancient Porcelain Kiln Ruins are located in Hutian village, 2.5 miles (4 km) away in the eastern suburb, and cover an area of 99 acres (40 hectares). First built in the tenth century, these kilns are the largest private kilns in terms of production, the number of years in which they were in operation, and the superb workmanship carried out there. They serve as a vehicle to record the seven-century-old techniques, art, and development of the porcelain industry in Jingdezhen. They are also the first producer of such rare pieces as Yinging porcelain, Qinghua porcelain, and Youlihong porcelain. A great variety of artifacts have been found at the ruins, and are shown in the exhibition hall.

The Jingdezhen Museum of Porcelain History is situated in the Panlonggang Scenic Area. In the 64,600 square-foot (6000-square-meter) buildings, in the Ming and the Qing styles, you will see valuable ancient chinaware, ancient kilns and workshops, the porcelain stele gallery, and the demonstrations of the handmade porcelain technique. You may marvel at how the china clay is changed into such an amazing thing as a bowl, a cup, or a vase.

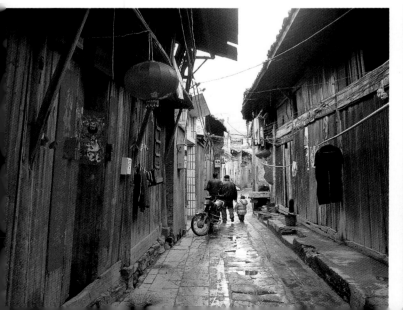

Shaoxing (Zhejiang)
A city of rich traditional culture in Zhejiang

LOCATION
Shaoxing is situated in the south of the Yangtze River delta, in the north of Zhejiang province.

CLIMATE
There are four distinct seasons and a moist climate, and the average annual temperature is 61.5°F (16.4°C).

OF SPECIAL INTEREST
There is an ancient cultural city in Zhejiang, the birthplace of many famous people. It is known as "the Land of Bridges" and "the Land of Wine."

MAIN ATTRACTIONS
Yu mausoleum, Lan Pavilion, Shenyuan Garden, Qingteng Study, Lu Xun Museum, the East Lake, and Keyan Rocks.

Shaoxing brings to mind a stone bridge, Tanglu, Lan Pavilion, village theatrical performances, Wupeng boats and aniseed-flavored beans, Mount Kuaiji, and Shaoxing wine. All of these are like old black and white pictures, taken with tenderness and revealing cultural richness.

Jiangnan region (in the south of the lower reaches of the Yangtze River) has an abundance of water. Shaoxing is a typical example of a city in that area, with widespread lakes and rivers. Water means both bridges and boats, just as an old local saying goes: "Leave home to take the boat and walk down to cross the bridge." Every visitor is advised to make the bridge crossing and to try boat travel while in Shaoxing.

The ancient bridges were made of Qingshi stone, a local product, and have maintained their endless charm, due to their arches. There are currently up to a hundred stone bridges in the city proper, and the total number may be found to be as many as ten thousand if the whole region is investigated. Because of this, the city is nicknamed "the Capital of Bridges," with the Bazi Bridge as its best representative. Situated at a site where three rivers join together (the larger one, running from north to south, is flanked by two smaller ones on its east and west), Bazi's main section spans the larger river. Its two sides cross smaller rivers, for which there are bridge openings underneath. The bridge was built almost seven hundred years ago during the Southern Song dynasty (1127–1279 AD) and has maintained its unique appearance ever since.

What is more extraordinary is the ancient towpath, called Tanglu, which is actually a watercourse connected by stone underwater bridges. At the river's bottom slabs of stone were piled up to form bridge piers, on which larger slabs were laid side by side, to form the ancient towpath. It was designed to be used for towing boats, and when people are walking on the bridge while boats are sailing by on the water. Today there remain two sections of Tanglu: one extends 1640 ft (500m) with 149 openings, and the other covers 1237 ft (377m) with 112 openings.

Shaoxing people rely on boats as a major form of transport. If you visit Shaoxing, be sure to take a ride on the Wupeng boats, which are small black sampans. Wupeng's boatmen, in felt hats and sitting on the stern, usually row the boats by using their hands and feet simultaneously. With their hands they do the steering, yet it is the skill of their feet that produces the power. Keeping a rhythm between their hands

and feet and rowing along with the stream leisurely and slowly, the boatmen direct their boats a long way along tributaries of the river.

The city's residences still retain the traditional style, and are called *Taimen* by the locals. They have the following distinct features: a black door and wooden window, light blue stone floor, moss-grown courtyard, and a position between a street in front and a river at the back. There are both large and small Taimen for different purposes, and they include official residences, retail shops, workshops, and private houses in which several families may live together. In a word, any size of residence built in the local style may be termed Taimen. It was from his family's Taimen that Lu Xun, a modern Chinese writer, left his home town. Shaoxing's Taimen currently houses groups of households ranging from half a dozen to several score. Visitors seldom realize, however, that each Taimen has its own distinct history hidden behind its door.

An enormous amount of cultural evidence is to be found among Shaoxing's flowing rivers. At the foot of Mount Kuaiji is the Dayu mausoleum, the tomb of Emperor Yu of the Xia dynasty (which lasted from about the twenty-first to the sixteenth century BC) according to legend. The platform and the hall of Yue's king are on Mount Fu. Both of them are reminders of the historical stories about King Goujian of the Yue kingdom of the Spring and Autumn Period (770–476 BC). Lan Pavilion is at the foot of Mount Lanzhu, with luxuriant trees, bamboos, and clear streams around. It was at this pavilion that distinguished artists of the Eastern Jin dynasty (317–420 AD) once gathered, and the calligrapher Wang Xizhi was aroused to write down his masterpiece at that moment in time. In Baicao Garden of the Lu Xun Museum, although Lu's footprint has long since faded away, his heavy steps can still be sensed. Qingteng Study has a small and serene garden consisting of two old-style houses, from which Xu Wei, a poet of the Ming dynasty (1368–1644 AD) – dubbed "a Person with Mixed Accents" – emerged. A love tragedy was set in Shenyuan, a well-known local garden on Yan'an Street. Lu You, a poet of the Southern Song, had to break from his lover Tang Wan because she was unacceptable to his mother. They met again here in the garden over a decade later, and the poet was so heart broken that he wrote a poem on the white wall of the garden, expressing his distress and remorse.

A view of Jianhu Lake
(above, left)

The ancient town of Anchang in Shaoxing
(above, right)

Sanwei Study, a traditional private school in Shaoxing
(center, right)

Wupeng boats
(below, right)

The Great Wall (Beijing)

Stone upon stone made the Great Wall

A song of the Great Wall
From then on the frontier remained strong;
From soldiers and horses went up a roar,
How desolate both sides of the wall are now.

The Great Wall, the longest man-made defense structure in China, is known as one of the Seven Wonders of the World. Its magnificence has deeply impressed anyone who has been there, as well as those who have simply heard about it. From Jiayuguan Pass in Gansu province at the west end to Shanhaiguan Pass on the shores of Bohai Bay at the east end, the Great Wall stretches for 4000 miles (6400km). From local measurements comes its name of the "10 000-*li* Long Wall." For several thousand years, it has witnessed the vicissitudes of China's northern frontier. In the past, sol-

diers stationed along the wall devoted their lives to warding off intruders from the north. Today, buffeted by the roaring winds that sweep over the wall, tourists may imagine themselves back in that ancient battlefield.

As the emperors of the Ming dynasty were fully aware of the military importance of defense structures, no effort was spared for over two hundred years under the dynasty in enhancing the wall. The superb workmanship, the scale of the project, and the faultless construction are incomparable in history. The Badaling section and the Mutianyu section of the Great Wall are noted tourist attractions, while the section at Jinshanling Ridge has added luster to it as well.

The Huanghuacheng section is under repair and will be opened to visitors. It snakes along the ridges, meeting a clear stream that cascades

down the steep valley. Along the wall stand precipitous cliffs, and below lies the valley dotted with mosses, withered vines, and yellow flowers. It is enveloped in white clouds, and all this makes up the unique picture of the northern frontier. To climb the wall – the base of which is built of stones about 4 ft (1.2m) long and 2 ft (0.6m) thick – it is necessary to follow the broken stone steps and make a way through lush grass. At the top is a watchtower with five openings that command a panoramic view of peaks rising one upon another, with hawks circling against the clear sky and pale clouds. Viewed from a distance, the wall going up abruptly and going down the same way looks like a big inverted "V." It is the very spot to have a dialogue with nature.

Along the Huanghuacheng section there are stone tablets inscribed with the achievements of the former

A distant view of the Jinshanling section of the Great Wall (above, left)

A beacon tower on the Great Wall (above, right)

A view of the the Great Wall's Huanghuacheng section (below, right)

governor Tan Lun, who supervised the construction of the Great Wall in the Ming dynasty, as well as the names of many well-known craftsmen and artisans. They will live as long as the wall, which represents the indomitable spirit of the Chinese nation.

LOCATION
The nearly three-mile-long (4700m) Badaling section of the Great Wall is situated 37.5 miles (60km) northwest of Beijing, stretching from the Seventh Watchtower in the south to the Twelfth Watchtower in the north, with Wencheng as its center.

CLIMATE
This area enjoys hot summers, cold winters, and a mild spring and fall (the golden season). The best months to visit are May, September, and October, although the air is rather dusty in spring.

OF SPECIAL INTEREST
The Badaling section, rebuilt in the mid Ming dynasty, is the best part of the Great Wall. It is on the World Heritage List.

MAIN ATTRACTIONS
The Badaling section, the Mutianyu section, and the Simatai section.

Dunhuang Mogao Grottoes (Gansu)

A rarity of far more than one thousand years

When in Dunhuang, the first thing you see is a vast sea of yellow. It is so yellow all over that if you looked down from an airplane, you would have a sense of despair. The yellow is so vast, so massive, so quiet and so confident, that it almost makes you breathless. No other colors, no other signs of life can be seen. Occasionally, there are anomalous white lines on the sand that seem to be ancient dried up lakes. Or you may see some fine curved lines left by the wind. Here we see only the footsteps of nature. Two thousand years ago, there used to be a prosperous oasis, there were riotous routes full of caravans, silk products, official documents and swords and spears, and performances of secular dances and songs and religious chanting. Now all are submerged in the boundless sand. All the music and prosperity, trades and diplomacy, wars and campaigns, were so vulnerable, so flimsy, in the face of the vast yellow, with the eternal shadows left over on the Dunhuang stone walls.

The Echo Sand Mountain is to the southeast of Dunhuang city, with precipices at its east end. People began to dig caves here in 366 AD, and it became prosperous during the Sui and Tang dynasties. It seems a giant engineering enterprise, regardless of age and dynasty. From East Jin and West Jin until the Yuan dynasty, people worked on it continuously. Take Mogao Grottoes as an example. Here seven hundred caves, three thousand statues, and huge murals stretching 48,450 square feet (4500 square meters) were left behind. In Chinese terms, the murals would extend 60 *li* if laid out one after another. What they depict is mostly related to religion and mythology, and includes stories about Buddha, fairytales, scenes showing the conversion of worshipers, and so on. Others include paintings showing spirits, animals,

landscapes and buildings, and social life at different times in history, as well as different artistic features. We can find out something about the demise of the North Wei Dynasty, the gentle Sui dynasty, the magnificent Tang dynasty, the serene Five dynasties, and the elegant Song dynasty. On visiting the caves, you feel as if you are experiencing the vicissitudes of history. The narration of the stories is three dimensional and chronological. Dunhuang is an accumulation of generation after generation. History is active here. These dark and cold caves are in full bloom because of the art they reveal.

According to one book, in Chinese Dunhuang means "the thriving earth." This book was written in the Han dynasty, but the definition was proved only after two thousand years had passed, namely, at the end of the Qing dynasty. It seems that all the chisels, all the strokes of brushes, and the long, long time were just preparations for that evening, in the summer of 1900.

Wang Yuanlu was a native of Macheng in Hubei province. At first he enlisted in the army, and then he became a Taoist. In 1897 he made a journey to Dunhuang, where he stopped to build Taoist temples. He hired a poor local man named Yangguo as his secretary to copy some Taoist scriptures to sell to passersby and those who were on pilgrimage.

One day, Yangguo was sitting in the passage of Cave No.16 smoking. He began to knock off the ash on the wall behind him, and he suddenly realized that there seemed to be an echo from the wall. A hidden cave, maybe? People still remember the day this happened: May 25th, 1900. With the fall of an ax, the riddle was finally solved, and it caused a sensation throughout the world.

Now we turn back to 1035, in the Song dynasty. Then Dunhuang was on the route to the famous Silk Road, a strategic point, and the scene of constant battles. When a riot of the West Xia broke out and spread to Dunhuang, the monks here decided to flee from the disaster. Before leaving, they sealed in Cave No. 16 the scriptures, documents, embroideries, and paintings that it was not possible for them to carry with them. The monks never came back. All the treasures were safe for eight hundred years.

They are treasures, some 50,000 pieces of them, from several different dynasties. But to the wretched Taoist Wang, they were worth just a few coins. They were scattered all over the world. Only some four thousand rolls of them are left in Beijing Library.

The great calamity made Dunhuang world famous, but today in Echo Sand Mountain, we can still hear bitter weeping.

LOCATION
Located at the extreme west of the Hexi corridor, the junction of Gansu, Qinghai, and Xinjiang, and enclosed by desert. The Danghe River originating in Qilian Mountains is the river of its life. People call it the Oasis of the Gobi.

CLIMATE
The climate is dry, and there is a great difference in temperature between day and night. Rainfall is low, and there is plenty of sunshine. This is a typical continental arid climate.

OF SPECIAL INTEREST
Mogao Grottoes, or Dunhuang Grottoes, are the biggest in China. Most of the murals depict religious stories, but there are some relating to customs, farming, hunting, and festivals. The sculptures and paintings are so fine that they are recognized to be world treasures of religious art.

MAIN ATTRACTIONS
Mogao Grottoes, Echo Sand Mountain, Crescent Moon Stream, West Thousand Buddha Cave, Yulin Grottoes, West Hill Buddha Cave, and many more.

An external scene at the Dunhuang Mogao Grottoes (left)

The Big Buddha Temple at Mogao Grottoes (below, right)

Mount Wudang (Hubei)

A sacred mountain with ancient architecture

LOCATION
Mount Wudang is located southwest of Danjiangkou city in the northwest of Hubei province.

CLIMATE
Conditions are subtropical and monsoonal. Here we are on the buffer zone between the Subtropical Zone and the Warm Temperate Zone. Owing to its vicinity, close to the reservoir of the Danjiang River, it is quite misty and humid high up on the mountain.

OF SPECIAL INTEREST
Mount Wudang is the largest complex of Taoist palaces and temples in China.

MAIN ATTRACTIONS
Taihe Palace, Nanyan Palace, Ziyun Palace, Fuzhen Temple, the Stone of "Zhi Shi Xuan Yue" (meaning "managing the world high up on the sacred mountain"), and many others.

Sometimes ingenious craftsmanship is more extraordinary than the work of nature. The large complex of ancient architecture on Mount Wudang in Hubei province adds to the uniqueness of the mountain. The complex of ancient architecture contains structures built over the three dynasties of Yuan, Ming, and Qing, among which those of the Ming dynasty are in the best condition. Considered a miracle of architecture, the group of historic buildings on Mount Wudang has been included in the UNESCO World Cultural Heritage List.

This archeological site comprises more than two hundred structures. It includes four palaces – Taihe, Nanyan, Ziyun, and Yuzhen – the ruins of Yuxu Palace and Wulong Palace, the Taoist temples of Yuanhe and Fuzhen, and a large number of nunneries, temples of worship, cave temples, and so on. The complex was devised with such an ingenious layout that all the structures are closely adapted to the mountain's topography and integrated into one harmonious system, despite their individual features. The vision to combine the imperial power and the power of gods is revealed by the structures perching on peaks, ridges, slopes, and cliffs, all of them taking full advantage of the physical features of the mountain. All in all, the majesty of imperial power and the divinity of

the gods have been embodied through the integration of natural beauty and human creativity in a single mountain.

The stone-paved sacred way, 44 miles (70 km) long, starts at the foot of the mountain and stretches to the Golden Palace of Tianzhu peak, flanked by 8 palaces, 2 Taoist temples, 36 nunneries, 72 cave temples, 39 bridges, and 12 pavilions. During the 12 years over which this complex of ancient structures was constructed, Emperor Zhudi of the Ming dynasty was so concerned about the project that he issued more than 36 orders, ranging from such important matters as the provision of labor to more trivial ones like the disposal of redundant building materials. Besides, he insisted on many occasions that the works should take account of nature and the slightest change to the

mountain should be avoided; this testifies to the fundamental tenet of Taoism to let things be, and reveals an acceptance of what nature offers. This last is an outstanding feature implicit in the ancient structures on Mount Wudang.

Making full use of the towering peaks, the grotesque and precipitous cliffs, and the deep caves, the structures of Mount Wudang are perfectly fitted into the physical environment. They are blended with forests, rocks, and streams around them in great harmony.

As an eminent Taoism mountain, Mount Wudang continues to have great allure for a growing number of pilgrims. The ancient palaces and temples that have withstood time, the melodious music of Taoism, the rich legacy of legends and stories – together with those loyal pilgrims – il-

lustrate a time-honored and profound Taoist culture.

Though many of the palaces have been reduced to rubble, those that continue to exist have retained their stateliness and elegance. One cannot help marveling at the innovative minds that underpin these structures. For instance, what is distinctive and outstanding about the five-story Fuzhen Taoist Temple is its frame, with a single pillar supporting 12 beams. The zigzag Yellow River Wall, similar to the Echo Wall in Beijing, can transmit sound. When the huge bell strikes in the Zhuanshen Hall, silencing everything else, the echoes of the ringing bell resonate far beyond. The Golden Hall, with bronze casting and gilded in gold, perches high on the mountain top and is a masterpiece of high artistic value. It is related to several spectacular phenomena,

one of which is known as the Golden Hall tempered by Thunder and Fire. In ancient times, when there was no modern protection against lightning, during storms the hall was exposed to thunder and encompassed by sparks and fireballs caused by light-

ning. The hall remained intact, and looked even more splendid in the aftermath of torrential rain. This is more evidence to have us marvel at the ingenuity and knowledge of our ancestors.

Golden peak on Mount Wudang (above)

Huangjingtang Hall, one of Mount Wudang's ancient buildings (below, left)

Complex of ancient buildings on Mount Wudang (below, right)

129

Longmen Grottoes (Henan)

Extending along cliffs on either side

The poet Bai Juyi once said, "Among all the landscapes in Luoyang city, Longmen is the best." He settled down in Xiangshan, facing Longmen, in his later years and was buried there. Maybe he was fascinated by the beauty and mystery of the Grand Vairocana Buddha.

Longmen is the natural gate to the south of Luoyang. Here cliffs tower aloft, with the green Yi River flow-

ing between them. Sculptors began to work here after the emperor of the North Wei moved his capital to Luoyang, and continued right through the successive dynasties of East Wei, West Wei, North Qi, Sui, Tang, and North Song. Their day-to-day work left on the mountain precipices nearly 110,000 stone Buddhist images and 2800 stone tablets, together with about 70 Buddhist pagodas. The

caves they dug and the niches they constructed are concentrated like beehives. They stretch for about half a mile (1 km) on the west bank of the Yi River. Longmen Grottoes is one of three places in China to see magnificent grottoes. The statues, carved in different periods, are varied both in appearance and in style. These Buddhist images produced by anonymous ancient artists have now be-

Buddhas at the Longmen Grottoes in Luoyang (above, left)

Groups of "Grand Vairocana" stone grottoes (above, right)

come an important source for those who want to carry out research into ancient Chinese art. The elegant statues, the green hills, and the blue waters harmonize in one scenic spot what may be termed Longmen landscape, and are the most important of Luoyang's eight scenic areas. Longmen Grottoes offer examples of the religious art produced under the political influence of the ancient powers of China. They feature a royal style owing to the fact that two imperial houses, the Wei and the Tang, took the lead in sculpture. The starting and stopping of individual structures usually reflects the political situation of the time.

The Grand Vairocana niche is the biggest open niche in the Longmen Grottoes and displays some extraordinary representatives of the stone sculpture of the Tang dynasty. After you climb up the steep steps, the Grand Vairocana Buddha appears before you. She is 56 ft (17.14 m) high. She has a plump face, and from under arched eyebrows her merciful and supremely beautiful eyes gaze out. Her long ear lobes hang down, and with her kind, serene, and inscrutable smile she shows her divine wisdom, her unrivalled experience in judging, and her constant care for the human world. From any angle you will feel she is looking at you. You will be greatly moved, and will perhaps suddenly think of the broad mind of the Buddha – "to deliver all living creatures from torment." This figure is the eastern Venus. Anyone who stands before her for the first time will be enchanted by her elegant face, beautiful eyes, and stately and generous manner. What she presents is a confident smile that never repulsed foreign cultures in the heyday of the Tang dynasty. It is said that the statue was modeled after Empress Wu Zetian. According to the Account of the Grand Vairocana Niche Project, printed in the tenth year of Kaiyuan of the Tang dynasty, Empress Wu Zetian once made a contribution of 20,000 *guan* for the project, from her savings for cosmetics. On each side of the Grand Vairocana, there are two disciples, two bodhisattvas, two heavenly kings, and two guards, all vivid and impressive, and all manifesting the eternal appeal of art.

There are many other caves that were dug in the North Wei dynasty –

such as Guyang Cave, Binyang Middle Cave, Lotus Cave, Stone Grottos Temple, among others. The main ones are Guyang Cave, Binyang Middle Cave, and Stone Grottoes Temple. Of these, Guyang Cave holds groups of stone images of imperial nobility and ministers, reflecting the historical fact that the whole country worshiped the Buddha. All the grotesque and versatile sculptures are the record of a Gandhara Buddhist artistic style, and also of a site where there was a merger of traditional culture and foreign civilizations, for Indian stone carving techniques was passed into Luoyang. The colorfully painted Apsaras – some flying freely between moving clouds, some holding sacrificial fruits or dispersing flower rain in the sky – are forever vivid in their expression and graceful in their movement. The famous "Longmen 20 Articles" is an outstanding representative of North Wei stone tablet calligraphy. There are 19 articles in the form of stone tablets in this cave. The calligraphy of the inscriptions is extremely majestic and rigorous. These are all national treasures.

Here the tourist can appreciate the art of stone carving, and become aware of the inclusivity and profundity of the Chinese Buddhist culture. There is also the opportunity to find out about such things as the politics, economy, and social conditions. A large number of objects of historical value that relate to religion, fine arts, calligraphy, music, dresses, medicine, architecture, and many other areas are displayed here and there modestly, so that the visitor may feel as if he is in a museum.

LOCATION
The grottoes are located to the south of Luoyang, 8 miles (13km) from Luoyang city.

CLIMATE
This area is in the transitional band from the south subtropical border to North Temperate Zone, there being a clear contrast in temperature between the four seasons.

OF SPECIAL INTEREST
One of the great treasure troves of stone carving art in China, the grottoes are listed by UNESCO as a World Heritage site.

MAIN ATTRACTIONS
Grand Vairocana Statue, Guyang Cave, Binyang Cave, Lotus Cave, Stone Grottos Cave, and so on.

Potala Palace (Tibet)
The sacred shrine of Tibetan Buddhism

LOCATION
Potala Palace is located on the Red Hill in northwest Lhasa, Tibet.

CLIMATE
There is a cold highland climate here with a long winter and no summer. The air is thin and there is plenty of sunshine.

OF SPECIAL INTEREST
Potala Palace is a renowned architectural complex that embodies the quintessence of ancient Tibetan architecture.

MAIN ATTRACTIONS
Potala Palace, Jokhang (Dazhao) Monastery, the Red Palace.

The world-renowned Potala Palace is an architectural complex that embodies the quintessence of Tibetan architecture. Having capitalized on the collective wisdom of the Tibetan people and witnessed the cultural exchanges between the Han and Tibet, this ancient architectural complex has become the hallmark of the Tibetan ethnic culture owing to its massive and imposing structure and its being the sacred shrine of Tibetan Buddhism. In 1994 Potala Palace in Lhasa, Tibet, was put on UNESCO's World Cultural Heritage List.

Potala Palace was initially built in the seventh century, during the reign of Songtsan Gambo, the thirty-second successor to the throne of the Tubo kingdom. Songtsen Gambo commissioned the construction of the palace for Princess Wencheng of the Tang dynasty, whom he was soon to marry. The palace was named "Red Hill Palace" at the time. It was later reduced to ruins with the decline of the Tubo kingdom. In the eighteenth century, the fifth Dalai Lama ordered the construction of a new and imposing structure that was named Potala Palace. Since then, the palace has assumed the role of a political and religious center for Tibet.

The stone and wood structure of Potala Palace is 12,140 ft (3700 m)

above sea level and covers an area of over 3,875,040 square feet (360,000 square meters), with its 13-story main building measuring 387 ft (118 m) in height. Complete with palaces, stupas, chambers for worship, chambers of scriptures, living quarters, and courtyards, the palace is the highest above sea level and the biggest architectural complex in the world. It is referred to as the Holy Palace in the Highlands.

Potala Palace consists of two sections: the Red Palace and the White Palace. The Red Palace, right at the center of the complex, has a religious function. The White Palace, with its white polished walls, incorporates the

offices and living quarters of the Dalai Lama.

With an exterior of 13 stories and an interior of 9 stories, the Potala contains chambers for worshiping, chapels, living quarters, stupas, and courtyards. The Red Palace is where all kinds of religious ceremonies take place. It houses stupas that contain remains of previous Dalai Lamas. All the stupas look magnificent as they have been plated with gold and inlaid with gems.

The most magnificent stupa is that of the fifth Dalai Lama. Standing three stories tall inside the palace, this stupa was covered in gold and countless gems from top to toe. A plate bestowed by Emperor Qianlong was hung in the palace, bearing inscriptions that read, "Where the Lotus Flower Emerges" (Yong Lian Chu Di). The palace also houses a huge pair of brocade drapes, a rare treasure. The legend goes that Emperor Kangxi ordered a weaving fac-

tory to be built in order to make them, and that it took workers a year to finish them.

The Red Palace has a large collection of valuable cultural relics and various types of Buddhist sculptures, thankas, and utensils for religious ceremonies. The palace that flanks the Red Palace is the White Palace, which is predominantly used as the Dalai Lama's offices and living quarters. The halls in the White Palace, especially the Dalai Lama's living hall, are extravagantly furnished. On display in the living hall are an exquisite gold teapot and jade tea bowls on a tea table and resplendent embroidered bedding made of brocade.

Rising up from the eastern foot of the mountain, zigzag steps ascend to the Pengcuoduo Gate, giving way to meandering corridors that lead to the grand East Platform of Deyangxia, where religious activities and performances used to be staged during festivals.

Today, the unique value of the Potala – stemming not only from its architectural structure of stone and wood but also from its cultural significance – seizes the gaze of every visitor. The granite walls, the wooden roofs with flared eaves covered with gilded bronze tiles, and the carvings of birds and animals on the beams are perfectly combined to lend a touch of majesty to the palace as a whole.

The frescoes inside are another treasure of the Potala Palace. These are a collection of paintings and other art forms of huge dimensions. They not only tell the history of Tibetan Buddhism, but the personal history of the fifth Dalai Lama and the story of Princess Wencheng's marriage in Tibet. They also depict ancient architectural structures and a large number of Buddhist characters. It is no exaggeration that these frescos are a valuable historical record in painting.

Potala Palace viewed from the Beijing Road in Lhasa, Tibet (above, left)

The golden roof of Potala Palace (above, right)

A magnificent view of Potala Palace at night (below, left)

The 11-faceted silver statue of Guanyin (Mother Buddha) (below, right)

The Ruins of the Guge Kingdom (Tibet)

Creation and destruction by war

The ruins of the Guge kingdom (above, left)

Buddhist pagodas in front of the ruins of the Guge kingdom (above, right)

The blockhouse, in front of the ruins of the Guge kingdom (below, right)

From Lhasa westward, almost all the way across the Tibet Plateau, are the ruins of the Guge kingdom, a mysterious territory in the west part of Ngari with Gar as its political center, and to the west and southwest Nepal and India.

The Guge kingdom, whose past glory and civilization is represented only by the Tsada earth forest, is one of China's first national monuments. It was founded in about the tenth century by a descendant of King Lang Darma, who fled from Lhasa after the collapse of the Tubo kingdom. The ancient kingdom played an important role in the second renaissance of Tibet and sur-

vived for some seven hundred years before disappearing mysteriously in the seventeenth century.

The ruins, lying on a hilltop near a river, cover 1,937,500 square feet (180,000 square meters). Houses, cave dwellings, monasteries, and stupas were all found on the hill and in the surrounding area. Palaces were

With an area extending about 119,700 square miles (310,000 square kilometers) – one quarter of Tibet – and an average elevation of 14,760 ft (4500 m), Ngari has seven counties and also includes the town of Gar. These are inhabited by a population of about 70,000. Known as "the roof of the roof of the world," it boasts many scenic places, such as the ruins of the Guge kingdom, the Pabghong Tso Lake, Mount Kailashi, Mount Namonani, and the holy lake of Manasarovar.

Ngari is also a paradise for animals, including Tibetan donkeys, Tibetan antelopes, and wild yaks. It is the second biggest base for animal husbandry in Tibet.

Tibet
Autonomous Region

● **The Ruins of
Guge Kingdom**

LOCATION
The ruins of the Guge kingdom, with the average elevation of more than 14,760 ft (4500m), are located in Ngari in the west of Tibet, 11 miles (18km) from Zanda county proper.

CLIMATE
It is very cold throughout the whole year, the best months being May, June, September, and October.

OF SPECIAL INTEREST
The Guge Kingdom, which was established around the tenth century, came to an end in the seventeenth century. Its natural and cultural attractions remain a major interest for international tourists.

MAIN ATTRACTIONS
The ruins of the Guge kingdom, Tsada earth forest, Tholing Monastery, Mount Kailash ("Sacred Mountain," Gang Rimpoche in Tibetan), Lake Manasarova ("Holy Lake").

set at the summit, while monasteries were perched on the hillside and cave dwellings for the common people were at the foot. The kingdom was enclosed by tunnels and walls that acted as fortifications. Some structures have survived time and remain in good condition in this isolated region, though many structures have been reduced to dust. A one-and-a-quarter-mile-long (2 km) tunnel built of stone was used for a water supply by the Guge people.

The Guge kingdom is well known for its murals, sculptures, and stone inscriptions, which are to be seen on the surviving structures.

Among them, murals from the White Palace, the Red Palace, Yamantaka Chapel, Tara Chapel, and Mandala Chapel are preserved in good condition, although they are hundreds of years old. The murals feature the stories of Buddha.

The walls of Guge are like a library of stone inscriptions, which are as impressive as its murals are. Most sculptures in the Guge style are gold and silver Buddhas. Around the ruins are weapons of the Guge people, and there are mummies that are probably Guge soldiers, the only representations of people of a once glorious kingdom.

Jiayuguan Pass (Gansu)
A key pass in China's West

Jiayuguan's city
wall - the western
region (above, left)

The gate tower
of Jiayuguan's city
wall (above, right)

An internal view of
Jiayuguan (below, right)

136

A boundless expanse of sand and a vast area of the Gobi desert – both are preludes to the roads leading to west China. Endless yellow! Travelers become drowsy as their cars bump continuously over the yellow sands.

But then, in this vast expanse of desert, visitors suddenly come cross Jiayuguan, a magnificent and grand city under the background of snow-capped Mount Qilian. With Mount Qilian on one side and Mount Blackness on the other (only 9 miles/15 km apart), there is Jiayuguan, a former historic battleground. Located on a thoroughfare in the Hexi corridor, Gansu province, it is adjacent to Jiuquan – a strategic town on the ancient Silk Road – to the east, and to its

west lies a wide expanse of flat grassland. The city once witnessed count camel conveys passing to and fro and a multitude of battles at sunrise and sunset.

Jiayuguan was founded in the Ming dynasty (1368–1644 AD). Initially it was a pass that was not associated with a town, and later it was fortified with an earthen city wall. The city gate tower was not built until more than a century later. With the passage of another hundred years, the city wall was flanked, both to the south and west, with additional walls and beacon towers, both of these features being part of the Great Wall. Since then, Jiayuguan has become established as a pass with a complete city wall, including an inner wall, an

outer wall, a trench, and so on. The inner wall covers an area of 269,100 square feet (25,000 square meters) and the wall is 33 ft (10m) high with a three-story tower on top of it. On the city wall, there are also a dozen or so other structures such as a watch tower, corner tower, and sluice gate, all representing the defense-oriented military strategy of ancient China.

Five miles (8km) down the route to Jiayuguan to the north is what was formerly the Great Wall, and there still remains a significant stretch of the original wall, even today. From the north slope of Mount Blackness, the Great Wall runs steeply downward along the mountain ridge (this stretch is 94 miles/150km long and 45 degrees steep). With the yellowish

white wall against the greenish black mountain, it looks as if an iron hand has hung the wall up high. The loess-rammed city wall was constructed in 1539, and has remained in its original shape for over five hundred years. Here at Jiayuguan the Great Wall truly demonstrates its historical significance.

Despite being a place far away from the empire's center, a variety of realistic dramas, with subjects encompassing war, journeys, money, and time, used to be performed around the city. This would all have

been a chapter in a grand symphony – for diversified sounds from hoof beats, camel rings, reed instruments, and ancient flutes, together with the sound of arrows whizzing by, are consonant. However, all of these sounds have either been silenced or have vanished in the widespread expanse of grassland and desert.

Approximately 5 miles (7.5km) from Jiayuguan is the end of the western part of the Great Wall. Here may be seen what is called "No. 1 Mount of the Great Wall," which looks like a dragon's head rearing

above the wall and rises high in the desert. This is a square-shaped beacon tower, part of which is already in a state of collapse as a result of erosion by wind and rain, which makes the remainder look even more distinctive. According to the pictures of the Great Wall displayed in the museum, those beacon towers are made from reed and earth, with the reeds as long as 3 ft (1m).

Naturally, the countryside along the Silk Road would have been green, but what remains in this area today is nothing but boundless sand. Only the remains of the city wall stand lonely on the ground, witness to the history and the burial of the past under the vast desert.

Unexpectedly, an old stage remains in the city. Can you imagine what was performed on that stage? Maybe it was a romance or a tragedy, but one thing is certain: regardless of what was running, the garrison's soldiers were the intended audience. With the next daybreak, they once again had to step onto the city wall and walk down to the beacon tower at the west end. Looking far into the southern sky under which their homelands were located, they would have made a beacon fire. Its smoke rose high in the air. Did they want to signal the alarm, or just to tell their families they were well?

Today, no trace of the beacon fire has been left on the mottled tower, and there is nothing left around. Surrounding the earthen tower is nothing but a vast expanse of the Gobi.

LOCATION
Situated at the midpoint of the Hexi corridor in Gansu province. The visitor attractions have been developed since the establishment of Jiuquan Iron & Steel Corporation in 1958.

CLIMATE
Hot in summer, cold in winter, dry all through the year. There is a big temperature difference between day and night.

FEATURES
A key city on the ancient Silk Road, with the exquisite and intact city wall, No. 1 Mount of the Great Wall, a zigzag section of the Great Wall, and the surrounding vast desert.

MAIN ATTRACTIONS
Jiayuguan's city wall, No. 1 Mount of the Great Wall, ancient tombs (totaling 220-420), cliff paintings on Mount Blackness, and snow-clad Mount Qilian.

Zhouzhuang (Jiangsu)

Tender feelings embracing the water town

LOCATION
Zhouzhuang is 38 miles (60km) from Shanghai, and 24 miles (38 km) from Suzhou. Transportation here is easy.

CLIMATE
There are clear differences between the seasons.

OF SPECIAL INTEREST
The primitive simplicity and water town scenery of this small town in the southern part of the Yangtze River.

MAIN ATTRACTIONS
The Twin Bridge, Fu An Bridge, Shen's Hall, Zhang's Hall, The Confusing Building.

To tourists, Zhouzhuang is something of a leisure center. Wherever they come from, as they approach Zhouzhuang they slow down their pace. They will either hire a boat to go onto the water, or take a walk in the lanes of the town.

It is a town of which water draws the outline, for water encircles it on four sides. Four water lanes cross each other in the shape of a hash symbol, serving as the main transportation system for the town. Here all the lanes are by the water, and all the houses are built alongside the water, too. It seems that lives here proceed along with the flowing water. There are endless scenes of small bridges, ever flowing water, and the daily life of the households here.

First there are the rivers, then the lanes. The flagstone-paved lanes extend alongside the rivers, worn down over the years by all those passing feet. Tourists will very often come across the stone-arched bridges within walking distance of where they are staying. They look ordinary, but they have all lasted for hundreds of years. Of course, the most renowned one is the Twin Bridge. There are in fact two bridges at this particular point. One is an arched bridge with a single opening, the other a flat bridge, also with a single opening. One is angled, and the other is straight. The two bridges join here over the T-shape river course. The Twin Bridge assumes the shape of an ancient Chinese key, and it therefore has acquired another name: the Key Bridge. In 1984, when the Zhouzhuang natives didn't care as much about the

bridges here as they do now, Chen Yifei, the famous painter, came to Zhouzhuang and by putting the local scenery onto canvas carried it to the United States, bringing the world's spotlight onto the Twin Bridge.

Most of the ancient bridges in Zhouzhuang are simple and unsophisticated in style. But they are exquisite. Take the Fu An Bridge as an example. It was built in 1355. What is extraordinary is the detail of the structure. At either end stand tall buildings facing each other, with upturned eaves and painted railings, carved beams, and ornamented pillars. Such architecture, combining bridge and building, is quite rare in the southern parts of the Yangtze River, especially in waterside towns.

At this bridge there is a teahouse and a restaurant serving tourists. When you are tired, you can take a seat here and enjoy both the tea and the scenery, looking out across the railings. The water lanes below the windows, lined on both sides with rows of dwelling houses, flow quietly in the humid atmosphere year in and year out. Zhouzhuang has 14 of its ancient bridges left. Be sure to stop for a while when passing these bridges. Take a look at the women squatting and washing on the stone steps by the river, the people leisurely walking along the old lanes around the bridge, and the old men sitting on the pier contemplating the water. Nine hundred years is but an instant here. The bridge seems to be the place where history lingers on.

Residents of the small town usually have their dwellings close to the water, with their doors facing the lanes and their backs facing the water. A boat is the only means of transportation. The houses have black tiles and white-painted walls, wooden windows with carved frames, and under the eaves hang strings of red lanterns. Sixty percent of them were built in the Ming and Qing dynasties. Nearly a hundred classic courtyards are concentrated here within an area of 0.15 square miles (0.4 square kilometers). What interests visitors most is Zhang's Hall, which has the reputation of "having sedans entering the front door and boats passing through the houses." It was built in the Ming dynasty. On entering, you can see wing rooms on both sides, equipped with French windows downstairs and smaller windows upstairs. Alongside the hall there is a sunken entrance lane that unexpectedly leads to a rivulet. This is the starting point for a boat trip by the ladies and the unmarried girls, and boats would bring provisions of all kinds for the household to this point.

Shen Wanshan, the richest resident in the southern parts of the Yangtze River in the Ming dynasty, was at one time the master of Shen's Hall. He endowed large sums of money to build or repair one third of the city walls of Nanjing, making the emperor envious. He had many industries and property, but Shen's Hall in Zhouzhuang was his headquarters. It covers an area of more than 21,530 square feet (2000 square meters), with seven courtyards and five gate buildings, amounting in all to a hundred rooms or so. To Shen Wanshan in his heyday all this seemed unworthy of mention. But it must have been a place he often dreamed of when he was sent into exile in Yunnan province, where he died later.

Zhouzhuang is praised as "The First Water Town in China." The best way to appreciate it is to take a boat. You will enjoy hearing the boatwomen's local tongue, as well as seeing the enchanting scenery and sensing the congenial atmosphere. You can reach out to the windows overlooking the water, and be hypnotized by the monotonous repetition of the oars.

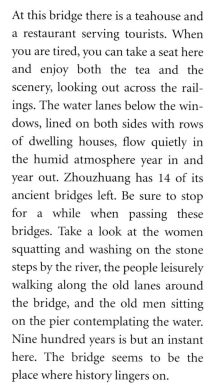

Zhouzhuang, an ancient waterside town (below)

A water lane in Zhouzhuang (above, right)

Taishan Mountain (Shandong)

Where natural scenery harmonizes with history and culture

The "sea of clouds" in Taishan Mountain (above, left)

The Eighteen Mountain Bends in Taishan Mountain (above, right)

A view of Taishan Mountain overlooking the East China Sea (below, right)

Huge stone carved with Chinese characters, which read "the Taishan Mountain is ranked first among five famous mountains" (below, far right)

Taishan Mountain is a marvelous attraction displaying both majestic natural scenery and brilliant historical sites. Its magnificence lies in the rugged geographical features, huge pine trees, gigantic rocks, and the changes in its enchanting landscape. Its cultural achievements are indicated by the civilization that has flourished here for several thousand years and its rich historical legacy.

At the foot of Taishan Mountain, in the northeast, stands the Tianzhu peak, to which a serpentine road runs from below. Circling around the peak are many majestic hills, and creeks run down the ravines here and there.

From Baizhang Cliff there is a huge waterfall, as sonorous as thunder. The continuous rushing of the water has resulted in a pool called the Black Dragon Pool – a dragon is said to swim freely between the pool and the East China Sea. A poet of the Qing dynasty wrote on his tour: "The endless source makes the waterfall, which dashes from the highest hill. Overlooking the fathomless pool, I think a dragon is hidden down below." The waterfall over the Dragon Pool is regarded as a major attraction here, and it will inspire the tourist's imagination and fancy.

Fan Cliff looks as steep as an extended fan standing upright, hence its name. On the cliff the three Chinese characters *xianrenzhang* (which means cactus) were carved during the Ming dynasty. On the west flank an iron ladder has been erected to get to the top. From there Jiunu village to the north, the Aolai peak to the west, and Longtan Reservoir to the east are visible. Sun Baotong, a poet of the Qing dynasty, produced a poem about these features, as follows: "The peak like a sword seems to pierce the sky while other hills are also towering. Overlooking the ghost valley, I have the steep crag to support my side."

Lying on the west side of Taishan Mountain, the Peach Valley features

wooded hills, clear water, and pleasantly fresh air. Zhang Zhicun, a Taoist poet of the Yuan dynasty (1206–1368) commented, "The flowing water comes from the heavenly cave to the human world. Peach Valley, not far away, is betrayed by bundles of red blossoms."

As well as all this, there are four natural wonders on Taishan Mountain. They are called the Sunrise, the White Clouds, the Forest in Ice, and the Blue-red Sky Aureola.

The sunrise on Taishan Mountain is both splendid and exciting. Choose a fine day, get up early, and climb to the Tianzhu peak. The eastern sky turns a little white when the first ray comes into being. Then the sky becomes red, then golden yellow, and it is radiated with brilliance as a fire ball jumps out of the horizon and rises high. It is a mind-blowing scene!

Try a visit on a sunny and calm day, a short while after a shower in summer. Standing atop the hill, you may come across a sea of white clouds. They look exactly like a huge jade plate, hanging between the sky and the earth. When the wind comes all of a sudden, the huge plate is changed into a dragon that dances and flies wildly.

The Forest in Ice is a very special natural scene on Taishan Mountain. It usually happens when the temperature stands around 32ºF (0ºC). The forest is bathed in ice, a transformation created by the cold air. Covered with something between ice and frost, the forest shines with crystal branches and leaves in gusts of wind, presenting a new and unparalleled view.

If you stand on the peak early in the morning or in the evening on a foggy day, you may spot the blue-red Sky Aureola, which occurs in the misty clouds. It is a large circle, blue in the center and red further out. The aureola may reflect your whole figure or your head, and the effect will be similar to the aura above the Buddha in a temple.

Yungang Grottoes (Shanxi)

A treasure trove of stone sculpture

Located 10 miles (16km) west of the city of Datong in Shanxi province, the Yungang Grottoes became a famous tourist attraction in the 1980s. The image of Buddha in the twentieth grotto has already become popular, and is available in pictures and souvenir albums, and on postage stamps. The big statues in the grottoes are known as a landmark scene, while small statues behind the big ones – ignored by many – attract the attention of the discerning visitor, especially those in the fifth and sixth grottoes.

The statues covering the cliff catch your eye upon entering. The most representative grotto is No. 6, which features the story of the spreading of Buddhism, together with Buddha, Bodhisattvas, arhats, and flying Apsaras.

Also known as the "Grotto of Sakyamuni," it is dominated by a huge square pillar some 49 ft (15m) high. The 20-odd statues on the four sides of the pillar depict scenes from the life of Sakyamuni, from his birth to his attainment of nirvana.

In the Chinese-style pavilion, some of the figures play flutes, others play stringed instruments. Still others invite reclining men to have more to drink. Above these are two figures sitting hand in hand, who are presumably talking lovingly to each other.

Groups of standing or kneeling Bodhisattvas and arhats are reminiscent of sculptures in ancient India, Greece, and Egypt.

The stone statues of Buddha in the Gown style are characteristic of Chinese images of Buddha. Those in other styles are foreign, even western. According to *The Chinese History of Art* by Wang Xun and *The Cambridge Introduction to the History of Art* by Susan Woodford, *et al.*, both the Chinese and the western-style sculptures are equally impressive, despite their different techniques and clothing.

The atmosphere of Grotto No. 12 is enlivened by statues of flying Apsaras that dance on the ceiling and walls. Of these, perhaps the most captivating is a group carved on the northern wall. One Apsaras is known as the "Chinese Venus."

With a history of 1500 years, the Yungang Grottoes were first built in the Northern Wei dynasty (386–534 AD). The whole area extends about two thirds of a mile (1km) from east to west. The existing 53 grottoes are home to an amazing total of more than 5100 stone statues.

Historians of Buddhism regard the grottoes as a treasure trove. The Northern Wei dynasty is an important period during which Buddhism was fairly popular, and instrumental in the emperors' rule of the country.

In a word, the Yungang Grottoes are both a scenic spot and a valuable historical resource.

LOCATION
The Yungang Grottoes are situated at the foot of Wuzhou Mountain, 10 miles (16km) west of Datong on the loess plateau.

CLIMATE
In this area there is a weather pattern of cold winters and cool summers, with a big difference in temperatures between day and night. The two best seasons to visit are spring and summer.

OF SPECIAL INTEREST
The grottoes date back some 1500 years to the Northern Wei dynasty. In the existing 53 grottoes, which stretch about two thirds of a mile (1km) from east to west, there are 5100 or so statues. Grottoes Nos. 16-20 are the earliest, the giant statue of Buddha in the open at Grotto No. 20 being the representative work of Yungang. Noted as one of the four most famous grottoes in China, this particular one is of very high artistic merit.

MAIN ATTRACTIONS
Giant Buddha at Grotto No. 20, Grottoes Nos. 5 and 6, and Grottoes Nos. 16-20.

One of the stone statues of Buddha at Yungang Grottoes (left)

The stone statue of "Buddhism Guanyin with One Thousand Hands" in Yungang Grottoes (below, right)

Qingdao (Shandong)

A coastal city of Taoist and European architecture

Badaguan beach at Qingdao (above, left)

Red trees on Laoshan Mountain (below, left)

The Qingdao local carnival (above, right)

No. 1 Beach (below, right)

A beautiful coastal city, Qingdao impresses tourists most on account of the sea. Moreover, Qingdao is an intriguing city because of its proximity to Laoshan Mountain, an important breeding ground of Taoism in this country, and also because of its long history and its exotic architecture.

As you walk by the sea you encounter many buildings in modern German style. The church is a typical German Gothic building, featuring hard granite walls, solemn and rough. The Governor's Building, which took six years to finish in the style of the European Imperial Palace, used to be the office for a German governor when he worked in Qingdao. It is said that the governor was impeached by the German Parliament because of his huge expenditure on the building.

It is interesting to note that some architectural styles exemplified in Qingdao no longer exist in Germany. Therefore, some buildings seen here are regarded as important specimens of world architecture. Constructed in 1930s, the Badaguan holiday zone includes examples of the architecture of more than 20 countries. When taking a stroll through the zone, which is given a tranquil atmosphere by the dense trees there, you may feel as if you are on a pleasant European tour.

One hour's travel from downtown Qingdao will bring you to Laoshan Mountain, a well-known state-level tourist attraction. Lying on the east coast and overlooking the Yellow Sea, Laoshan Mountain with its 3717 ft high (1133m) peak is the highest point along the 11,250-mile (18,000km) coast of the country.

Then there is the Beijiushui Stream, on the mountainside. The name of the stream is said to come

from a story. Once upon a time, a farmer went to Laoshan Mountain to cut some firewood. He was worried that he might go astray on his way home, so he left nine marks along the stream as he went upward. Later on, a route was made in his wake. The seven-mile (11km) long stream is now a big attraction for city dwellers, who gain great delight in walking uphill alongside the meandering stream, which offers a temporary escape from urban noise. The gurgling water and picturesque landscape lead you all the way to the peak. On one side you can enjoy the sea, and on the other side you may take in the fresh air and experience the excitement of seeing numerous outlandish rocks which catch your attention from time to time.

With its views of rough granite scenery, Laoshan Mountain offers a good assemblage of odd-looking stones. If you take a cable car, feast your eyes on a variety of hills over

an altitude of over 1640 ft (500m). The stones stand out in a variety of forms. Collectively, they are called the Park of Natural Sculpture. The granite on Laoshan Mountain is famous for its beautiful streaks and unusual hardness. The main part of the Monument to the People's Heroes in Beijing's Tian'anmen Square is made out of a huge granite rock from Laoshan Mountain.

Laoshan Mountain is the cradle of Taoism in the country. Starting in the Tang dynasty (618–907 AD) and continuing down to the Wudai dynasty (907–960), the mountain was a pilgrimage site for Taoist pilgrims. Moreover, a large number of Taoist buildings have been constructed in the long history of the development of Taoism. Most buildings are scattered at the foot of the mountain and in the valleys. Dozens of them are well preserved, in spite of the rain and wind, after more than a thousand years. The most famous monasteries include the Taiqing-

gong, the Mingxiadong, and the Mingdaoguan. You may well marvel at the magnificence of these time-honored buildings.

LOCATION
Lying on the southern tip of the Shandong peninsula, facing the Yellow Sea and circled by Jiaozhou Bay, Qingdao is an ideal natural port city, 219 miles (350km) away from Jinan, the capital city.

CLIMATE
Qingdao boasts a mild climate with an annual average temperature of around 54°F (12.2°C). You may enjoy sunshine and the beach all through the year here.

OF SPECIAL INTEREST
A key city with regard to economic development and trade with the rest of the world, Qingdao is also a state-level historical city, a scenic tourist attraction, and a holiday resort. With a total coast line of 539 miles (863km) and 69 islands, Qingdao's beach is home to millions of holidaymakers every summer.

MAIN ATTRACTIONS
The aquarium, Laoshan Mountain, the pier, and the Badaguan holiday zone.

Shanghai (Shanghai)
The Bund, as prosperous as ever

View of the Bund at night (below, left)

Exotic buildings in the Bund (below, right)

Yuyuan Garden, a famous traditional southern-style garden (below, far right)

Most of what is now Shanghai used to be a vast sea of nothingness before the Tang dynasty (618–907 AD), but by the Yuan dynasty (1206–1368) Shanghai county was formally established. November 17th, 1843 marks the date when Shanghai officially inaugurated its opening to the outside world, and thereafter it changed into the largest metropolis in the Far East by the early twentieth century. Shanghai has entered a new phase of high-speed development ever since the 1990s, shining like a dazzling pearl on the west coast of the Pacific Ocean.

Shanghai is now building a brand new tourist city with its unique characteristics of "metropolitan scenery, business, and culture." Here in the city, there are well-preserved lanes lined with old-fashioned stone-framed gated houses, the luxurious premises left by the former colonists, and the exotic building complex in the Bund – as well as the Old Town and the Yuyuan Garden. The city has been turned into a so-called Oriental aquatic metropolis on account of the surrounding landscape: the Huangpu River and the Suzhou River, plus Zhouzhuang and Zhujiajian. In addition, Shanghai's sky seems to have been lifted by the dense highrise buildings in the Lujiazui area, and its vivacity has been enhanced by urban transport, expressways, and magnetic suspension trains.

The 4920 ft (1500m) long Bund – which gathers together various buildings such as foreign companies, hotels, banks, and foreign consulates set up in the period between 1873 and 1947 – is the heart of modern Shanghai and a must-see on the itinerary of every visitor. Of these buildings, the former office of the Hong Kong and Shanghai Banking Corporation (HSBC), now Shanghai Pudong Development Bank, is considered one of the landmarks of the Bund. It is a Greek-style granite mansion in British neoclassical style, characterized by the pretty and delicate mosaic murals on the dome of the lobby. At the core of the dome is a picture of Apollo, the classical sun god, representing the then British Empire at its zenith. Surrounding Apollo are a variety of scenes depicting HSBC's local branch office buildings in the early twentieth century and a background of the following eight cities: Shanghai, Hong Kong, London, Paris, New York, Tokyo, Bangkok, and Calcutta. The principal feature of the mural is a representation of the goddess symbolizing the city, and the whole embodies the past splendor of the Bund.

The nighttime view at the Bund is rated one of the most beautiful of its kind in all China. Once darkness falls on the Huangpu River, a stream of tourist boats winds about, and neon lights radiate vivid colors. On the opposite bank of the river is Lujiazui Finance and Trade Zone in Pudong, representative of contemporary Shanghai. Meanwhile, the Oriental Pearl TV Tower, one of Shanghai's landmarks, beams brilliantly, and Jinmao Mansion – the tallest building in Asia and in third place worldwide – looks like a sparkling pagoda rising to the skies.

Pudong is the face of contemporary Shanghai, the Bund marks modern Shanghai, and from the Old Town a very dim picture of ancient Shanghai can still be sensed. The Yuyuan Garden, one of the famous gardens of Jiaangnan (south of the lower reaches of the Yangtze River), can be traced back to more than four hundred years ago when its construction started in the Jiajing years of the Ming dynasty (1368–1644 AD). The brick engraving in the garden, regarded as unrivaled in the garden arts of China, is exemplified by a section of walls engraved with dragons. These dragons wriggle and prance along the wall, stretching halfway through the garden. Crossing the Old Town, the Old Street of Shanghai was the earliest business section in the old city, where there were to be found private banks, gold shops, restaurants, teahouses, pawnshops, theaters, embroidery sellers, and so forth. The Old Street, with numerous tourists every day, is the ideal place to go to stroll about old Shanghai. In the center of the Old Town are Zigzag Bridge and Mid Lake Pavilion, which are surrounded by a wide range of Jiangnan-style snack bars, such as those well-known names Lvbolang, Songyunlou, Guifangting, and Laotongchun. Nanxiang Xiaolong Steamed Bun Bar, all through the year – regardless of weather conditions – is always seated to its full capacity in business hours, and simultaneously has a long queue of customers waiting for buns just outside the doors. The Xiaolong steamed bun, a famous local snack, features a juicy meat stuffing inside a translucent and delicate, floury skin. Shanghai is both modern and traditional, both Chinese and global, both unrestrained and restrained.

LOCATION
Situated at the converging point of the Yangtze River and the East China Sea, with the estuary of the Yangtze River to the north, Hangzhou Bay to the south, the East China Sea to the east, and both Jiangsu province and Zhejing province to the west.

CLIMATE
Shanghai's climate is representative of the subtropical maritime monsoon climate, with four distinct seasons and a pleasant climate. The best seasons to visit are spring and fall.

FEATURES
Shanghai combines the modern and the traditional, and displays a kind of coexistence of Chinese and western cultures.

MAIN ATTRACTIONS
The exotic building complex of the Bund, the Old Town, Yuyuan Garden, Nanjing Road, and the People's Square.

LOCATION
Dalian is situated on the southern tip of the Liaodong peninsula, facing the Yellow Sea and the Bohai Sea on the east.

CLIMATE
The city is endowed with a mild climate in four distinct seasons. The warmest place and the summer resort of the northeast part of China, its average annual temperature ranges from 46.4°F to 51.8°F (8-11°C), with the highest in August and the lowest in January.

OF SPECIAL INTEREST
Located on Liaodong peninsula, one of three large peninsulas in China, Dalian is listed as one of five hundred top environmentally aware places in 2001. The only city in the country on the list, it also takes the second highest place on it in Asia.

MAIN ATTRACTIONS
Binyu Island, Bangzhui Island, People's Square, Xinhai Square, Haizhiyun Square, and Shangya Sea World.

The golden beach in Dalian (above, left)

A colorful package ship off Dalian (above, right)

An impressive statue of a marine animal (below, right)

Dalian (Liaoning)
A coastal city full of Eastern and Western romance

Known as Hongkong of northeast China, and a famous port and important gateway to Beijing and Tianjin, Dalian stands out as the powerhouse of the Bohai marine economic zone.

About a hundred years ago a group of Russians traveled a long way eastward from Siberia and arrived here in a bid to build a new city on a swamp that was then called the Green Mud Lowland. It took them a long time to achieve any result. They named the place Daliney, which means, "a city far away from Moscow and St Petersburg" in Russian. The Japanese came to occupy the city about 70 years ago, renaming it Dalian to reflect Chinese pronunciation. In the past 50 years the Chinese have greatly developed the city, which is striving to become an international metropolis of its own.

There are many stories about Dalian's history. Nowadays, the city features a lot of squares. Why is this so? It is said that a century or so ago a team of Russian engineers who were heavily influenced by French culture were stationed here, and they hoped to transform the place into an Oriental Paris, which they attempted with a map of Paris in their hands. Consequently, their efforts turned Dalian into a city from whose numerous squares of different sizes radiate roads in all directions. As a matter of fact, the city has more than 80 squares, which often make tourists confused, so that they wander hopelessly about what seems to be a huge labyrinth.

In the squares you may take in the meadow, the pigeons, the sculp-

ture, and the fountains. Pigeons walk here and there, eager to peck food from your hands when they are hungry. Fountains spout water in different rhythms, creating interesting patterns in the sky. What is more, from time to time you may see a group of mounted police-women who cross town in tune to a light dancing melody, an urban scene unique in the country.

Dalian is also a land enraptured by football. Its city football team has won seven national championships since 1994, when Chinese football was reformed based on professional clubs. There are thousands of hardcore football fans, and they are eager to rush to the cities where their team takes part in national matches.

Women have their own outlet for letting off steam here. Dalian International Fashion Festival is a carnival for the local people, for ladies in particular. Up until now, the city has hosted more than ten annual festivals. Each is an attraction for fashion designers and models both at home and abroad. As the saying goes, "Canton has the best food, while Shanghai has the most amusement and Dalian has the best fashion." Dalian girls are lucky, and they are admired – dressed as they are like models every day; they have made the most of the festival, keeping themselves well-informed about the newest trends as soon as they become public.

Dalian is proud to have an eco-friendly environment with 30 per-cent green cover. As a result, it is a city hidden in a garden. Because of this, Dalian was designated within the five hundred top environmentally aware places in 2001.

Perched alongside the Yellow Sea, Dalian has come to be an enchanting city full of beauty, romance, and sunshine.

Lushun (Liaoning)

A city full of historical notes

LOCATION
Situated at the southern tip of Liaodong peninsula in Liaoning province, surrounded by the sea on three sides. The remaining side is adjacent to the city of Dalian, and faces Shangdong peninsula in Shangdong province, across the sea.

CLIMATE
There is a pleasant climate without severe heat in summer and harsh cold in winter. The best season is spring. From March every year, flowers such as winter jasmine, peach blossom, yulan magnolia, oriental cherry, and Chinese flowering crabapple take turns blooming.

FEATURES
One of China's famous historical and cultural cities, with natural reserves and national forest parks.

MAIN ATTRACTIONS
Wanzhong's Tomb, Lushun Naval Weaponry Museum, the Friendship Tower, and the Victory Tower.

In 1880, Beiyang Fleet was established here at Lushun by the government of the Qing dynasty (1644–1911 AD), and the city therefore became a military fortress with defensive facilities such as naval port, battery forts, shipyards, and barracks. The city was the battleground for two significant wars: the Japanese–Qing War of 1894 and the Japanese–Russian War of 1905, both of which have left behind bitter memories. It is said that to some degree Lushun can be regarded as an outdoor museum of China's modern history of China, and even for the world. Standing on the top of Mount Baiyu, you have a bird's-eye view of Lushun's naval port. There are two mountains: Mount Gold (to the east) and Mount West Jiguan (to the west), situated on the two sides of the port and demarcating the grand dividing line between the Bohai Sea and the Yellow Sea. Other scenes include the tiger tail-shape sandspits stretching across the port's entrance and the two nearby islands called Snake Isle and Bird Isle. Numerous relics ranging from the Neolithic Age to modern times demonstrate the long history that the city boasts. Located in the Taiyanggou district of the city, Lushun Museum is a huge three-in-one compound, namely a mixture of zoo, botanical garden, and museum, and it is one of the largest institutions of its kind in China. Lushun Museum is now a historical and artistic institution run by the Dalian municipal government. Founded in 1917 by the Japanese who then occupied the region, the construction of the museum was completed in 1918 at the cost of 300,000 Japanese

yen, and it was opened to the public in the same year. In 1945 it was taken over by the Soviet Union, who eventually turned it over to the Chinese government in 1951. Throughout its history, the museum has been known by several names, but its current name was adopted in 1945 and has remained the same ever since.

Lushun Museum, one of the best examples of modern architecture in China, has a total collection of nearly 100,000 pieces, including some examples of exquisite workmanship in bronze, cultural relics from Xinjiang, calligraphy, painting, and ceramics. In particular, the museum collects foreign artifacts that are rarely seen in other domestic museums, and its Indian works made of carved stone, among other things, constitute the only collection of its kind in China. The museum has a variety of exhibition halls displaying bronze arts and crafts, Korean and Japanese porcelain, Japanese painting, and foreign stamps as well as unearthed artifacts discovered in Dalian itself.

The museum's buildings have been maintained and extended by both the National Cultural Relics Bureau and the local government in the late 1980s, with an investment totaling two million RMB. In accordance with the comprehensive reconstruction program of the museum, a thorough renovation project was carried out between 1999 and 2000 at the cost of 30 million RMB, involving setting up a new branch of the museum and improving the surrounding environment. The branch enjoys a system of central air conditioning and artificial lighting,

and there are a number of fully equipped multifunction lecture rooms. An open-air exhibition of works of art and artistic sculptures is part of the complex, and the original trees growing on the site are preserved. All these features have made this one of the largest garden-style museums in China.

Just opposite the museum, in the square, there stands the Sino–Soviet Friendship Tower, a landmark built in 1951 to represent unity and friendship between the Chinese and Soviet peoples. The tower is 73 ft (22.2 meters) high and its body is a polygon of 12 straight sides. Its two-story base is made of granite, on which steps have been constucted all around. The tower and the surrounding railings have been finished with inset snow-white stones. On the base of the tower there are four relief sculptures, the Sino–Soviet Friendship Badge appears right at the top of the tower, and the surrounding area is covered with verdant cypress trees.

Lushun has much history that is well worth knowing; a study of the past helps us value what we have today.

The old prison during the period of Japanese and Russian occupation (below, left)

Baiyushan Hill scenic area in Lushun (right)

150

LOCATION
Situated in northeast
China, Shenyang
is the capital city
of Liaoning province.

CLIMATE
With four seasons,
Shenyang is very cold
in winter. The lowest
temperatures are likely
in January, with -46.4°F
(-8°C) the average.

FEATURES
Its long history adds
luster to the old capital.
In spring, which starts
in April, various
beautiful flowers
are in full blossom.

MAIN ATTRACTIONS
Shenyang Imperial
Palace, Nu'erhachi
mausoleum, Zhao
mausoleum, General
Zhang's villa, the bizarre
slope, and the ancient
meteorites.

Shenyang (Liaoning)
Origin of the Qing Dynasty

Around Shenyang there stand four pagodas, beside each of which is built a monastery that houses lamas. Each pagoda and monastery is constructed in the same style and on the same scale, except for differences in name and shrine. To some degree the four pagodas symbolize the starting point for the rise of the Qing dynasty.

As the cradle of the Qing, Shenyang was the place from which the Manchu minority on horseback embarked on an epoch-making journey to the Forbidden City in Beijing, from whence they ruled China for over two hundred years. In 1625 Nu'erhachi, the first emperor of the Qing, began work on his grand palace. In 1644 Emperor Shunzhi, his grandson, settled down in Beijing, leaving behind him the evacuated palace in Shenyang, which was later called the Shenyang Imperial Palace and is one of the two groups of palace architecture still existing in the country today.

Covering an area of more than 645,840 square feet (60,000 square meters), much smaller than that in Beijing, the Shenyang Imperial Palace is built in a unique architectural style and preserves traces of the grassland culture of the nomadic tribe. The palace is made up of three sections. The east section was completed in the time of Emperor Nu'erhachi and the middle section was constructed during the reign of Emperor Huangtaiji, while the west section was finished by Emperor Qianlong. The most attractive part is the east section where there are 11 "pavilions." The biggest, the octagonal one called Dazheng ("major administration") Palace includes the seat of Emperor Nu'erhachi. It is sandwiched between two groups of ten smaller pavilions, five on each side to create a Y shape. These are of the type called "ten-duke pavilions," each of which used to be the offices for eight ministers. All the 11 pavilions look like tents, which would have reminded the emperor and his ministers of the remote but familiar grassland they had come from long before. All these fixed pavilions took

the place of the portable tents, which indicated that the herdsmen settled down and switched to start a new, stable dynasty in the midland of China.

The tomb of Nui'erhachi in the east suburb of Shenyang is named the East mausoleum. Surrounded by huge pine and cypress trees, this red-walled, yellow-tiled, and castle-like building was completed within 22 years. It is a really gigantic project. As he struggled through his war-ridden lifetime, the emperor would never have expected that his resting place would turn out to be much more magnificent than his first palace in Shenyang.

Another recommended tourist spot in the city is General Zhang Xueliang's office building and villa. Zhang rose to fame in 1937 when he managed to put Kiang Kai-shi under house arrest, forcing him to fight against the Japanese invasion. This is called the Xi'an Incident by historians, and the event took the world by storm. Since then Zhang Xueliang has become a household name in the country.

This group of buildings was constructed in the Sino-European style. In the eastern part of General Zhang's villa all the structures have traditional Chinese architectural features, except for the Daqing building, which is Gothic in style. In the western part there are six western-style buildings, where some important historical events took place, as it happens. All the heroes are gone, however, and the buildings serve as the best witnesses of each story.

What is more, there are two natural wonders in the city. These are very

much worth seeing. One is The Slope, which is 263 ft (80m) long and unique in China. The slope has made many tourists puzzled and excited. The amazing thing is that any vehicle on this bizarre slope tends to glide uphill, and a vehicle needs pushing when it goes downhill. Another natural miracle is the ancient meteorites, which are estimated to have fallen upon Shenyang 1.9 billion years ago. It is said that each meteorite on the Taizi Mountain measures 108 (100m) long and 164 ft (50m) wide, and weighs 200 tons. In an area of 3,229,200 square feet (300,000 square meters) on Mantou Mountain lie 18 ancient meteorites. Imagine how spectacular the meteorite showers which brought these stones to earth 1.9 billion years ago must have been.

**Shenyang Imperial
Palace (above, left)**

**General Zhang
Xueliang's office
building (center)**

**Shenyang Imperial
Palace (below, left)**

**Shenyang's Central
Square (right)**

Guangzhou (Guangdong)
Mount Baiyun, standing out in spring

LOCATION
Guangzhou is situated in mid Guangdong province, south China, in the northern part of the Pearl River delta, bordering on the South China Sea. Mount Baiyun is behind and the Pearl River runs through the city itself.

CLIMATE
There is a subtropical monsoon climate here. Temperature and humidity are on the rise in spring, and in summer the temperature is as high as 91°F (33°C) and the humidity 90 percent. There is no winter season.

FEATURES
A key port city in China's coastal region, the starting place of ancient China's "Sea Silk Road," and the venue for the China Export Commodities Exhibition.

MAIN ATTRACTIONS
Five-ram Statue, Sun Yat-sen Memorial Hall, Mount Baiyun, former site of Huangpu Military School, Shamian, and Chen Family's Temple.

Boasting an all-spring climate and dotted with splendid flowers all through the year, Guangzhou is indeed "a City of Flowers." It is particularly renowned for the winter jasmine at its flower fair, held annually during the run-up to the Chinese Lunar New Year's Eve. Mount Baiyun is one of the first provincial scenic places officially authorized by Guangdong provincial government. Against its backdrop of blue sky and white clouds, Baiyun really is a picturesque and lush place, where a view of beautiful mountain flowers and fragrant wild fruits can be seen throughout the year. In addition, a number of poems appreciative of this very scene, written by poets and celebrities throughout history, enhance the mountain's splendor and fame. Mount Baiyun is perhaps best portrayed by the following poetic lines: "Clouds are everywhere over the famous mountains, but the cloud here stands out in spring." Guangzhou's landscape is generally described as "Pearl Sea and White Clouds."

Mount Baiyun, situated just under 5 miles (7.5km) north of Guangzhou city, consists of a range of mountains and hills, and covers an area of 10.8 square miles (28 square kilometers). In the middle of the mountain range lies its highest peak, the Moxingling (925 ft/382m), also dubbed "No. 1 Mount in the Southern Sky." Part of another mountain range to the north called the Dayuling, Mount Baiyun is the branch that winds down southward. Towering over the Pearl River delta, it is known as the highest mountain in south Guangdong. Baiyun, literally meaning "white clouds" in Chinese, was named after the white clouds floating above its peak, as described in an ancient poem: "Clouds and wind sighing in the pines." One of the Eight Famous Scenic Spots in Guangzhou, the venue for this is located right here on the mountain, and acquired its description owing to the esthetic concept of a string of clouds amid the mountain's pines.

If you climb up Mount Baiyun and look down over the landscape below it, the panorama of Guangzhou will be immediately visible on the horizon. Mount Baiyun has for a long time been a well-known scenic spot in Guangzhou. In history, many famous poets and scholars came to visit it and many poems have been written about it. It is a place endowed with a profound cultural atmosphere, right up to the clouds above. Around the Mount

Baiyun area, there are several scenic places and historical sites, including the Eight Famous Scenic Spots in Guangzhou, all of which contribute to the mountain's renown.

Mount Baiyun also functions as a natural park and summer resort, both of which are the result of development over a thousand years. It is now divided into six touring areas: Mingzhulou, Moxingling, Santailing, Mingchungu, Feieling, and Luhu. Features of these include those named or now known as Moxingling, Looking at Clouds at Dawn, Looking at Clouds at Dusk, No. 1 Peak in the Southern Sky, Clouds and Wind Sighing in the Pines, the Mountain Inn, the Courtyard, Wind Sighing in the Pines, Mingzhulou, Luming Restaurant, and Baiyun Fairy Residence. New attractions and facilities have been developed over the past decade, including Baiyun Cableway, Mingchungu (the largest birdcage in Asia), a golf course, and Baiyun Slide.

Nine Dragon Spring lies right at the center of the park set up on the mountain's peak. According to legend, this spring was created by the Dragon King's princes. There was no spring water here until An Qishen of the Qin dynasty (221–207 BC) came and lived in seclusion nearby. He witnessed the spring begin to flow, which happened immediately after the appearance of nine young boys, whom he assumed to be the incarnation of the Dragon King's princes. And from that comes the name Nine Dragon Spring. The spring area is now surrounded with hexagonal granite railings and the spring itself is encircled with a pro-tective fence incorporating dragon-engraved posts. And next to the spring stands a stone tablet with Chinese characters expressing the name "Nine Dragon Spring" on it. The water from the spring is clear and tastes sweet. To the north, east, and west, the spring is surrounded by towering mountains, whereas to the south it faces a mountain stream that runs nearby, its water warm in winter and cool in summer. The Tinglang Pavilion is dotted with a variety of facilities including a teahouse and a vegetarian restaurant.

Guangzhou looks like a bunch of flowers blooming in the sky to those who view it from above.

The beautiful night scene at Zhujiang River in Guangzhou (below, right)

The Sun Yat-sen Memorial Hall, Guangzhou (below, left)

Huanghuagang Martyrs' Cemetery (above, right)

Harbin (Heilongjiang)

An exotic city of ice in the northeast hinterland

Heilongjiang Province

Harbin •

Harbin has a history of more than a hundred years. In 1898 the Russian Railway Engineering Bureau was opened in a small fishing village near the Songhua River. Several years later, when the railway had been completed, the city of Harbin came into existence. Then, in the wake of the operation of the railway, thousands of immigrants from 33 countries flocked to Harbin, which was an open city from its foundation.

Central Avenue (since 1925) has witnessed the birth, development, and flourishing of the city. Originally called Chinese Avenue, it has become the downtown area of the city and is the longest pedestrian street in Asia. It is exotic because the granite-paved street is lined with more than seventy buildings of different architectural styles. Some are Romanesque, while others are Baroque, and others still are Art Nouveau. The black-painted nineteenth-century-style lamps in sconces are turned on when night comes. You might think you are walking in the Victorian age all of a sudden.

In Harbin another highlight full of exotic flavor is Saint Sophia's church, which was built in 1907 and occupied by Russian troops for a period of time. It is a perfect example of Byzantine architecture, and its refurbishment was completed in 1932 following a large-scale renovation project that started in 1921. The onion-shape ceiling in the middle links several canopies of different sizes around it. The red-tiled wall and the deep blue ceiling combine to present a splendid view against the blue sky. The church's elegant and detailed carving adds more luster to the architecture. In addition, on the top of the gate there stands a belfry that houses seven huge copper bells. It is interesting that when the bells are struck by well-trained musicians the sound makes seven musical notes. And the melody can be heard far away.

The city hosts an ice lantern festival every year, which brings the local people a lot of enjoyment. The making of ice lanterns dates back to the Qing dynasty (1616–1911), when sculptors "made the lantern of longevity" out of 10 ft (3m) thick blocks of ice. Two lighted candles were placed inside each. The lantern looked like a crystal man and shone forth on the fifteenth day of the first month, according to the traditional Chinese lunar calendar.

At the lantern festival of 1963 Harbin held its first Ice Lantern Display, and there were a thousand or so ice lanterns and other ice sculptures. Since then the display has become a regular event. In winter sculptors carve different objects from huge blocks of natural ice dragged out of the frozen Songhua River. Zhaolin Park is then the home of thousands of ice lanterns, featuring castles, ice figures, and stories. It is a world of ice. Whether in daytime or at night, it is like a fairyland decorated with crystal ice lanterns.

In recent years the city has held a snow sculpture display several times, too. On Sun Island you may enjoy a splendid ice exhibition that lasts as long as two months.

In winter you must not miss Yabuli, the biggest place to ski in China. Formerly the hunting enclosure for the imperial family in the Qing

dynasty, it covers an area of 630 acres (255 hectares) at an altitude of 4508 ft (1374m). Yabuli boasts snow that is 12–20 in (30–50cm) in this enclosure, and in the mountains it is 3 ft (1m) deep in winter. You may enjoy such events as mountain skiing, sled skiing, and dog-sledging there.

LOCATION
Harbin is situated in the south of Heilongjiang province.

CLIMATE
The city is cool in summer and cold in winter, with four seasons. The coldest month is January, when the temperature falls to -68°F (-20°C) on average.

OF SPECIAL INTEREST
This is a winter resort, renowned as the City of Ice throughout the country.

MAIN ATTRACTIONS
Central Avenue, Saint Sophia's church, Sun Island, Ice Lantern Display, Yabuli ski field, and the tiger reserve.

Saint Sophia's church, Harbin (left)

The Flood-fighting Monument in Harbin (above, right)

Harbin's famous ice sculptures (below, right)

157

Kunming (Yunnan)

Where spring stays all year round

Much of the land in the country is covered with snow or ice from December to March, while thousands of red-beaked gulls, flying over ten thousand miles (16,000km) from afar, settle down in Kunming. This is the city where spring stays all year.

In fact, Kunming has neither a hot summer nor a cold winter. Thanks to its unique climate and geology, the World Horticulture Exposition was held here in 1999.

It is evident that the World Horticulture Garden is something that visitors to Kumming must see. As professional displays, the World Horticulture Expositions fall into four grades. The exposition held in Kunming was of the highest grade, and it has left behind the World Horticulture Garden as a permanent theme park in the city.

Lying in the Jindian scenic area in the northeast suburb of the city,

the garden covers an area of 539 acres (218 hectares), among which 297 acres (120 hectares) are slopes planted with luxuriant bushes and about 69 acres (28 hectares) are covered with water. Its green cover amounts to as high as 76.7 percent of the total area.

In the World Horticulture Garden, nine countries and international organizations have set up their own exhibition areas, and nu-

Seagulls flying over Cuihu Lake, Kunming (left)

Daguan Tower in the World Horticulture Garden, Kunming (below, right)

merous provinces and cities throughout the country have also built special gardens to show off their horticulture. There is no doubt that this is a superb park, a collection of much of the world's horticultural practices today.

Dianchi Lake, which is said to extend over 140 square miles (370 square kilometers), is a typical attraction in Kunming. Perched on the Yungui Plateau, the lake is a pearl. White sails drift over the expansive blue water circled with wooded mountains. It is a spectacular view!

What is more, Dianchi Lake boasts a long history. Originally, a tribe called Dian lived around the lake. In the Warring Period (770–256 BC) the lake witnessed the culture of the kingdom of Dian. During the reign of Emperor Wudi (140–88 BC) in the Han dynasty, the prefecture was established in this area. In the Yuan dynasty (1206–1368) it was named Kunming after Yunnan province had been set up.

Consequently, many historical sites are related to Dianchi Lake. The well-known places include the Huating Temple, the Taihua Temple, the Sanqingge Tower, and the Daguan Tower. The high mountains around the lake serve as a backdrop. The extensive fertile soil and the plentiful yearly rainfall have worked together to make Kunming a famous producer of rice and milk in Yunnan province.

Another attraction in the city is the limestone forest – a miracle of nature's engineering. This is the result of unique karst geology. Covering an area of 150 square miles (400 square kilometers), the limestone forest is filled with more than a hundred groups of huge stones, each group like a grove in a black forest. Some stones form part of the view on their own, while others seem to be interwoven with each other. Some stones stand high into the sky, and others reveal intricate patterns.

He Tanyun, a poet of the Qing dynasty, presented an ode to the stone forest of Kumming. His lines go as follows: "Extending into the far distance, at the first glance the forest seems gray and mysterious. The high stone seems to pierce the sky. Its foundation is like the blue jade planting into the land."

Liziqing Forest is the highlight in this scenic area. It has the biggest collection of limestone with the most beautiful views of the stone landscape. At the Torch Festival, which falls on June 24th, the local people of the Han and the Yi will hurry to gather at the stone forest to celebrate this great day. In the daytime they are wild with excitement, joining in many recreational activities such as wrestling, pole climbing, and bullfighting. At night they usually perform the dragon dance and the lion dance, and sing folk songs around a big bonfire.

LOCATION
The capital city of Yunnan province, Kunming is situated in the middle of the Yungui Plateau.

CLIMATE
Lying in the plateau's monsoon zone and benefiting from warm and humid currents from the Indian Ocean, Kunming is a pleasant city without an overhot summer or cold winter.

OF SPECIAL INTEREST
Kunming is a good tourist city, with a perfect combination of natural scenery. It has the World Horticulture Garden at its core and local customs of various ethnic groups abound.

MAIN ATTRACTIONS
The Yunnan Village of Ethnic Groups, Kunming Museum, Yuantong Temple, Woyun Mountain, Heilong Pool, Xishan scenic area, and Jindian scenic area.

Changchun (Jilin)

A city on a green corridor

LOCATION
The capital city of Jilin, Changchun is situated in the hinterland of the Songliao Plain in the northeast of the country.

CLIMATE
With four seasons, Changchun is cold in the long winter, with a short warm summer. It is dry and windy in spring, and sunny and variable in fall.

OF SPECIAL INTEREST
Changchun boasts a European-style urban landscape. It is heralded the spring city in northeast China.

MAIN ATTRACTIONS
Jinyuetan scenic area, the Imperial Palace of the puppet Manchurian state, Changchun Movie City, and the ancient pagoda of the Jin in Nong'an county.

Two colors could be used to paint Changchun in northeast China. One is white, since the city is covered with snow for five months of every year. The other is green, for at other times it is a scene of green land, green streets, and green lakes.

The City of Forests boasts a green cover rate amounting to 40 percent. Meadows abound in the city. Every avenue is lined with pine trees and cypress trees. Parks, squares, and courtyards teemed with green trees, all of which makes the city seem to be hidden in a forest.

Moreover, the suburb is surrounded by green belts. The expressways that encircle the city have been planted with trees that stretch as far as 56 miles (90km) and form a green way as wide as 1800 ft (550m). They make Changchun seem to be sandwiched between long green corridors when viewed from afar.

In addition, there is one more green attraction, about 6 miles (9km) away from the city proper. It is called Jingyuetan, and it is a state-level forest park where you can take delight in the lake and the wooded hills. Both the lake and the forest nourish each other.

Changchun is also renowned as the city of movies. Changchun Film Studio, established in 1945, is almost synonymous with the city. In the studio you can visit the Film Art House, the Multi-functional Movie Shooting Sheds, and the 2151-square-foot (200-square-meter) Film World. In a word, you may find almost everything related to the country's movie industry here.

On the other hand, in Changchun there are many historical sites that are concerned with one thing, the puppet state of Manchuria. This used to be the capital city of its government; Changchun is the very place where Aixinjueluo Fuyi, the last emperor of the Qing dynasty, ascended to the throne for the third time. He spent the 13 years from 1932 to 1945 in the Changchun Palace as a self-styled emperor. And this is the place where, without a struggle, he handed the sovereignty of northeastern China to Japan. The city has a large number of historical sites, some of which relate to the puppet Manchurian government and may remind people of this cause for national shame.

If we go back to a little earlier, Changchun had something to do with historical events in the Song dynasty. More than nine hundred years ago, the Song government was often troubled by the northern tribes of the Jin, which carried out a series of raids and were a permanent menace. Eventually, the Jin took two emperors of the Southern Song dynasty captive after fierce battles. Yue Fei, the famous general of the Song, managed to defeat the northerners by launching some effective attacks. Once, hoping to encourage his troops to gain more victories, he announced to his soldiers, "I shall drink to the full with you if we fight all the way to Huang-longfu." Nong'an county, 44 miles (70km) northwest of Changchun, used to be the Huanglongfu referred to by Yue Fei, and it rose to prosperity in the age of the Liao and Jin (907–1234 AD).

Today, in the county there is a 13-story ocatagonal-shaped pagoda that was built in the Jin, a witness to the ancient warfare. The sound of the wind-stirred bells on the time-honored pagoda at twilight hints at the general's promise to his soldiers and the historical stories related to it.

The long and severely cold winter in Changchun (below, left)

Thick snow covering the trees lining Changchun's expressways (right)

Hong Kong

A pleasant night by the Oriental Pearl

The magnificent night scene of Hong Kong, viewed from the Peak (below, left)

A sailing ship in the Victoria Marina, Hong Kong (below, right)

Hong Kong, the dazzling "Oriental Pearl," is a lamp that never burns out. Hong Kong is renowned for its diversified and exciting nightlife. Once you experience it, you never forget it.

The nightlife spreads all over Hong Kong and each area has its own characteristics. It is concentrated in Tsim Sha Tsui, Yau Ma Tei, and Mongkok in Kowloon peninsula, and in the central district and around Wan Chai and Causeway Bay. Lan Kwai Fong is full of exotic atmosphere. It is the most renowned place for nightlife in the central district.

The small area between Wellington Street and Wyndham Street is quiet and uninteresting at daytime, but when night falls the most fashionable people in the city gather here. On both sides of the narrow street, bars and restaurants of European style take the people inside their doors. When the young men from the nearby offices finish work, they enjoy the remainder of the day here. They may choose a restaurant to eat in, or arrange to go with some friends to a bar for a drink, or even go somewhere to enjoy live music and dancing until dawn.

The adjacent Soho food district, which is located between the Central and Mid Level Escalator, houses the flourishing multitude of excellent and well-decorated bars and restaurants offering all kinds of exotic food under the sun. Hong Kong is really a gourmets' paradise. Not only high-class restaurants, but small family-run businesses are also worth a visit. In the neighborhood around Nga Tsin Long Road, Nan Kwok Road, and Prince Edward Road in Kowloon lots of Asian eateries offer all kinds of delicious and inexpensive southeast Asian delights, including Cantonese and Chiu Chow dishes.

Wan Chai is the most famous spot for nightlife of all in Hong Kong.

The area is crammed with bars, nightclubs, and night spots of different kinds, offering live music and dancing. Take a walk along Jaffe Road, or Lockhart Road, or Luyard Road. You are sure to find a place to enjoy yourself. You can also go to an exciting concert or show to have a special night out in Hong Kong. Internationally famous groups and solo performers land in Hong Kong to offer exquisite shows that suit all different kinds of taste.

Causeway Bay is a good place to pass the time and go shopping. Around the shopping center, there are a lot of bars and karaoke bars to attract your attendance. Sharp Street East and Yiu Wa Street near Times Square, and the areas around Hoiping Road and Sunning Road just opposite to the Lee Gardens, are where the bars are concentrated. All of them are within walking distance of the Causeway Bay MTR Station. The resplendent neon signs on Tsim Sha Tsui shine over Kowloon peninsula. Along Hart Avenue, Prat Avenue, and Knutsford Terrace and Step there are lines of fashionable bars and restaurants. On the east side of Tsim Sha Tsui, you can find many karaoke bars, nightclubs, and other attractive places. The deluxe nightclubs are mostly found on the east side of Tsim Sha Tsui and Wan Chai.

If you enjoy the thrills of gambling, you can pay a visit to the Happy Valley Race Course and Sha Tin Race Course run by the Hong Kong Jockey Club. There is racing every Wednesday evening during the season, from September to June. If you happen to be there during this period, be sure to attend a race to test your intuition and fortune, as well as to enjoy the ambience.

Besides its fascinating night scenes, Hong Kong has its famous ocean park. This is a top place for eating and shopping.

LOCATION
Hong Kong is on the east side of the Zhujiang River estuary, by the South China Sea. It consists of Hong Kong island, Kowloon peninsula, and the New Territories (including Lantau island and 230 other islands, large and small). It is connected with Shenzhen Special Economic Zone across the Shenzhen River, in Guangdong province. On the west, it faces Macau across the sea - it is only some 38 miles (60km) away.

CLIMATE
The finest season is fall. The annual average temperature is 73°F (22.8°C), and Hong Kong enjoys warm weather all year round. There is long daylight in summer. The area is susceptible to monsoons.

OF SPECIAL INTEREST
Hong Kong is the Special Administrative Region of the People's Republic of China, as well as a famous international financial center, trade center, and free harbor. It is praised as the "Oriental Pearl" and the "Forever Active City."

MAIN ATTRACTIONS
Ocean Park, Repulse Bay, the Peak, Lan Kwai Fong, Times Square, Avenue of Stars, Temple Street Night Market, Tsing Ma Bridge, the Tian Tan Giant Buddha, and so on.

Xidi (Anhui)

A village that is like a rural garden

The enchanting scenery of the famous Hu Wenguang Stone Archway in Xidi in spring (above, left)

A view of the ancient village, with peach blossom in full bloom (above, right)

Xidi is a village that is 2300 ft (700m) from east to west, 980 ft (300m) from north to south, with over three hundred households and totaling more than a thousand villagers. It is said that the village looks like a boat: the closely linked private houses are the cabins, and the stone archways are the mast and sail, while the mountains that surround the place are the waves. The groups of households and the extensive fields round them look exactly like a huge ship perched on a quiet harbor.

Built in the Northern Song dynasty (960–1127 AD), Xidi is an ancient village circled with wooded hills. Two creeks run through the northern section and the eastern section of the village before they converge at the Huiyuan Bridge in the south. The village is constructed on a framework crisscrossed by a main road in the east and two roads extending northward and southward along the creeks. All the roads and lanes here are paved with stone slabs. It was customary to construct the ancient buildings of

wood or brick, decorated with various carvings that convey manifold cultural meanings.

There are three main roads, over forty lanes, and two creeks, which divide the village into many square sections. The ancient mansions featuring pink walls, blue tiles, and outstanding eaves look magnificent. Row upon row, the long deep lanes between them lead you to more excitement and mystery.

The old stone archways in Xidi are worth mentioning. Hu Wenguang Stone Archway, which mea-

sures 43 ft (13m) in height and about 33 ft (10m) in width, presents a splendid view with exquisite carvings full of traditional symbolic connotations.

Today, the village contains over 120 ancient private mansions, most of which were built in the Qing dynasty. Generally speaking, every household is composed of an inner square, a rectangular courtyard, a main hall, a side hall, a front chamber, a study, some bedrooms, and a yard. In addition, you may find smooth slabs, an old-fashioned wooden gate, high and spectacular eaves on the corbel-stepped walls, furniture in the Ming and Qing styles, stone benches, jewelry, and jadewares and plaques decorated with couplets – all of which give

some indication of the simple local customs and strong cultural atmosphere.

Hu Wenzhao's Private Mansions, Taohuayuanli Mansions, Taoliyuan Garden, and the Yuleyuan Garden are examples of the typical architecture of the Anhui school. Some have a pond, some boast lower walls with delicately carved window frames, and some are decorated with stone carving. Others are furnished with a stone bench and a stone table, or a stone vase.

It is the blood ties that keep Xidi together, and it is dominated by families of the Hu. The village was built in the eleventh century. It developed and flourished from the fourteenth to the nineteenth centuries. Little disturbed by any intrusion of war and inaccessible to any outside challenge from the modern economically developed world, the village has been well preserved in its primitive condition. What is more, its architectural style is outstanding in terms of its workmanship, which is of the well-established Anhui school. The mansions usually feature fine stone carvings, wood engravings, and brick sculptures. They serve not only as research objects for the scholars who specialize in Qing architecture, but also as primary sources for researchers in economics, architectural history, and art. Consequently, the village is praised as a living museum of private mansions of the Ming and Qing dynasties and the best-preserved center of ancient private architecture in the world.

LOCATION
Xidi village is situated 28 miles (45km) from Tunxi, another ancient village, and 5 miles (8km) from Yi county in Anhui province.

CLIMATE
With four seasons, conditions for sightseeing in the village are pleasant throughout the year.

OF SPECIAL INTEREST
The village boasts over one hundred mansions of the Ming and Qing dynasties, and it is regarded as the premier historic village in the land.

MAIN ATTRACTIONS
Hu Wenguang Stone Archway, the Lufu Hall, Taoliyuan Garden, Jing'ai Hall, and the Zhenshixiaozhu Mansion.

Hongcun Village (Anhui)

A village in a traditional Chinese painting

Built in 1131 at a high geographical vantage point, Hongcun village looks like a strong ox lying along the river. It is a grotesque ox-shape ancient village in Yixian county, Anhui province. Its crescent-shape pond is the "stomach," and the 1310 ft (400m) zigzagging creek in the "belly" seems to correspond exactly to the "intestine." Four wooden bridges on the Yushan Creek are the "legs." In all, this "ox" is made with the mountain as the "head," the trees as the "horns," the houses as the "body," and the bridges as the "legs."

From 1131 to 1163 the villagers made the most of their advantageous natural environment when they dug the eco-friendly irrigation system. Numerous streams run throughout the village in all directions. Private mansions dot the terraced land in the picturesque surroundings. It is the intricate arrangement of mountains, water, and houses that have made Hongcun village different from other groups of buildings around.

Nowadays, the village boasts more than 140 well-preserved private houses of the Ming and Qing dynasties. Perched on the Yangzhan Ridge and Leigang Mountain, they are often bathed in colorful clouds, like those reflected in traditional Chinese paintings of different styles. Hundreds of ancient private houses featuring pink walls and blue tiles are lined, row upon row, along the creek. The most striking ones include Chengzhi Hall (praised as the folk imperial palace), Jinxiu Hall, Dongxian Hall, and Sanli Hall.

Nearby there are the mirror-like Yuezhao Pool and the expansive Nanhu Lake, the antique shops on the slab-paved street, the ancient towering trees on Leigang Mountain, the ivy creeping across the wall, the century-old peony garden, the solemn Xurenting, the Shangyuanting Ancestral Temples, and the Nanhu Academy of Classical Learning.

Many creeks run through the village, like silvery silken belts viewed from afar. The crescent-shape pool and Nanhu Lake offer amazing reflections of the blue sky, the white clouds, the green trees, and the pink walls. The village has a different view in spring, summer, fall, and winter, and therefore it has for many years been compared to the countryside in traditional Chinese paintings.

Stone bridge on Nanhu Lake, Hongcun village (above, left)

One of Hongcun village's deep and quiet lanes (above, right)

Yuezhao Pool, Hongcun village (below, right)

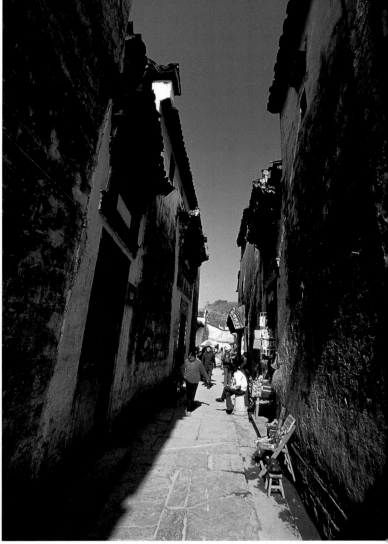

Chengzhi Hall is certainly a masterpiece of ancient private architecture in southern Anhui in terms of grandeur and workmanship. Built by a salt trader of the Qing dynasty and covering an area of over 21,530 square feet (2000 square meters), the hall is spectacular and exquisite. The wood carvings on the horizontal beams, arches, latticed doors, and window bars are composed of many figures with different expressions, and praised as the best of their kind in the Anhui school. In fact, the hall is such a good example that it serves as a showroom for the best local wood carving, which depicts such popular story pictures as the Group of Officials at Dinner, Fisherman, the Woodcutter and Farmer Reading, the Gods of Fortune, and the Romance of Three Kingdoms, which are all full of typical connotations and symbols of traditional Chinese culture.

Generally speaking, Hongcun village's architecture is more charming than that of other ancient villages in this region because the green mountains in the background serve as a screen to ward off any cold current from the north, and to prevent flooding in summer. It is fortunate that its ancestors were smart enough to set up a water conservancy system from which the villagers benefit greatly in both farming and day-to-day living.

LOCATION
Hongcun village is situated 7 miles (11km) northwest of Yixian county and 41 miles (65km) from Tunxi in Anhui province.

CLIMATE
The village is in the subtropic monsoon area, with four seasons and relatively high humidity all year round.

OF SPECIAL INTEREST
Hongcun village boasts picturesque natural scenery.

MAIN ATTRACTIONS
Nanhu Academy of Classical Learning, Spring Dawn at the Yuezhao Pool, the Meandering Brook, the Double Creeks, Chengzhi Hall, and Shuren Hall.

Huangyao (Guangxi)
Nine hundred years of history

Huangyao was a prosperous small town nine hundred years ago.

Southward from Yangshuo is Huangyao, a small town 125 miles (200km) south of Guilin. Huangyao is located in the lower reaches of the Lijiang River, within the border of hill-surrounded Zhaoping county. It boasts a complete range of the ancient architecture of the Ming (1368–1644 AD) and Qing (1644–1911) dynasties. All of the following may be seen: temples, towers, pavilions, bridges, stone-paved streets, and memorial halls. Because of the karst topography and the subtropical climate across the region, this small town features

a pleasant climate all year round, hills covered with green woods, and magnificent caves. The small town is a place with an eventful past and with quaint features in the present.

There are several important buildings: Wenming Pavilion, Baozhu Tower, Xingyu Temple, Shizi Temple, the Ancient Stage, the Wu Family Memorial Hall, the Guo Family's Memorial Hall, Zuolong Temple, Jianlong Temple, Dailong Bridge, Hulong Bridge, and Tianran Pavilion. Experts and scholars of historic buildings have a glow of excitement in their eyes when they visit this town.

The layout of the town was arranged according to the Book of

Changes, one of the five classics of ancient China, and mainly written for divination. Its compilation began in the early Zhou dynasty (about the eleventh century BC), and it was completed in later dynasties in history. It is built in line with the pattern of Nine Palaces and Eight Diagrams from the book.

Today, there are eight so-called big scenes and twenty-four small scenes in the town. Its population is currently within about six hundred households, most of which maintain the style of the Ming and Qing periods. The town has a total of eight streets, all of them are paved with dark blue stone slabs. The ancient architecture of Huangyao

LOCATION
Situated in Zhaoping county of Guangxi, and 44 miles (70km) from Zhaoping county proper.

CLIMATE
There is abundant precipitation, a mild climate, and an average annual temperature of 66°F (19°C). Throughout the year there are, on average, 335 frost-free days.

OF SPECIAL INTEREST
The unique sight of "small bridges and running water."

MAIN ATTRACTIONS
Wenming Pavilion and the Zhou family's reservoir. On March 3rd of the lunar calendar, local operas are performed on the Old Stage; on July 14th and 15th of the lunar calendar, the custom of holding a memorial ceremony in honor of the god of the river is observed. Lamps are put into the river at night after being lit. The ceremony usually lasts from two to three hours.

town is figuratively described in a popular poem that sums it up in numbers.

Both the green vegetable gardens and the laundry used by the local people prompt thoughts about what occurred here in the remote past. The small rivers with blue ripples, the long and lonely lanes, the courtyards still full of classic taste – all of these seem far away from earthly hustle and bustle. Those old shops along the street have been empty for a long time, but people can still sense the past bustle and prosperity from the engraved railings and door lintels.

The Old Stage, a richly ornamented building, is the liveliest place in town. Whenever March 3rd of the lunar calendar comes round, the ancient town celebrates the occasion on the old stage by performing local operas.

As for the local people, they don't think that there's anything

different about their town in comparison with others anywhere else. Every day, they go to work in the fields, and then they return to the homes, where they eat the home-cooked sweet potatoes, rich porridge, rice flour noodles, and glutinous rice cake. If a visitor wants to have a meal with the locals, he just has to express such a wish and he will certainly be invited by a local family to do so. Bean curd and fermented salty soybean, two local specialties of Huangyao, are famous both locally and in the neighboring areas. Other towns and villages around are unable to prepare bean curd as delicious as Huangyao's, and maybe the secret of Huangyao's products lies in the excellent quality of its water. Plump chickens and tender fish are very commonplace around the town too.

At dusk, smoke curls slowly upward from the kitchens of every

household. The dark blue stone-paved street is filled with the fragrances of the dishes cooking across the town. This small old town is serene, elegant, and unforgettable.

The garden-like ancient town (above, left)

Former shops reveal their past prosperity (below, left)

A tranquil morning in the ancient town (above, right)

Peasants having a rest on Xingmi Bridge (center, right)

The ancient theatrical stage built in the Ming dynasty (below, right)

Langzhong (Sichuan)
Where legendary ancestors lived

LOCATION
Langzhong is situated in the north of the Sichuan basin, on the middle reaches of the Jialing River, 188 miles (300km) from Chengdu, the capital of Sichuan province.

CLIMATE
The area has four seasons with an annual average temperature of around 64.4°F (18°C).

OF SPECIAL INTEREST
As the cradle of the Ba culture, Langzhong is a model of harmony between heaven and man, representing the best choice of location for a town for ancient Chinese people.

MAIN ATTRACTIONS
Zhang Fei's Temple, the Yong'an Temple, the Wulong Temple, and the Jingpingshan mountain scenic area.

A view of local residences in Langzhong (above, right)

Langzhong wharf (below, left)

An old street and ancient gate tower in Langzhong (below, right)

The oldest legend about Langzhong concerns Hua Xu, the goddess, who is said to be the mother of Fu Xi, the first human. Langzhong is regarded as the birth place of Hua Xu. Mythology being the shadow of history, the mysterious stories concerned with Langzhong have something to say about the origins of humanity.

The name of Langzhong came into existence in 314 BC, and it has remained unchanged for over 2300 years. Surrounded by mountains and rivers, Langzhong is endowed with amazing scenery. As a Chinese character, *lang* means a high gate, which here refers to the high mountains around. The name of the ancient town means a city perched on the mountains.

An ancient city preserved in perfect condition, Langzhong is built on a checkered layout with its architecture featuring a combination of the southern and northern styles. A street named Guanxing (star keeping) and a tower named Guanxing (star watching) are related to an interesting story about astronomical research in ancient China. When Emperor Wudi of the Han dynasty (206–220 BC) ascended the throne, he accepted advice from Sima Qian, a great historian, who proposed to solicit opinions from men of letters about reforming the calendar. Luo Xiahong, a native of Langzhong, hurried all the way to Xi'an, the capital, to submit his

plan. Among 18 reforming options, Luo's was outstanding and accurate in calendar calculation since he combined agricultural science, astronomy, and mathematics in his system. As a result, Luo's plan was accepted by the emperor. In 104 BC the new calendar was proclaimed and put into use in the country. However, giving up the coveted official status he had gained, Luo petitioned to go back home, preferring to carry out research in astronomy on his own. It is interesting that more and more renowned astronomers came from Langzhong after Luo Xiahong was there.

In West Street stands Zhang Fei's Temple, which was built to remember Zhang Fei, a famous general of the Period of Three Kingdoms (220–280 AD), who was stationed in Langzhong as magistrate. He stayed in the town for seven years until he was murdered. The local people established the temple in front of his tomb to honor the general for his loyalty and bravery. In the following 1700 years the temple suffered a lot of destruction and reconstruction.

Today's temple was built in the Qing dynasty. It has an ancient compound structure. The external part looks magnificent, and the internal part is exquisite.

In Xuedao Street there is a building called Gongyuan, the place where the imperial examination to select civil servants in the

Ming and Qing dynasties was held. Langzhong people have a tradition of working hard at reading. As a result, this town produced four *zhuangyuan* (the name for the winner in the nationwide imperial examinations for civil servants), and it is therefore acclaimed as the home of *zhuangyuan*. There is no historical record of when Gongyuan was constructed. However, it is certain that there were 40 examination rooms here in the Ming dynasty. Later Gongyuan was expanded and renovated, and stood high above the private houses nearby.

High on Yutai Mountain, the Tengwang Tower was erected. It was Tengwang, son of Emperor Gaozu

in the Tang dynasty, that ordered the tower to be built. But what is remembered in history is Du Fu, a great realistic poet of the Tang, he wrote a poem during his tour to Langzhong in 764.

Du spoke highly of the tower in his verse: "The duke made the structure on the Bashan Mountain, and the tower is too high to climb without a huge ladder." Since then, the fame of the Tengwang Tower has spread near and far.

Wuyuan (Jiangxi)

A picturesque town

The Caomen ferry crossing (left)

The ancient Rain Bridge in Qinghua (above, right)

A view of Jiangshan village in Wuyuan (below, right)

Wuyuan is geographically in Jiangxi, but culturally in Huizhou. Its streams, valleys, mountains, waters, cottages, trees, flowers, and plants all remain in the memory.

In the misty autumn rain, this time-honored town enveloped in greenery is dimly visible to the naked eye. Drops of rain from the bamboo drip down to the roofs of the houses with their plaster walls and black tiles. The whole building seems to hang in mid air, its foot being reflected in the pond. Roosters can be heard, awakening villagers from their dreams.

Clinging to the whitewashed walls are some dark green ivies. On the black tiles atop the wall grows a cushion of moss. Weathered for years, the old wall slants slightly, but is held up by a hundred-year-old Chinese tallow tree with some red leaves, which dance in the breeze.

A stone-slabbed old post road leads to Raozhou, a historic town in Jiangxi, and Huizhou, a cultural town in Anhui. The road goes across fields and villages, up hills and down valleys, winding its way past pavilions at long or short intervals. It has seen scholars going all the way to the capital for the imperial examinations, retired officials, who returned home with honor in their sedan chairs, small tradesmen and porters, who hurried from day to day for small gain, painters and writers, who created artistic works to their hearts' content.

In the mountain village of Jiangling it becomes cool by the late fall. Jiangling appears attractive in the dimly visible mountain scene and the late red autumn. Several dozen old houses are scattered around the mountain, along with bamboo groves. Streams flow past the houses, some forming ponds and others channels, and there children play in the water while the women do their washing. On the cliffs beside the streams grows a carpet of wild chrysanthemums. The natural environment – range upon range of hills, streams, thatched cottages, and the southern mountain slope covered in flowers – reminds you of Tao Yuanming, hermit poet and chrysanthemums-lover dating back more than 1400 years.

Suddenly, I found myself back in Wuyuan in a dream, only to wonder whether it is my home town or a strange land.

LOCATION
Wuyuan, under the Shangrao Prefecture in Jiangxi province, is located where Jiangxi, Zhejiang, and Anhui meet.

CLIMATE
With an annual mean temperature of 61°F (16°C), Wuyuan enjoys four distinct seasons, with spring and summer the two best seasons.

OF SPECIAL INTEREST
Known as Shangri-La, the town features mountains, bamboo, stone, trees, shoals, and ancient private houses.

MAIN ATTRACTIONS
The eastern tour: Likeng-Wangkou-Xiaoqi. The northern tour: Yancun-Enxi-Rainbow Bridge (Qinghua township)-Likeng.

Yangshuo (Guangxi)
Mountains and rivers of Yangshuo: the finest in Guilin

LOCATION
Yangshuo is 41 miles (65km) from the south of Guilin City, in the golden district of Lijiang's scenery.

CLIMATE
There is a subtropical monsoon climate, with an annual average temperature of 66°F (19°C), the temperature being pleasant all the year round.

OF SPECIAL INTEREST
The landscape is a combination of hills, peaks, water, and different features of interest to visitors. People say the mountains and waters in Guilin are the finest under heaven, while those in Yangshuo are finer than those in Guilin.

MAIN ATTRACTIONS
Green Lotus Hill, Boy Student Hill, Moon Hill, Lotus Flower Cliff, West Street, and so on.

Caoye, a poet of the Tang dynasty, would not have imagined a return to fame after 1200 years owing to the beautiful landscapes in his home town.

Caoye was a Yangshuo local in the Tang dynasty. He achieved success in the fourth year of the highest imperial examination in Dazhong, then had a brilliant official career in the following years until becoming the governor of Shanxi. Caoye was a practical person, and he took care of his people's livelihood. He was fond of music and poems and also wrote poems himself, in a simple and refined style reflecting social reality and the sufferings of the people. During the late Tang dynasty period, he was a poet with a considerable reputation. After 1200 years, he is mentioned by people because of his home town, Yangshuo, with its clean and elegant landscape.

Yangshuo is located in the southeast of Guilin in Guangxi province, under the renowned Green Lotus peak (Bi Lian Feng). In the east of Yangshuo, Lijiang River winds around and, in the west, Yulong River and Jinbao River echo each other in the distance. With craggy peaks all about, the town is within the scenery and the scenery is within the town. Yangshuo was founded in the tenth year of Kaihuang of the Sui dynasty, and it has existed for more than 1400 years.

Lijiang scenery extends 30 miles (48km) and presents a beautiful landscape gallery, with crystal clear water, famous hills concentrated in a thousand postures, and villages and houses setting each other off in the green bamboo and trees. There are more than twenty unique and wonderful landscapes around here, such as the Peach Source Fairyland (Taoyuan Fairyland), the Wavy Stone Scenery (Langshi Scenery), the Nine Horses Drawing Hills (Jiuma Hua Hills), the Seven Fairy Sisters (Qijie

Xiafan), and Snail Hill (Luosi Hill) – all are unique and fantastic.

This is also the biggest rock-climbing base in the country because of its karst topography. Among them, the Moonlight Cave (Yueliang Cave), the Butterfly Stream (Hudie Stream), the Passing through Peak (Chuanyan Feng), and the Gold Cat Cave (Jinmao Feng) are the most famous.

Yangshuo is renowned for its West Street, too. There are a lot of westerners lingering here because of the fascinating landscape. On West Street you can find stone slab paving, the dwelling houses of northern Guangxi, bars and rock-climbing bars, and restaurants and hotels – everything you would expect to find.

In the western-style stalls on West Street there are traditional ornaments, totemic cloth dyed in cloisonne colors, purses of artificial embroidery, personal hangings, Chinese knots, and peaceful charms of different kinds, one after another. It is all just as in a small town, where condensed Chinese culture and universal intelligence attract hundreds of thousands of foreigners who are eager to know China – like the Chi-

nese knots hanging and swaying on every corner of the street.

On several occasions, when you reach the ends of the streets you will come across buffalo in the fields or the footpaths between them.

The Green Lotus peak (Bi Lian Feng) facing Lijiang River is the symbol of Yangshuo. It is like a lotus flower coming out of bathing water, or a flower bud just ready to burst. The Green Lotus peak has a pointed top and a round base, and is tall and straight.

Boy Student Hill (Shutong Hill) is just over a mile (about 2km) away from the southeast of the town, where Tianjia River and Lijiang River join. It stands lonely and high up. On the hillside there is a rock that resembles a boy student in loose clothes with wide sleeves, holding a book and reciting. The hill acquired its name from this rock.

You can ride a bike from Yangshuo through the Puyi Highway to Aishan village. After a right turn along the footpath, the landscape of Tianjia River comes into sight. It presents a pleasant view, with reflections of peaks in the clear, calm water. Yulong River is praised as Little Lijiang, where you can take a mud

bath at Moon Hill. Foshui Cliff is another interesting place. You can get perfect service and guidance about rock climbing and camping in Yangshuo. Equipment for rock climbing can be bought or rented from shops on West Street.

The enchanting scenery of Yangshuo (above)

Picturesque rural scenery (below, left)

Boy Student Hill (below, right)

Tunxi (Anhui)

An ancient town spanning three rivers

Tunxi is a picturesque mountain town on the southernmost tip of Anhui province. Three rivers converge here and run through the town, which is perched on the wooded Huashan Mountain and the Yangmeishan Mountain.

As the southern gate to the Huangshan Mountain Scenic Area, Tunxi is the first leg for most mountain climbers. History has it that in the Period of Three Kingdoms (220–280 AD) a general called He Qi stationed his troops along the rivers in order to suppress the local rebellion that was under way. The name of the town, Tunxi (which means "a troop stationed on the banks of the creek"), comes from this event.

With a long history, Tunxi is a tranquil and elegant ancient town, which used to be an important place for Anhui businessmen. It boasts both a rich cultural heritage and beautiful natural scenery. To be seen here are Old Street, the Tunxi Bridge of the Ming dynasty, Riverside Park, Daizhen Park, the Fairy Cave, and Xiaolongshan Mountain. Historical sites include Cheng Dawei's Former Residence, Dai Zhen's Memorial Hall, and the Huangshan Museum. Huashan Hill, in the eastern suburbs, is where many mysterious caves, fine stone carvings, and grottoes are hidden along the crags.

Built in the Southern Song dynasty (1127–1279 AD), the 4920 ft (1500m) long and 7 ft (2m) wide Old Street looks like a narrow line in the distance. Meandering along the northern bank of the Xin'anjiang River in the lower town, it retains some of the best-preserved architecture of the Southern Song, the Ming, and the Qing styles in the country. In the 1930s and 1940s the street saw flourishing commerce and trade, and was therefore praised as a lesser Shanghai.

In Old Street you find a different world, for the street is lined with traditional mansions of the Anhui school. Built in the shape of a fish skeleton, with the main street as the backbone and the horizontal side lanes representing the lateral bones, this area is linked with the river, the mountain, and the residential quarters to the rear. The old architecture featuring whitewashed walls, blue tiles, and corbel-stepped walls extends along the streets, one after another. Exquisite lofts carved with fine patterns, small gates, main halls, courtyards, and narrow deep lanes are connected with each other, all of them highlighting the unique architectural style of the Anhui school.

The whole area is full of hustle and bustle. Most shops are two-storied and include an open blue-tiled house, while a few have three stories. The corbel-stepped walls link pairs of shops. Every shop usually has three sections: the external one is the shop front for the sale of craftwork, the middle one is for processing goods or storage, and the rear one is a bedroom or a kitchen. Very few of the shops have a back yard with a garden.

Cheng's Private Mansions are regarded as among the most unusual architectural examples throughout the country in terms of their long history, superb carving, and rich cultural connotations.

Professor Fu Xinian, an expert in ancient architecture from the Beijing Imperial Palace Museum, has conducted a detailed on-the-spot study of the style of the buildings, and has deemed them a treasury of private houses of the Ming dynasty.

The main walls of the mansions are built in an arched shape, a rare design for the Anhui school of architecture. What is particularly amazing is that on the first floor, a contract signed in 1621 may be seen, while the spacious main hall on the second floor retains well-preserved wallpaper of the Ming dynasty. In addition, on the gate tower such hollowed patterns as the "Phoenix pecking at a Peony" and "Two Lions scrambling for an Embroidered Ball," both of which are masterpieces of Anhui stone carving, are carved.

LOCATION
Squashed in among Anhui, Zhejiang, and Jiangxi and situated on the upper reaches of the Xin'anjiang River, Tunxi is the home of Huangshan city.

CLIMATE
Tunxi has plentiful rainfall and sunshine, with a pleasant temperature all the year round. Every season is good for sightseeing.

OF SPECIAL INTEREST
Tunxi is a picturesque old town with ancient and elegant private houses and culture-laden architecture of the Ming and Qing dynasties.

MAIN ATTRACTIONS
Huangshan Mountain, Old Street, Cheng Dawei's Former Residence, Cheng's Private Mansions, and Dai Zheng's Memorial Hall.

A traditional shop in Old Street of Tunxi (left)

Old Street, built during the Song dynasty (below, left)

A traditional herbal medicine store in Tunxi (below, right)

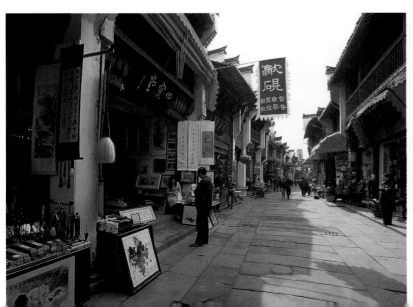

Nanping (Anhui)

An ancient village full of ancestral temples

This village is named after the Nanping Mountain to its southwest. The village has expanded rapidly since the Ye family moved here from Baimashan in Qimen in the late Yuan dynasty (1206–1368 AD). Then during the Ming dynasty (1368–1644) the village was dominated by three families: the Ye, Cheng, and Li. The competition among them pushed the village to its apex after the Qing dynasty.

In this village of a thousand or so people, there are over three hundred well-preserved buildings of the Ming and Qing dynasties. Besides, it boasts 36 wells and 72 alleys, which turn the village into a labyrinth. The longest alley is over 330 ft (100m), while the shortest is only about 66ft (20m). Every alley leads to its neighboring one. It's easy to become confused about which alley to take when sightseeing without the help of a guide.

In the waterside village a 130 ft (40m) long stone bridge with three arches spans the Wuling Creek. Three Chinese characters denoting Wansong Bridge, handwritten by Yao Nai, the master writer in the Qing dynasty, are carved on the front of the bridge. On the opposite bank are the Leizu Palace, the Wen-chang Pavilion, and the Wansong Tower, behind which stand nearly a hundred ginormous old pine trees. The Nanyang Academy of Classical Learning and Liquan Spring are hidden in the forest. On the gate of Leizu Palace an ancient couplet reads "Those who make a contribution to the people will be remembered, while those who act in an honest and upright way will be respected." The palace is decorated with a fresco which is renowned for its lively design and magnificent craftsmanship.

The most striking architecture in the village is the ancestral temple. In

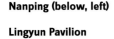

ancient China people attached great importance to their clan, and every big family built its own ancestral temple where later generations could show their respect for their forefathers.

Today there are eight ancestral temples here, most of which stand on the 660 ft (200m) long axis of Hengdian Street, which is prominent in the village. Some are grand "clan temples" that belong to the whole clan, some are "branch temples" for a sub-clan, others are small "family temples" used by one family or shared by several families. All of these somewhat mysterious ancestral temples are ancient and elegant.

Built in the Ming Dynasty, the ancestral temple called Xuzhitang, of the Ye family, is a splendid building situated in the village center, facing west. High on the front gate are hung several plaques that indicate the high-ranking positions offered by the emperor because of the owner's excellent performance in the imperial examinations.

These plaques not only show the exploits of the ancestors, but also bring grace and glory to the generations that followed. Moreover, the front gate is flanked by two finely carved stone drums, which are both imposing and powerful. Supported by 80 large round pillars, the temple is composed of three main halls. The first hall was for receptions and the second was used for sacrificial rites, while the third was the place where a band would play or a stage could be erected for theatrical performances.

In addition to the ancestral temples, ancient private gardens and houses abound in the village. Constructed during the reign of Guangxu (1875–1908 AD) in the Qing dynasty, the garden called Bancunyuan was financed by Ye Zhizhang, a rich businessman, and intended to be a place where his children could learn to read. Inside there are three spacious studies and a half-moon-shape courtyard. A couplet displayed here reads: "Pleasant reading in tranquility may make you forget fortune and fame while the stroll around may outstrip silk and satin."

Another famous garden, called Xiyuan, was built in 1791. Its is famous because of *The Story of Xiyuan* by Yao Nai, a well-known essayist of the Qing dynasty. Located in front of the ancestral temple of the Ye family, the garden formerly had four sections in which children were educated. Unfortunately, the original Xiyuan has been destroyed. All that is now to be seen are such relics as the plaque from the front gate, the brook, the bridge, and the camphor tree.

LOCATION
Nanping is situated to the southwest of Yixian county, about 38 miles (60km) from Tunxi, in Anhui province.

CLIMATE
There are four seasons, with abundant rainfall and plentiful sunshine.

OF SPECIAL INTEREST
The village is listed as the Chinese Museum of the Ancient Architecture of Ancestral Temples.

MAIN ATTRACTIONS
The clan temples, subclan temples, and family temples.

Mudu (Jiangsu)
The houses near small bridges and rivers

The waterside pavilion in the Yan Family Garden (below)

Ancient carved window in the Yan Family Garden (above)

Mudu, 6 miles (10km) southwest of Suzhou city, is situated where the Xujiang River and the Muguang River join, and is a serene ancient town in a region of rivers and lakes. Here also lies Taihu Lake, 3 miles (5km) further southwest of Mudu.

In this area Fuchai, king of the Wu kingdom in the Spring and Autumn Period (770–476 BC), arranged to have the Guanwa Palace and the Gusu Platform constructed to show his great love for his favorite concubine, called Xishi. Some time after that, water flowing here from around the countryside brought a deposit of timber that blocked the rivers which used to flow below the hills. The jam lasted for three years, and gave the ancient town the name of Mudu (from *mu*, meaning "timber," and *du*, meaning "ditch").

The stories that are part of legend seem far away from us now, and today's Mudu is peacefully surrounded by hills. Its people live at ease here, where it is warm and there is plenty of water. This is a leisurely and carefree place to live, exemplified by the crisscross pattern of the rivers, the connecting streets and bridges, and the houses made of light blue bricks, white walls, and black tiles.

Xiangxi Stream and the Xujiang River converge within the town. One legend tells us that Xishi once lived on Mount Lingyan, and her bathing water flowed into the stream below and made it fragrant – so the stream was named Xiangxi (fragrant stream). The Xujiang River was originally a canal cut under the supervision of Wu Zixu (a government minister of the Wu) to connect Taihu Lake and the Yangtze River, and the river was the last resting place of the body of Wu Zixu following his death. The river and the stream come together here at Mudu, running further down in

a single watercourse. Nowadays, amid Mudu's waterways, it is virtually impossible to track the rivalry between the ancient foes and the stories of heroes. Beauty has long since gone with the wind and rain of times past.

Shantang Street, one of the examples of Mudu's antique charms, is connected to the river at one end, and to the flourishing business sector at the other. Along the street is an assemblage of private gardens, such as the Yan Family Garden, as well as

Xianzhitang and the Hongyingshan House. All of these are the work of ancient masters, and most of them are ingeniously designed and comfortable places in which to live.

It is mild and moist in Mudu in springtime. You may stroll down the streets as you please, or just stand by the arched bridges with rivers running below. As the wooden boats pass to and fro, the sound of current, oar, and clock blend together under the warmth of the sun in the afternoon.

Set up in the Qing dynasty (1644–1911 AD), the Yan Family Garden is located near the Wangjia Bridge in Shangtang Street, and was well known in Jiangnan (the south of the lower reaches of the Yangtze River). It was bought by the Yan family from the late Qing. They enjoyed a good reputation because of their philanthropic deeds. Their descendants later moved to Taiwan. The garden is well worth seeing for the sense of peace and tranquility it imparts upon entering.

The Bangyan Residence (Bangyan is the person taking the second place in the imperial examinations of ancient China), located at Xiatang of Mudu, was where a Bangyan surnamed Feng once lived. A prodigy when he was in his teens, he had a promising official career, but decided to resign and return to his home, living a quiet life there from then on. We have no idea of what did happen at this house in the past. For visitors, what remains is the elegance of the setting and a sense of aloofness from the world.

Mudu is not always as tranquil as this. At the time when Xishi was living on Mount Lingyan, Mudu was a prosperous small town. It observed all the festivals of the Wu region (now Jiangsu province), half of which were temple fairs. A picture of Mudu as it was shows the following features: rivers crisscrossing the town, connecting bridges, West Street, Xiashatang and Shantang Street, and also the verdant private gardens of celebrities, countless bridges on the Xiangxi Stream, and a steady stream of boats under bridges. Mudu's life was certainly lively.

"Qianshengyuan" jujube paste cake, a special kind you can buy in Shantang Street, is a unique local snack of Mudu offering fragrance, crispness, and softness. In the town's theater, you may enjoy a pot of tea, eat a slice of jujube paste cake, and watch a performance by the local opera, thus immersing yourself in the life of Mudu.

Mingyue Bay (Jiangsu)
A haven in the real world

LOCATION
Situated in the west of Mount Shigong, a hill located at the south end of Mount West in Suzhou. Its landscape looks like the surface of a bright moon and is it thus named Mingyue, which means "bright moon."

CLIMATE
There are four distinct seasons throughout the year, a mild climate, and abundant precipitation. The average temperature in January is 37°F (2.8°C), and in July it is 82°F (28°C).

OF SPECIAL INTEREST
One of the extant ancient villages in China with the characteristic features of Jiangnan (south of the lower reaches of the Yangtze River).

MAIN ATTRACTIONS
Yuantouzhu, the Tang city, the City of the Three Kingdoms, the City of the Land of Outlaws, and the Lingshan Buddha Statue. Both the The Three Kingdoms and The Land of Outlaws are titles of two of China's literary classics.

An old house in the ancient village (below, left)

A lane in the ancient village (below, right)

Stone bridge (right)

Situated on the shore of Taihu Lake, Mingyue Bay is the oldest village on Xishan island and is almost as old as the ancient city of Suzhou. The village, renowned as a haven of peace and well-being, is surrounded by hillocks and thus landlocked, with only one opening in the southwest, leading to Taihu Lake. The village was first inhabited in the Spring and Autumn Period (770–476 BC), and according to legend the king of the Wu kingdom, which flourished then, used to carry his lover here to see the beautiful scenery around the village. The village is characterized by towering old trees, paths paved with stone slabs, and moss-grown walls, as well as orange and pomegranate trees planted nearly of everywhere. Also, there are courtyards of outstanding splendor and delicacy.

Most residents in what was then Mingyue Bay were actually from the Yue kingdom, an ancient kingdom in the late Spring and Autumn Period, with its territory in modern Jiangsu province and Zhejiang province. They were exiled to this area following their defeat by the Wu kingdom in war. Here they had to serve the Wu kings. A famous beauty named Xishi, one of the four most famous beauties in China's history who came from the Yue, was said to live at Mingyue Bay at that time, and used to make up her face in the reflection in a pond in spring. Today there still remains an ancient reminder left by Xishi: a pond called Huamei Pond on the nearby Mount Shipai.

As early as the Tang Dynasty (618–907 AD), the village began to assume its chessboard-shape pattern, which has lingered ever since. During the Qianlong Years of the Qing dynasty (1644–1911), Mingyue Bay's residents made great fortunes by planting flowers and fruit here, and their prosperity enabled them to build sumptuous and exquisite courtyards and temples. In terms of the architecture of those Qing-style ancient houses, they feature a three-row compound with the central row lower than the other two. Specifically, the

first row is a two-story building comprising living rooms, the second row is a round hall, and the third row is another two-story building. This is considered an exceptionally good place to see the Ming (1368–1644) and Qing architecture of the Taihu Lake region.

In Mingyue Bay, it is pleasant to get up early to watch the sunrise somewhere near Taihu Lake. And you may also enjoy a view of the orange trees, the ancient wharf, the bridge, the old camphor tree, and the crescent-shape pond. In addition, behind Mount West Dongting there are many tea and orange trees, and on the shore of Taihu Lake there are groves of reeds, among which wild ducks can occasionally be spotted.

It is said that the old camphor tree in the village has an age of over two thousand years. The original tree had only half of its trunk left after surviving a blaze, and the villagers planted a new one behind the remaining trunk. The two have grown by embracing each other ever since. As a result, the current camphor tree looks as if a grandpa is carrying his grandson on his back and the trunk is so large that it takes as many as six people to span it with their arms linked.

If you are strolling around Mingyue Bay in the rain, you will ex-

perience the pure and fresh air, under the green trees and red flowers setting off the white walls and black tiles, indeed an enjoyable feeling, both physically and mentally. When the rain becomes increasingly heavy, the streams from the surrounding hills pour their water down so that the level in the slabstone-paved street rises. It is an artificial waterway designed to gather and divert the stream's water to the ponds in the village. Old documents tell us that the street at Mingyue Bay was 4590 ft (1400m) long and laid with 4560 slabs of granite in total. Both the street and the courtyards constitute unique sights in the ancient village of Mingyue Bay on Xishan island.

Changting (Fujian)
A Hakkas village near the Tingjiang River

The experiences of the ancients may have been much deeper than ours, as they were very particular about the naming of the areas in which they were living. The Chinese word ting, for example, was used by the forefathers to designate a stretch of flat land close to water. After the ancient people had gathered to live on such a flat area, it gradually developed into a town with a name that is based on "Ting", for example, Changting.

Changting is now at a junction of three bordering provinces: Fujian, Guangdong, and Jiangxi. It is located in a basin surrounded by precipitous mountains, with a long river running through it. This is where the ancient ethnic Yue used to live and multiply four thousand years ago. When Central China's culture transferred southward after that, a city named Changting was established here and was predominantly inhabited by the forefathers of the Hakkas. Now Changting has the largest population of Hakkas in Fujian province.

The Tingjiang River, running by the city of Changting, is the longest river in the west of Fujian, with a length of 178 miles (285km). It flows via Guangdong and, converging with other rivers, ends in the South China Sea. Changting came to public light as an ancient city of the Ming (1368–1644 AD) and Qing (1644–1911) dynasties. The style and characteristics of the ancient Hakkas architecture in Jiangnan (the southern part of the lower reaches of the Yangtze River) have been preserved outstandingly in Changting. And such examples of this architecture are a key compo-

nent of what make Changting one of China's most historically and culturally appealing cities.

The Hakkas not only established Changting, but created its own unique culture. Traditional houses in Changting display one of the striking feature of the Hakkas culture. Some of the houses are large enough to hold dozens of households representing a number of families under one roof. Others simply have the typical archway above the gate and storied living quarters at the back. All the houses are elegant and distinctive. This kind of Hakkas house is exemplified by the Weiwu House in Changting. The Yunxiang Pavilion is a good example of the ancient storied building of south China. It was set up in the Dali Years of the Dang dynasty (618–907 AD). It combines the following elements: hill site, blue water, ancient tree, bridge, and storied building – all embodying the wisdom and superb architectural style of the Hakkas forefathers. One of the traditional buildings in Changting, the Tianhou Palace,* demonstrates another characteristic of the Hakkas' architectural tradition. It inherited the mansion-style architecture of Central China, with its buildings spreading out to both sides along an axis and connected with each other, one by one. This kind of building was rigorously structured in order to achieve symmetry from both left to right and from front to back.

The unusual ancient well at Shuangyin Pagoda in Tingzhou is matchless, and it in fact comprises two wells in combination: one of the Dang dynasty, and the other of the Song dynasty (960–1279).

According to the tablet inscription, the pagoda was built to guard the writing style then in use, rather than just to house a water supply for drinking. Today, it continues to guard two wells, which still have a clean supply over a thousand years after the water was first protected here.

The traditional ancient neighborhood of Changting took shape largely in the Tang, Song, and Ming periods. The construction of the town began in the Dali Years of the Tang while the city was being built, and was gradually completed by the Song dynasty. Its streets are 20–26 ft (6–8m) wide and laid with cobblestone. The houses are mostly wooden and earthen structures, in the form of a front shop and a rear house.

Throughout the city, the buildings beside the streets extend along toward the gates of the city wall. Quadrilateral pavilions were set up at crossroads in the traditional neighborhood, both as shelters from the rain for passersby, and to hang lights in at night.

Changting is not a coastal city. It has Tianhou Palace, which is so outstanding that it is clear that the Tingjiang River deserves the honor of being accredited as the major river of the Hakkas in China.

Note:

*Tianhou Palace: according to traditional Chinese folklore, Tianhou is the name of the goddess of the sea. A building that is called the Tianhou Palace was usually established in each coastal city or region in ancient times.

LOCATION
Changting, or Tingzhou, is situated in the west of Fujian province. To the north are Xiamen, Zhangzhou, and Quanzhou, all also in Fujian province. To the west is Jiangxi province, to the south is Guangdong province, and to the north is Sanming city in Fujian province.

CLIMATE
There is a subtropical maritime monsoon climate in the hilly land, and an average annual temperature of 65°F (18.3°C).

OF SPECIAL INTEREST
One of the most famous historical and cultural cities in China, Changting is the capital of the Hakkas, the ancient site of the famous Tingzhou region, and the birthplace of the ancient civilization of Fujian province.

MAIN ATTRACTIONS
The ancient well of Tingzhou, the Shuangyin Pagoda, Mount Wolong, the Yunxiang Pavilion, the Mother Garden of the Hakkas, Tingzhou Confucius Temple, and Zhuzi Temple.

Tingjiang River and the old city wall of Changting (below, left)

Tianhou Palace in Changting. Changting has the largest population of Hakkas in Fujian province. (below, right)

Peitian (Fujian)

An ancient village secluded in Fujian Province

The beauty of Fujian province, also known as Min, is multifold. Apart from the natural landscape of mountains and rivers, Fujian has a number of ancient residential houses with distinctive features. Among them, the village of Peitian is an architectural wonder with its mysterious ancient residences built during the Ming and Qing dynasties.

With a history going back over eight hundred years, Peitian boasts one of the well-preserved complexes of ancient residential houses of the Hakka that remain in the western mountainous areas of Fujian province. They include 30 magnificent residential houses, 21 ancestral temples, 6 schools, and an old street 1080 ft (1000m) in length. The largest structure in the complex contains 9 halls and 18 wells, covering an area of 74,270 square feet (6900 square meters). Each building, covered by cameos, couplets, inscribed boards, stone carvings, and other decorations, demonstrates great craftsmanship and majesty.

These ancient buildings of the Ming and Qing dynasties, with gray tiles and white walls, are so exquisitely constructed, so well preserved, and so deeply rooted in culture that they strike visitors with awe and amazement. The elderly of the village are considered to be the best tourist guides here, owing to their profound knowledge of the history of these ancient buildings.

The ancient residential houses in Peitian were laid out in an orderly fashion, well arranged and properly distributed, as is typical of the architectural style of the Ming and Qing dynasties. Though the old houses in Peitian are in sharp contrast in style to the clay buildings of the Hakka in

Yongding, both styles are important elements of the Hakka ethnic culture. The ancient residential houses in Peitian inherited the essence of architecture from Central China and carried it further by imbuing it with the creative thinking of the ancestors of the Hakka.

Visitors going from one courtyard to another will be warmly greeted with smiles and nods from local residents, who are by nature open and sincere.

Dafudi, the biggest residential house in Peitian, was also named the Hall of Heritage with a view to advocating filial piety. More than 170 years old, the first stages of his house were built during the reign of Emperor Daoguang of the Qing dynasty and it was completed 11 years later. The most outstanding feature of the building is that its Hakka courtyard with 9 halls and 18 wells was built by adapting the general layout of courtyards in Central China to the rainy and humid climatic conditions of the south. The skilled use of a frame of beams and columns provided solid support for the house and carried it through a number of earthquakes of a magnitude ranging between 5 and 6.9.

Every detail of the construction of these residential houses in Peitian was accomplished with the assistance of the wisdom and fine workmanship of Hakka craftsmen; such things as the fire-proof bricks on all exterior walls, the clay sculptures and stone carvings on the archways, colored ceramic glaze on ridges and eaves, wooden carvings, and lacquer paintings on window panels.

The old residential houses of Peitian are symbols of a time-honored history, the profound Hakka culture, and the rich Hakka legacy.

LOCATION
Peitian is located in Liancheng county, to the west of Fujian province. It is 69 miles (110km) from Longyan city.

CLIMATE
The climate is the tropical and oceanic monsoonal one typical of Central Asia. There are mild winters and summers, with an annual average temperature of 66°F (18.9 °C).

OF SPECIAL INTEREST
Peitian has well-preserved ancient residential houses of the Hakka, who cling to the Hakka philosophy of "worshiping ancestors instead of gods" and "prioritizing farming and education."

MAIN ATTRACTIONS
Dafudi House and its courtyard, ancient ancestral temples, ancient schools, and Old Street.

Peitian Village is one of the best-preserved ancient villages of the Hakkas. (below, left)

Old Street in Peitian Village (above, right)

Peitian Village is a symbol of the rich Hakkas culture (below, left)

Yongding Hakka earth buildings (Fujian)

Where square rivals circle

LOCATION
Yongding is located in Yongding county, Longyan city, in Fujian province. It is 28 miles (45km) southwest of Longyan.

CLIMATE
There is a clear temperature contrast among the four seasons. The summer days are hot and rainy, and the visitor should try to avoid them.

OF SPECIAL INTEREST
This is very special as far as oriental construction is concerned. It boasts a long history, and a unique harmony with nature.

MAIN ATTRACTIONS
Zhencheng Building, Chengqi Building, and Huanji Building.

Owing to the fact that this area is densely inhabited by the Hakka people, a feature that is well worth seeing is what are called Hakka Earth Buildings. They sit on the mountainsides and riversides, connected up in chains and combined into complexes, some square and some circular – with a unique style, and in picturesque disorder.

The West Fujian area is the first place of settlement of the ancestors who migrated from Central China to Fujian. The buildings are highly characteristic of Central China: usually a palace and hall-type residence with a single-story closed courtyard. When the Hakka people spread toward the southeastern areas, the square building and the Wufeng building – which are a combination of courtyard and earth building – appeared. And then at last the circular earth building was developed. It was the result of adaptation from the plain area to the mountainous area, and also the result of ever increasing emphasis on the defensive function of the buildings. The earth buildings originated in the Tang dynasty, and spread to the surrounding areas during the late Yuan dynasty and early Ming dynasty. These days, the county as a whole claims to have four thousand of the square buildings and 360 of the circular ones, the latter ones having the most outstanding characteristics.

Zhencheng Building is a representative example of the Hukeng communities of Yongding. Facing the courtyard is the central hall, a square, and an open type room with a tapered roof. Paintings and calligraphy works hang on both sides. The balusters and pillars are of western classical style. The exquisite cloisters on the second floor are made of cast iron, while their ornamentation is a mixture of western and Chinese tradition. With a lily in the center, encircled by orchid, jade green bamboo, plum blossom, and so on, the patterns imply long-lasting harmony and good fortune. The wooden doors of the hall bear sculpted decorations including magic fungi, clouds, and bats, and form a sharp contrast with the iron balusters.

All the buildings have names, regardless of their importance. Usually there are rhymed couplets of calligraphic work hung inside the hall to convey the meaning of the title that the building bears. For example, in Zhencheng Building, *zhen* means "discipline and law," and *cheng* means "successful career." Together they convey pulling yourself up to take more responsibility for the country. You can see such couplets with meanings like this example as decorations here and there around the building.

Around this area, there is a history of planting tobacco that has lasted for four hundred years. The long-cut tobacco grown here is claimed to be "the first brand of its kind." The manufacture and trading of tobacco processing equipment is also very successful. In Hongkeng, the Sunrise Tobacco Process Equipment factory that belonged to the Lin family is particularly well known. Descendants of the family built the Zhencheng Building in 1909, symbolizing the economic position of the local district. Generally speaking, the ancient residential community was very closely related to local entrepreneurs throughout the village's history. Examples are the salt traders in Anhui, the bankers in Shanxi, and the tea traders in Jiangxi. They all left impressive private buildings behind.

Behind Zhencheng is the Fuxin Building. There is a mortar and pestle displayed at the front. The smooth wooden handle and the deep mortar boast its long history. It is a square building, much earlier than the Zhencheng, with simple construction – no stone was used in constructing it. Beside it there is the Yucheng Building, again of the square type. And the building opposite Zhencheng has been renovated to become the Earth Building Museum.

Next comes the Chengqi Building, which was built in the years of the Kangxi emperor in the Qing dynasty, and is the most outstanding representative of earth building in the history of ancient construction in China – that information was once even printed on postage stamps. It used to have four hundred rooms, accommodating eighty or so households and six hundred people in its heyday. It is said that a newly wed woman would spend two years in getting to know all the relatives living in the building by acquainting herself with a new one each day. And it was also said that it would take a guest a year to sleep in every room in the house, if he were to change rooms every night.

Through this journey, you will come to realize that the Hakka people really are the descendants of people from Central China. You can see the reflection of this in the Dragon and Lion Dance, in the worship of the goddess of mercy, and so on. Of course, there is also a mix of local cultural elements, in earth buildings, in language, and in textile patterns, too. Here they embroider decorations on the bottoms of trouser legs, and fasten their garments on the right side. Women wear their hair in a bun. These particular customs come from the She minority. The phenomenon of the women working and the males spending much of their time in leisure is ubiquitous among the Hakka people, a trace of the matriarchal society of the aboriginal people.

Nanjing Earth Buildings, revealing the unique architectural style of this type of Fujian building (right)

Inside an earth building (below, left)

Qingyan (Guizhou)
A place in the reaches of the Huaxi Stream

Qingyan, an ancient town with a population of several thousand, is located in the frontier area where the Han, Miao, and Buyi nationalities now live.

After the southward advancement to the hinterland of central Guizhou province in 1381 by the troops of the Ming dynasty (1368–1644 AD), some of the new settlers were stationed at Guiyang city in order to reclaim the wasteland–thus the formation of Qingyan town began. Later a town located about two thirds of a mile (1km) away from the Qingyan Fort was established by the garrisoned troops and inhabited by both the military and civilians. The town was then called "the Royal Town," and it was the embryonic form of what is now Qingyan town. Originally set up for military purpose, Qingyan town, now situated on the cliff 7.5 miles (12km) south of the Huaxi Stream in Guiyang, has a history of over six hundred years.

The karst topography has developed in its typical way within the Guiyang area, and a scene of the natural accumulation of rocks is frequently seen here. Qingyan town itself was constructed with stones and rocks, and four gates were set up on the city wall, on which huge rocks in square shapes were used to build look-out towers, crenellations, and battery.

Dotted about Qingyan, the ancient buildings belonging to the Ming and Qing (1644–1911 AD) dynasties total 37. Three out of eight stone tablets still exist, all of them exquisitely designed and delicately engraved.

Featuring four pillars, three rows, and a quadrilateral roof, the stone Memorial Archway is highly prized by the distinguished contemporary master of arts Liu Haisu. Wanshou Palace, one of the three leading palaces in Qingyan, lies at the end of a small lane and its wall, above the gate, is inlaid with clay sculptures. Of course, this is not the whole story of Qingyan. Qingyan's uniqueness lies in its adaptability: church, memorial archway, monastery, and temple all gather here in this small rock-based town. The antique architecture of the Ming and Qing Period means that the small town enjoys a flavor of the bizarre and fanciful.

The Qingyan people live peacefully in their home town. Usually they sit in front of their houses, watching the backpackers passing hastily to and fro. And sometimes, they greet visitors warmly, invite them to sit on their cane chairs, and serve them with Rose Candy and Small Bean Curd. In return, they are told stories by their guests, who come from all over the country and further afield. With a floor space of more than 8610 square feet (800 square meters), the Ciyun Temple is located on a back street of Qingyan town and is adjacent to Wanshou Palace, the guildhall of Jiangxi province on West Street. The temple is acclaimed on account of its superbly engraved stone pillars and mounds.

Rose Candy is a special local snack. It is prepared with rose flowers and brown sugar. These are mixed thoroughly and the preserved fruit that results is exposed to intense sunlight for one month. Then, the fully dehydrated preserved fruit is selected to be added to a glutinous rice, and a sweet gruel is formed by adding sesame and walnut. The aromatic and crisp Rose Candy and Qingyan's long history are both things that are unforgettable.

LOCATION
Qingyan is situated in the Huaxi district of Guiyang city, Guizhou province.

CLIMATE
It is springlike through out the year. The average annual temperature is 59°F (15°C) or so, and in winter some days are overcast and rainy.

OF SPECIAL INTEREST
The ancient town of Qingyan is enclosed by city walls, all of which were built on the natural cliff, and it is characterized by its stockaded village and fortress.

MAIN ATTRACTIONS
Zhuangyuan Residence, Zhao Lilun's 100-year-old Memorial Archway, Mount Qianling, and Huaxi Stream.

The ancient city gate of Qingyan (left)

One of Qingyan's old alleys (above, right)

A memorial archway in Qingyan (below, right)

Zhaoxing (Guizhou)
A land inhabited by the Dong nation

According to folklore, the ancestors of the Dong nation initially lived in the upper reaches of the Yellow River, but they were later forced to move to south China because of the chaotic effect of the war in Central China. Some of them arrived in Zhaoxing in Guizhou province and began to settle down there, while others continued in their journey and went further south. Now Zhaoxing is the largest autonomous region of the ethnic Dong in China.

Zhaoxing, formerly known as "Zhaodong" (*dong* means "cave"), is dubbed "700 Guandong and 1000 Zhaodong." It is renowned for its Zhaoxing villages, in which 98 percent of the residents are from the ethnic Dong and share the same surname, Lu. They are divided into 12 large branches, each of which has its own internal common surname, namely: Ying, Guo, Meng, Bai, Cao, Bao, Deng, Ma, Xia, Man, Long, and Yuan. People are not entitled to in-

termarry. These 12 groups settle down in a total of five settlements in the region, and each settlement is called "Tuan" or "Zhai" (village) by the locals. Meanwhile each section has its own specific title, namely: Kindness Village, Justice Village, Courtesy Village, Wisdom Village, and Trust Village – the drum-tower of each settlement shares a similar name.

The drum-tower is a landmark that represents the unique ethnic culture of the Dong nationality. When some great event faces the

whole Dong people, the drum will be beaten at the tower, and then the people will amass there to hold a consultation.

These five drum-towers look rather like bamboo shoots sprouting from the Dong villages, which together are named the Drum-tower Group. They are distinguished from each other by their different heights and styles, but they share the same unique architectural feature in that all the components are connected only by wooden joints, rather than by nails or rivets. In addition, the decoration of the drum-towers expresses the very strong characteristics of the ethnic Dong.

Of the Drum-tower Group, the Kindness Tower, 71 ft (21.7m) in height, is a structure of seven eaved tiers and an octagonal spire. The Justice Tower, measuring 85 ft (25.8m) high, is a building with 11-tier eaves and an octagonal spire. The Courtesy Tower is a 76 ft (23.1m) high construction with 13-tier eaves and an octagonal spire, and the Trust Tower shares the same architectural structure as the Courtesy Tower. The colored sculptures and paintings of these drum-towers are diversified.

Last but not least, the Wisdom Tower is considered to be the most beautiful of the group. The Wisdom Tower was rebuilt in 1982, and its framework is composed of 16 pillars. The four in the middle penetrate into the top floor. The foundations of the tower cover a floor of about 754 square feet (70 square meters), with a fire pit in the center. Some wooden benches are placed all around for the use of the local people for resting, playing, singing, and talking. With a height of 49 ft (14.8m), this is a tower with nine-tier eaves and a quadrangular Xieshan[1] top supported by a Dougong[2] structure. Under the heads of those Ruyi, an S-shape ornamental object, traditionally used as a symbol of good luck by the Chinese, all the tiers are octagonal in shape with the side edges turning upward. There is clay sculpture in the form of gourd-shape bottles on the ridge of the tower roof, and on the side edges of the ridge there is exquisite and elegant sculpture in the form of

small birds. Each tier of the tower eaves is covered with small dark blue tiles with white ridges, on which there are sculptures of lions, tigers, phoenixes, and so on. Inside the building, the interior is also richly and delicately decorated.

In Dong villages, there are singing groups that present the Dong's folk songs, and theatrical troupes that perform the Dong's local operas. From within Zhaoxing villages and the bordering Dong villages as well, throngs of local people usually gather at festivals around the singing ground of the drum-towers. They put on "Caigetang," cheerful and enthusiastic performances of song and dance by the Dong people. Featuring beautiful melodies, the Dong's folk songs are popularly known outside their community – in particular the exhilarating performances by their mixed choruses. In general, Zhaoxing deserves its renown as the land of the drum-tower of the Dong villages.

Notes:

1. Xieshan: a traditional house roof in Chinese architecture, it is a mixed structure of double slopes with a horizontal ridge and quadrangular slopes with four sloping ridges.

2. Dougong: a traditional architectural system of brackets inserted between the top of a column and a crossbeam (each bracket being formed of a double bow-shape arm called *gong*, which supports a block of wood, called *dou*, on each side).

LOCATION
The Dong villages of Zhaoxing are located southwest of Liping county in Guizhou province and 44 miles (70km) from Liping county proper.

CLIMATE
There are four distinct seasons each year, and the annual average temperature is 61°F (16°C).

OF SPECIAL INTEREST
The largest naturally inhabited village of the Dong nationality in China, and also the famous land of the drum-towers.

MAIN ATTRACTIONS
Wisdom Drum-tower, Kindness Drum-tower, Justice Drum-tower, and Courtesy Drum-tower.

A view of Justice Village in Zhaoxing (below, left)

Courtesy Village in Zhaoxing (above, left)

Local residences in Wisdom Village (below, right)

Stone Village (Guizhou)

The home of wax printing

LOCATION
Located in Biandanshan town, Zhenning Bouyei, and Miao Autonomous County in central Guizhou province, Stone Village is 4 miles (6km) south of Huangguoshu Falls (the biggest falls in China).

CLIMATE
Stone Village has a pleasant climate with a moderate temperature all year, averaging 63°F (17°C). The best season to visit is when spring is changing into summer.

OF SPECIAL INTEREST
Stone Village boasts distinctive natural scenery and ethnic customs, and is the home of wax printing in China.

MAIN ATTRACTIONS
Enjoying the natural landscapes, visiting the stone houses, watching wax printing by the women.

L ocated in central Guizhou province, Stone Village is only 4 miles (6km) south of Huangguoshu Falls (the biggest falls in China). In Stone Village, you do not hear the roar of the falls, but you can see the stone houses built from the sedimentary rocks deposited by the water, and get in touch with the distinctive natural scenery and ethnic customs.

Stone Village is the home of wax printing in China. It is said that men of the village know how to enclose their family with solid stones, while women of the village know how to disclose the figure with gorgeous batiks.

The cultural charm and ethnic tradition exist in a context of duality, of toughness and gentleness, solidness and softness, crudeness and fineness. The river named Whitewater leads the way to Stone Village, which is on its banks.

The 600-year-old village features houses, walls, porches, pillars, tiles, gates, windows, paths, stairs, bridges, and steps all made of stone. To these are added troughs, mortars, mills, bowls, stoves, benches, chairs, tables, and vats as decorations.

While the stone houses appeal to visitors at first sight, the wax printing has a story behind it: After Revered Fubao and nine other sages had created heaven, earth, and the rivers, they tried to keep heaven up with a wormwood stem, but failed. Then they asked Wuashuang, a dab hand at weaving, to make a "heaven sustainer".

Wuashuang wove 99 fine pieces of cloth, and washed and starched them. When the cloth was being dried under a pear tree, however, the bees that were collecting nectar above in the tree dotted the cloth with their spit, which turned into beeswax over time.

What was more, the decomposed leaves and petals dyed the cloth black. Wuashuang had to wash

the cloth in the river. After being washed, the black color turned into dark blue while the wax spots remained glisteningly white.

After 13 years' work, Wuashuang managed to make an umbrella whose rod was able to sustain heaven firmly. The blue canopy decorated with white spots became the azure sky and sparkling stars.

Because of this, Wuashuang was given the title "Fairy of Flowers," and from him girls of the Bouyei and Miao learned wax printing and

adopted the fashion of dressing in pretty wax prints.

The Whitewater River, with an ancient stone bridge on it, embraces Stone Village nearby and mirrors the distant green hills. In the river, there are women on the rising stones washing clothes, and ducks paddling in the water. Water adds to the enchanting beauty of such idyllic scenes as this, just as it contributes to the making of wax prints. In the pastoral world of Stone Village, stones mean life to the Bouyei men while

A distant view of Stone Village (above)

Miao women washing wax-printed textiles at the waterside (below)

wax printing represents folk arts to the Bouyei women.

Besides Huangguoshu Falls – the most majestic sight in the vicinity – the river and the people add charm to Stone Village, the home of wax printing.

Nanshe Village (Guangdong)

A small 800-year-old village

Dongguan, a city in the east of Guangzhou, is named after a grass called guanaco (Scirpus) that is widely grown in the region. And now, Nanshe, a small village in the Chashan area of Dongguan, expands a legend from its history, which extends over eight hundred years.

Founded in the early days of the Southern Song dynasty (1127–1279 AD), Nanshe Village was initially inhabited by villagers with the surnames of Qi, Xi, Mai, Chen, and Huang. While the invading Mongolian troops were marching southward in the late Southern Song, Xie Shangren, a Song subject from the Jiangsu and Zhejiang region, escaped from his homeland and transferred his family to this area, ultimately settling down here in the village.

As one of the offspring of an intellectual family, Xie never overlooked the education of his children despite his poverty, and placed a high priority on reading and farming. Later on, descendants of high caliber from the Xie family came forth in great numbers, and the family flourished, making it the premier clan in Nanshe Village. Owing to the strong cultural atmosphere in the village and the fact that most of the Xie family's later generations held government posts, the village has become filled with mansions, tablets, and memorial archways. In total, there are currently 25 memorial archways and over two hundred houses built in the Ming Dynasty (1368–1644) or Qing dynasty (1644–1911). Nanshe is in-

deed a village made up of a variety of ancient buildings.

The present Nanshe Village, as shown to visitors, is centered on a rectangular pool in the middle, which is flanked by buildings scattered on the natural slopes of the surrounding hills. The village has an orderly, well-designed layout and a fresh, pleasant environment. There are numerous ancient buildings in the village, including houses, ancestral temples, classical houses of learning, shops, family temples, storied buildings, village walls, wells, lanes, memorial archways, and so forth – all of which constitute a cultural scene with the strong characteristics of the Pearl River delta.

Nanshe Village has the largest ancient building complex extant in

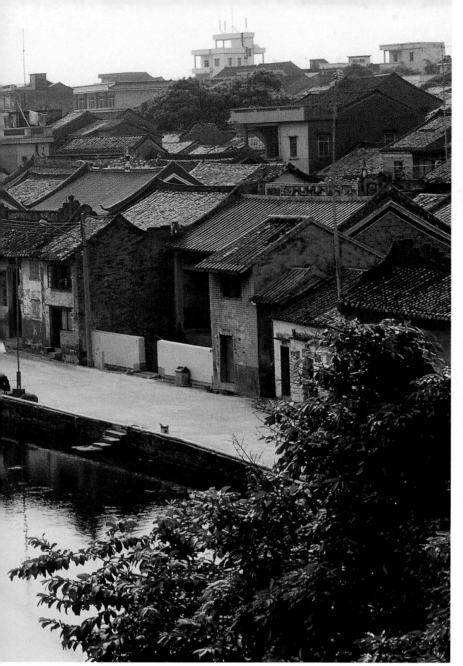

LOCATION
Nanshe Village is situated in the Chashan area of Dongguan, Guangdong province.

CLIMATE
The climate is mild, with heavy precipitation. It is green all the year round, and conditions are of the subtropical moist monsoon type.

OF SPECIAL INTEREST
One of the largest ancient building complexes in Guangdong. Individual buildings are simply designed and classically appealing.

MAIN ATTRACTIONS
The Village Wall, the Xie family's ancestral temple, the Century-old Men's Memorial Archway, the Xie Yuqi Family Temple, and Zizheng Residence.

Dongguan, and also one of the largest of its kind in Guangdong province.

Besides ancient architecture, the village also enjoys a history of longevity on the part of its residents. The long life of the locals is probably related to the quality of its drinking water. In the past, there was a time when four villagers were aged over 100 years, and the emperor of the time issued an imperial edict ordering a memorial archway to be set up to commemorate this. At another time the house of a 100-year-old man was transformed into a memorial hall for him after his death. Nowadays, of the old people in the village, up to thirty are more than 90 years old.

The construction of the ancient village wall began in 1644, the last year of the Ming dynasty. The foundations of the wall were made from either rammed earth or red stones, and its lookout towers are built on a base of light blue bricks, totaling

21, each bearing its own name and yinglian, a traditional Chinese couplet written on scrolls and hung on a pillar of the house. As for the Xie family's ancestral temple, it features a compound of three rows of houses and courtyards. The houses in the first row have pottery sculptures on the roof ridge; while the houses in the next two rows have clay sculptures on their ridges. All the houses have a style of roof rarely seen here in Dongguan. The century-old Men's Memorial Archway was constructed between 1592 and 1598 of the Ming dynasty, and was approved by the then imperial government in honor of the Xie Yanjuans, a pair of men in the village who were both over 100 years of age. Zizheng Residence is located halfway up a nearby hill, and the crossbeams of its side corridors have been superbly designed and constructed.

Of the houses in Nanshe Village, most of them have a brick and stone archway-style structure consisting

of four pillars, three rooms, and three stories. Such a structure usually has a Xieshan roof and Dougong-shape* eaves, as well as delicate wood-engraved lintels. As many as a hundred local houses dot the village, displaying their classical appeal among the dense tree groves.

Notes:

*Dougong: a traditional architectural system of brackets inserted between the top of a column and a crossbeam (each bracket being formed of a double bow-shape arm called *gong*, which supports a block of wood, called *dou*, on each side).

A distant view of Nanshe Village (above, left)

Stone carving on a local residence (below, left)

Sculptures on a local residence (above, right)

Ancestral temple in a private house (below, right)

Qiaoxi Village (Guangdong)

Hidden in mountains with the Hakka people

LOCATION
Qiaoxi Village is an unspoiled village in the northeast of Lumei county, near Yanyang township and 31 miles (50km) from Meixian county.

CLIMATE
There is a subtropical climate, with a hot temperature in summer and fall.

OF SPECIAL INTEREST
This enchanting village is where the folk customs of the Hakka people can be experienced.

MAIN ATTRACTIONS
Jishan Hall, Wucailin, Shi De Hall, Qiaoxi Reservoir, and others.

If you are tired of modern life and want to take a rest in a peaceful place, then you may want to come to Qiaoxi Village.

Qiaoxi is a small mountainous village located in Yinna Mountain, 31 miles (50km) from Meizhou city. Here the waters and the mountains, the forests and the ancient houses exude antiquity and mystery.

Qiaoxi Village is a well-preserved ancient village, and almost no signs of outsiders are to be seen. The village is hemmed in by steep mountains on all sides. The lofty Xianglu peak in the distance makes a dainty silhouette. The solitary Five Finger peak (Wuzhi Feng) keeps at bay all the distress, vexation, and grievance of the world. In such a mystic landscape, Tao Yuanming, a hermit of the Jin dynasty, surely would be satisfied if he were to come back into the world again. The mountain stream originating on Five Finger peak in Yinna Mountain flows westward through the village, nourishing the Hakka people who have lived here for four hundred years.

Besides a peaceful life and rustic charm, Qiaoxi Village has its own unique style.

Wherever there are humans, there are dwelling houses for them. Qiaoxi Village is hidden in a valley

of Yinna Mountain, and its locality is not like that of the plains people, who can boast of a vast expanse of flat land to build on. But the clever mountain villagers made the best use of the topography. They built houses of specific designs. Over the past hundreds of years, these houses have become groups of construction with a unique Hakka style. The houses follow the mountain slope. Sometimes they are on a platform by the water, sometimes arranged in picturesque disorder.

From the brook at the entrance of the village to Jishan Hall where the buildings are concentrated, there stand in turn four bar-type and two yard-type houses: Si De Hall, Baoshan Hall, and some other anonymous and one-story bar types that are largely ruinous now. They are built on stone-piled terraces running up the slope, one floor after another. A path winds through the village, with orange, peach, Longan, and citrus trees growing around. In the middle of the village there is a place called Wucailin ("colorful forest"), where you can find rare trees such as the red manmu and the white laurel which are listed by the government as second-grade protected species, as well as the Dragonhead tree, which is the biggest tree in Guangdong province. Not only are they rare, their leaves also present different colors, giving impressions of riotousness, quietude, and elegance. With different flowers blooming in different seasons, they exhibit a bright and charming picture in the rural landscape.

Through Wucailin, and halfway to Jishan Hall, there stands the western building known as Yi Lou (meaning of southeast Asian style), the Zhu family ancestral hall, and the Si De Hall, a semicircular loess

tamped structure that takes the highest position.

Of them, Jishan Hall is the most famous. Its construction began in the Guangshu Years of the Qing dynasty, and it took 12 years to finish it. It is a typical two-floor bar-type with an encircling hall, impressive door, stone pillars, and fine molded wooden eaves. There is a tablet and couplets of calligraphy. All these features divulge the past glory of the family. The inner decoration is refined and cultured.

The highest building, Shi De Hall, is built in an encircling form around the half-moon-shape pond in the front yard. The outer wall is

A distant view of Qiaoxi Village, a well-preserved Hakka settlement (above)

An antique stone-carved window (above, right)

The ancestral temple in a local residence (below, right)

loess tamped, and is unique in Hakka traditional dwelling-house construction. Standing on the wall, you can look over the whole Qiaoxi Village. Under a sky of cloudless blue, the Yinna Mountain in the distance is a stroke of light color, while the ancient Jishan Hall is nearby.

Let us think again about our own hometown, or to our own natural area. We are aware of the traces left by our own ancestors affecting our thoughts. This is the kind of experience we all have as tourists.

Dangjia Village (Shaanxi)

A perfect combination of village and castle

Gansu Province · Shanxi Province · Dangjia Village · Xi'an · Henan Province · Shaanxi Province · Hubei Province

LOCATION
Dangjia Village is situated 5.5 miles ((9km) northeast of Hancheng in Shaanxi province.

CLIMATE
The village is usually very hot and rainy in summer, and rather cold and dry in winter.

OF SPECIAL INTEREST
The village is known as a treasure trove of ancient private architecture in northern China.

MAIN ATTRACTIONS
Wenxing Pavilion, Kanjia Tower, Miyangbao Castle, and the archways of chastity and filial piety.

Down in the valley which is narrow from north to south and gourd-shaped from east to west, there is to be seen a village with ancient private houses set in row upon row. To the south runs a quiet river densely lined with fruit trees and vegetable fields. This is Dangjia village, which is composed of over 120 siheyuan (quadrangles, also meaning compound structures with square courtyards). In addition, the village has a castle and more than ten ancestral temples. It is interesting to notice that the slab-paved lanes are dustless on fine days and mud-free on rainy days. Many ancient structures such as pagodas,

pavilions, archways, and stele are to be seen, all of which makes the village's culture clear and shows it as very different from others.

With a recorded history of over 670 years, Dangjia Village was first built in 1331 by a certain family called Dang, who moved here from a far away place and settled down as farmers. Around 1420 one grandson of the family of Dang stepped into officialdom after doing well in the civil examinations. Then he drafted a plan to reconstruct his home village. Around 1480 the families of Dang and Jia worked together to start a big business. Following many years of hard work, they began

large-scale construction in the later Ming dynasty, funded with their huge profits from trading. In 1851 they built the Miyangbao Castle in a bid to prevent any robbers or bandits from intruding and to safeguard their lives and property, thus forming a combination of village and castle.

Walking in the stone-paved lane, you come across the magnificent gate towers of the quadrangle courtyards. Their auspicious inscriptions and fine stone, brick, and wood carvings serve as convincing evidence of how powerful and wealthy the owners must have been. It is said that there were hundreds of

quadrangle courtyards and dozens of watchtowers in the heyday of the village. When night fell, all the gates were closed, and armed men were watchful in their sentry positions around the castle. The whole village had become fortified against the outside world.

Now, most of the watchtowers have been pulled down. However, the solemn ancestral temples, the high Wenxing Pavilion, and the splendid archways of chastity and filial piety are left to become the best testimony to the glorious history of Dangjia Village.

The typical private houses in their quadrangle courtyards are both attractive and practical, built on sturdy brick foundations. Most of them have a single story based on a brick and wood framework, while a few have two stories. There are three styles: with the gate in the middle, on the side with two courtyards in the front, and in the rear.

The 130 ft (40m) high Wenxing Pavilion at the village primary school is a six-storied building that houses several shrines for sages such as Confucius and Mencius, both of whom were great educators in ancient China. In modern times, the pavilion serves as the most important building for the villagers after the ancestral temple. It is said that a pearl presented by the emperor was stored away in the top of the pavilion.

Built to the northeast of the village to guard against invasion, the castle is supplied with cannons on the surrounding walls. The highest point reaches 39 ft (12m). It is indeed a strong defensive fortress.

Dangjia Village is the best-preserved village with a castle of the Ming and Qing style in the country. Located in an ideal defensive environment, this boat-shaped village is built in accordance with the traditional theory of *yin* and *yang* and

eight diagrams. The quadrangle courtyards are decorated with wood, stone, and brick carvings of high artistic merit. The ancient inscriptions and daily utensils are ideal material for the study of the history of the region. Dangjia Village is a treasure of ancient private architecture in northern China.

A well-preserved local residence in Dangjia Village (above, left)

A section of the village (above, right)

An antique door-lock (below, left)

The well-preserved Baogushi stone in front of a local residence (below, right)

Zhuge Village (Zhejiang)
Built on the Nine-Palace and Eight-Diagram pattern

It is customary for ancient Chinese villages to be built in the most advantageous location, with families of the same clan together. However, Zhuge Village in Lanxi, Zhejiang province, is an exclusive example in the country, presenting a perfect combination of clan and home in a traditional cultural sense.

Originally called Gaolong, Zhuge Village extends within a superb layout featuring a wavy design, magnificent style, and exquisite structures. History has it that the village was first designed by Dashi, the lord of Zhuge, descendant in the twenty-seventh generation of Zhuge Liang, the renowned strategist in the Period of Three Kingdoms (220–280 AD). Inspired by the Nine-palace and Eight-diagram Pattern, Zhuge Dashi elaborated on the plan of the village in memory of his ancestor Zhuge Liang. This is the only ancient village of its kind in the whole country.

At present, villagers live a simple agricultural life. Their houses are characteristic of ancient architectural styles. What is the most striking thing is the layout within which the village has been constructed. The legend has it that Zhuge Liang was most expert in the tactics of the Eight Diagram in warfare. His unusual wisdom helped Liu Bei succeed in defeating the Wei and the Wu kingdoms. Therefore Zhuge

Liang is respected as the idiot-savant of devilish intelligence, as indicated in the Chinese proverb: "Three cobblers are equal to Zhuge Liang." Du Fu, the great poet of the Tang dynasty, once praised Zhuge's achievement in the words: "Zhuge's contribution comes first since he owed much to the Eight-diagram tactics."

Perched on a terrace, with the southeast section seeming to slide toward the northwest, Zhuge Village is surrounded by mountains in the background and facing the river, all of which represents the ideal natural environment, according to *fengshui* (geomancy). Moreover, the Zhongchi Pond in the center of the Nine-palace and Eight-diagram Pattern – made up of two parts: half water and half land – is flanked by two wells. The whole composition resembles the symbolic Taiji fish-shape *yin* and *yang* diagram. In addition, eight lanes radiate from the Zhongchi Pond, so that every household has its own position in the diagram. It is all the more amazing that eight hills, which together embrace the village, make up the external Eight-diagram Pattern naturally. The eight hills are at some distance from each other. As you explore the village, you may find yourself walking in a maze, crisscrossed with ancient lanes.

As a geomancy expert, Zhuge Dashi toured the country before he

discovered the dreamland of *fengshui* in Lanxi in Zhejiang province. He was content that he had found an ideal location for his clan to settle down. Then he invested huge wealth and manpower in shaping the village. His painstaking efforts led to Zhuge Village, boasting high mansions in rows and houses in a terraced array. The lanes are linked with each other in a responsive way.

Today, the village has dozens of buildings of the Ming and the Qing styles. They feature sculpted beams, painted pillars, and overlapped eaves in a good variety, embodying the designer's extraordinary wisdom, as reflected in the harmonious arrangement between man and nature.

Dominated by the ancient architecture of the Ming and the Qing, the village has over two hundred private houses and main halls in good condition. Surviving for hundreds of years, the layout of the Nine-palace and Eight-diagram Pattern has remained unchanged. The architectural style of blue brick, gray tile, corbel-stepped walls, thick beams, and small bedrooms has made Zhuge Village a unique model of an ancient Chinese village with traditional private houses.

LOCATION
Situated in Lanxi, in the hinterland of Zhejiang province, Zhuge Village is sandwiched between the Xin'anjiang River, the Fuchunjiang River, and Qiandaohu Lake. State Highway 330 runs by the village.

CLIMATE
With four seasons, there is abundant rainfall and plentiful sunshine. It is pleasant for sightseeing all year, with spring the best season to visit.

OF SPECIAL INTEREST
Eight radiating lanes divide the whole village into eight sections. Zhuge Village looks like a labyrinth with the traditional Chinese layout of the Eight-diagram Pattern.

MAIN ATTRACTIONS
Zhuge Liang's Memorial Hall, Zhuge Dashi's House, the Prime Minister's Temple, Yongmu Hall, Dajing Hall, and Sangu Hall.

Elaborated on the Nine-palace and Eight-diagram Pattern, Zhuge Village is the only one of this design in China. (left)

An ancient house with sculpted beams, painted pillars, and overlapped eaves in Zhuge Village. Mostly built in the Ming and Qing dynasties, Zhuge Village is representative of the ancient residences of China. (right)

Hibiscus Village (Zhejiang)

As beautiful as hibiscus flowers, indeed

LOCATION
Hibiscus Village is situated in Yongjia county, Zhejiang province.

CLIMATE
The village has four seasons. It is warm and humid and its annual average temperature is usually around 64.8°F (18.2°C).

OF SPECIAL INTEREST
Hibiscus Village is a picturesque ancient settlement that has stuck to the traditional idea of according equal importance to learning and farming since ancient times.

MAIN ATTRACTIONS
Xiufeng Mountain, the waterfall, and the Linmei area.

In Yongjia, Zhejiang province, in southeast China there stand three pinkish-white peaks that look like hibiscus blossoms – hence they are called the Hibiscus peaks. The nearby village is called Hibiscus Village since a big pond there show reflections of the peaks at twilight.

It is customary for the villagers here to attach great importance to learning and also to farming. History has it that in the Southern Song dynasty (1127–1279 AD) there were at one time 18 high-ranking officials, natives of Hibiscus Village, serving in the capital. Therefore, high in the ancestral temple were hung 18 portraits of the forefathers of these officials. These are extraordinary achievements, of which the villagers were once very proud.

The whole village lies on a rectangular plane with the main entrance facing southward. All the road crossings show up as square terraces, while the channel crossings form square ponds, all of them looking like stars dotted about the sky. The layout is said to be quite metaphorical in two ways. One is the corresponding location of each household to each constellation, and the other is indicative of the wish for more young talented people to come from the village, like stars.

Besides, the geographical arrangement is strategically defensive since the square terraces may serve as command platforms and the square ponds can be used to fight fire if the village should ever be invaded and any battle take place.

It is common for the private houses in Hibiscus Village to have pinkish walls and blackish tiles, which reflect the local architectural style. They match the surrounding mountains and rivers very well.

The main road extends through the majestic village entrance. In the rear there are village gates made of huge stone blocks, outside which may be seen green fields full of crops running as far as the foot of the Hibiscus peaks in the distance.

Therefore, the village is encircled with four gates in the east, west, south, and north. Beyond the south gate there is a brook, beside which the women start their day early washing clothes, quilts, and vegetables. Day in and day out, the men are accustomed to walking through the west gate and the north gate with their hoes and spades on their shoulders. They work in the fields and bring in the harvest in due time, thus feeding and supporting their families. They go out early in the morning and come back late at night. Their daily routine has remained unchanged for many generations.

The east gate is the highlight of the local buildings. It is a two-story tower decorated with exquisite carvings. When strolling along the main road, you may enjoy the reflections of the Hibiscus peaks and the Hibiscus Pavilion in the Hibiscus Pond, to which two stone bridges are linked. Behind the pavilion is the Academy of Classical Learning, which has desks and chairs in the courtyard, and a portrait of Confucius hanging in the main hall. As a rule, students are required to kowtow to Confucius, the great educator of the country, before they are admitted to study here.

From the main road radiate many lanes. Courtyards are tucked away in the bushes. Sometimes, a bunch of camellia flowers may greet you across the wall or beyond the fence.

In Hibiscus Village you will find that everything continues, easily and leisurely. This millennium-old village keeps going on its own. The elderly people may give you a smile, whether their experience of life is good or not. They have a calm attitude to everything that has happened to them. They have found the home for their souls. This is Hibiscus Village, as beautiful as the hibiscus flowers.

The Hibiscus Pavilion by the Hibiscus Pond in Hibiscus Village (below, right)

The villagers here have attached great importance to learning and farming, which is the traditional culture in ancient China. (below, left)

The village gate near the Hibiscus peak (above, right)

Wuzhen (Zhejiang)

A 2000-year-old water town in Zhejiang

Wuzhen is a time-honored water town in Tongxiang in Zhejiang province. It is criss-crossed with rivers and sited on the Hangjiahu Plain. Endowed with abundant rainfall, sunshine, and natural resources, the town has long been known as the land of rice and fish, and the home of silk and satin.

What is more, sandwiched between two provinces, three prefectures, and seven counties, Wuzhen is a strategically important place that has witnessed numerous battles, from the Spring and Autumn Period (722–481 BC) to the Tang dynasty and the Qing dynasty. It is a town coveted by any conflicting party in time of war.

Wuzhen has many historical sites. Such well-preserved relics as the Xiuzhenguan Monastery, the reading room of Prince Zhaoming, the ancient gingko tree of the Tang dynasty, Zhuanchuan Bay, and the double bridges are good tourist spots. Mao Dun's Former Residence is listed as a state-level key cultural location by the Central Govern-

ment. Nearby stands Mao Dun's Memorial Hall, where the modern master writer and translator studied in his childhood.

Having survived for over two thousand years, Wuzhen has retained the features and layout of an ancient water town. In fact, the whole town is built on rivers, which are used like streets. Houses, corridors, wharfs, pavilions, and courtyards extend along the rivers.

As a whole, the town is immersed in a tranquil and cultural atmosphere, featuring the perfect combination of bridge, water, and

house, and presenting a typical waterside scene in the Jiangnan region. In addition, the slab-paved roads, the antique log cabins, and the clear lake combine to generate an outstanding experience for tourists.

Walking in some old towns, you may be aware of their physical features only. However, things are different in Wuzhen. It is now divided into several sections, such as the traditional shopping area where the famous shops conduct their businesses in the way they are used to. There is a workshop sector where craftsmen expert in bamboo, fans, pottery, kettles, writing-brushes, Chinese paper, Chinese ink, ink slabs, wood carving, cloth weaving, and thread-spinning open up one after another. Elsewhere are the private houses which have been renovated to look as they used to. The elderly people you meet in the street are willing to tell you about the years they have spent in the town. Then there are the traditional cultural activities: you may tour the courtyard filled with blue-dyed cloth, enjoy the local opera on the ancient stage, and watch the shadow play as well.

In the old street stands a group

of buildings in the Ming and Qing styles, one of the best preserved of its kind in the country.

In addition to housing impressive local customs, waterside scenes, and exquisite private homes, Wuzhen is immersed in history and culture, which enhances all that may be seen there.

LOCATION
Wuzhen is situated in Tongxiang county, Jiaxing, Zhejiang province. It is not far from Hangzhou and Shanghai.

CLIMATE
Within the sutropical monsoon belt, it has four seasons with a relatively long and cold winter, and a short and cool fall.

OF SPECIAL INTEREST
Wuzhen is a typical town in the Jiangnan region that represents a realistic picture of flourishing crafts-manship and trade in China near the turn of the twentieth century. The town has a number of areas with different functions, which provide the opportunity to experience aspects of life as it used to be.

MAIN ATTRACTIONS
Xiuzhenguan Monastery, reading room of Prince Zhaoming, ancient gingko tree of the Tang Dynasty, Zhuanchuan Bay, the double bridges, and Mao Dun's Former Residence.

Corridor along the river in Wuzhen (below, left)

Night scene in Wuzhen (above, right)

One of Wuzhen's waterside residences (below, right)

PHOTO CREDITS

Translators: Qiu Hemin, Dai Hong, Yuan Qing, Tu Jingbao
Authors: Wang Zhen, Liu Yanli, Li Linzhi, Hu Minyan, Sun Ping, Mei Sheng, Gao Xing, Zhang Qunxing, Liu Xiaotian, Wu Jiahao, Dao Zi
Photographers: Mei Sheng, Xiao Yun, Guo Youming, Liu Shizhao, Bian Zhiwu, Yang Ying, Li Yuqun, Chu Xiaoqin, Zhu Chunshu, Yan Xinfa, Niu Aihong, Yu Jianyin, Yuan Zhu, Zhang Ziqiang, Ren Jin, Miao Jun, Zhao Zhijun, Xue Yao, Dong Jiancheng, Wang Jigang, Zhang Qunxing,